OPERATION HURRICANE

BOMBER COMMAND

OPERATION
HURRICANE

THE STORY OF THOSE WHO FLEW,
FOUGHT AND FAILED TO RETURN
ON 14 AND 15 OCTOBER 1944

• MARC HALL •

I wish to dedicate the book to my grandparents, Donald and Gladys Spooner, who sadly are no longer with us. They inspired the research into the family history and the book. Marc Hall, 2013

Published in 2013 by Fighting High Ltd,
23 Hitchin Road, Stotfold, Hitchin, Herts, SG5 4HP
www.fightinghigh.com

British Library Cataloguing-in-Publication data.
A CIP record for this title is available from the
British Library.

ISBN – 13: 978-0957116337

Designed and typeset in Monotype Baskerville
11/14pt by Michael Lindley www.truthstudio.co.uk

Printed and bound in China by Toppan Leefung Printing
Front cover design by Michael Lindley.

Contents

PART ONE • THE OPERATION

Chapter 1

The Volunteer

Ernest Bone was a mid-upper gunner in No. 626 Squadron.

I wanted to be a fighter pilot. As a 17-year-old in 1940, I watched, open mouthed, from the back of my garden, ten miles south of London, as our Spitfires and Hurricanes duelled, high in the summer sky, with Messerschmitt Bf109s and 110s during the Battle of Britain. It was perhaps inevitable, therefore, that, when I had to register for military service with my age group in November 1941, I volunteered to fly.

But so did thousands of other 19-year-old young men who had also been mesmerized by the feats of our fighter pilots, who, against tremendous odds, had put paid to Hitler's plan to invade and occupy Britain. I was sent home to await my turn to begin training. It was not until August 1942 that I received a letter from the King to report for duty in his Majesty's Royal Air Force. I was a few days short of my 20th birthday.

'So sorry, Laddie,' said the kindly medical officer at the Aircrew Reception Centre, whose faded wings on his tunic told me that he knew what he was talking about, 'so sorry, but with your astigmatism you would have trouble landing a plane, and we just don't have that many aircraft for you to practise on.' I was selected instead for navigator training. I had been in the Air Training Corps for a few months, and had a rudimentary idea of what that entailed, so in my youthful enthusiasm that was fine by me. I did well in the classroom work at Initial Training Wing, and passed the three months' course with good marks in January 1943. Because of the huge numbers of would-be aircrew passing through the system, there were bottlenecks that necessitated the setting-up of holding units where we 'marked time' with lots of drill, route marches and obstacle courses until we could move forward again.

It was not until June 1943 that I sailed in a troop ship, the crack liner the *Queen Elizabeth* in camouflage grey, for Canada, and in August I began my advanced navigation course in Winnipeg. But the air exercises were my undoing. I just was not quick enough in the air. Maths had never been my favourite subject at school. I felt my self-confidence draining away, and I was, in fact, relieved to be 'washed out' by November. Then another holding unit, where I was told that, as there was a nine-month wait for the bomb-aimer course, all that was left for me was the air gunner course. As the officer explained, 'They're always short of air gunners.' I had a good idea why, but at that moment I did not want to know more.

That was the instant when it really came home to me that I was just a small cog in a huge machine whose function it was to grind out as many 'bods' in the shortest possible time, to take the place of those who had gone before. So much for being a fighter pilot, I thought ruefully. I was rather doubtful that I, who had no mechanical aptitude (I had been a cub newspaper reporter before joining the RAF) and had no particular love for or interest in guns, would be a crack shot, but in my youthful innocence and optimism I told myself I would cross that bridge when I came to it. That bridge was still somewhere in the future.

The first thing I saw on entering the classroom at the gunnery school was a blackboard on which was scrawled the words 'You are here to learn to kill'. I soon learned to take apart and reassemble the Browning .303 machine gun. Then I was taught to do it blindfolded, for Bomber Command flew at night. Then I learned how to clear a stoppage at 5,000 feet in a now obsolete Fairey Battle (in 1940 it had been a front-line light bomber in the Battle of France) without taking my flying gloves off, because the temperature in the unheated machine was around -40°C at that height.

Target practice on the ground, I found, was one thing, but when firing from a moving platform at a drogue towed by another moving platform that was being deliberately flown at varying speeds in poor visibility, the chances of hitting the drogue, let alone the bull's eye painted on it, were frustratingly few. At times it was difficult to differentiate between the snow-covered ground and the snow-laden clouds. However, somehow I managed to pass the course with an 'average' assessment. Sitting on my bunk bed that evening, it was with some pride that I sewed my half wing and my sergeant stripes on my uniform. Hitler, here I come, I said to myself! Now we'll see who's who!

Things started to move pretty rapidly from then on. I arrived back in England in early April 1944, and, after a spell in another holding unit, I was posted to an Operational Training Unit (OTU), where I became a member of an aircrew. A couple of hundred pilots, navigators, bomb aimers, wireless operators and air gunners were told to 'sort yourselves out into crews'. It took about three days for my fellow gunner, whom I had known since our gunnery course, and me to find first a pilot, then a navigator, a bomb aimer, and a wireless operator. We began our training exercises on twin-engined Vickers Wellington bombers, just recently, and honourably, retired from active service. We did long cross-country flights up and down England, during which we familiarized ourselves with our equipment. As I was subject to airsickness, I [would later] opt for the mid-upper turret, while my fellow gunner happily took the rear turret. During these training flights we did air-to-air and air-to-sea firing, and fighter affiliation exercises to give our pilot opportunities to practise evasive action, the 'corkscrew' manœuvre. I had to take my turn in the rear turret and on landing would miserably have to clean up the rear turret of all traces of my vomit. Our graduation exercise was an initiation flight over enemy-held territory. We dropped leaflets over a French town two weeks after D-Day to give heart to the citizens that liberation was coming at last.

But we were not ready yet for the real thing. Our next stop was the Heavy Conversion Unit (HCU), where we made our first acquaintance with a four-engine bomber, the Handley Page Halifax. It was here we picked up the seventh member of our crew, a flight engineer. We were now a complete bomber crew; six untried and untested sergeants and a Flight Lieutenant pilot, who, we took comfort in knowing, had already done a tour in Coastal Command. We had a final week at the Lancaster Finishing School, where we thoroughly familiarized ourselves with the aircraft that we would soon be flying on an operational squadron, and then our training was over. In four short months, seven very diverse personalities had bonded into a fighting unit in which we had learned to trust each other's abilities and had come to know enough of each other's duties to give us a fighting chance to get back to base if one of us were to be incapacitated. '*Per ardua ad astra.*'

We were posted to No. 626 Squadron, RAF Wickenby, Lincolnshire, on 29 September 1944. We immediately got a week's leave. Having a pilot who had got 'some time in' was certainly paying dividends, we chuckled, and then we were allowed a week to get the 'feel' of the squadron, during which time we got some air time in, including fighter affiliation. Then, at last, we were included in a sequence of events that would become the very kernel of our existence for the next seven months. We found ourselves on the battle order for the following day, 14 October. Roused from our beds at 0230 hrs the next morning by our Flight Commander, we learned at briefing that it would be a daylight attack on Duisburg, a vital Ruhr port, by a vast number of Lancasters and Halifaxes, protected by a strong fighter escort. Back at base that afternoon I wrote in my diary: 'Flak fairly heavy. Shell bursts everywhere. Saw one kite go down. Felt scared. Flight Commander's kite is missing.'

It had been a tiring, adrenalin-packed day, and we put our heads down for a 'kip', as we called it, but were woken up at 1730 hrs by our Skipper, who warned us that we were on the battle order again for that night. Apparently Bomber Harris had not been too pleased with our work, and every crew that had been on the morning raid had to go back and do the job properly. So we were over Duisburg again at 0130 hrs the next morning. When we got back three hours later, I wrote in my diary: 'Impossible to keep up search over the target. Whole place lit up by flashes and flares. Bags of flak and searchlights effective but few. Down below, Duisburg was an inferno, very tired.'

We had been part of 1,000 bombers, sent to attack one city twice in less than twenty-four hours. Nearly 9,000 tons of bombs had been dropped on Duisburg for a loss of twenty-one aircraft, fifteen in the daylight raid and six at night. Because our Flight Commander was missing, and in fact had perished with his crew, our Skipper became Flight Commander.

We had completed ops Nos 1 and 2. Twenty-eight to go!

Chapter 2

The Birth of Operation Hurricane

Operation Hurricane, a comprehensive major bombing operation and aerial assault involving thousands of RAF heavy bombers and fighters, was planned to deliver a devastating blow on the enemy. (This was not just an RAF operation; it also involved the USAAF, but the focus of this book is on the RAF input.)

The initial operation, Hurricane I, focused on the non-damaged parts of German cities and industrial sectors, concentrating the maximum available force in time and space against the enemy, with the RAF attacking industrial targets and the US Eighth Air Force attacking synthetic oil and Benzol plants. The basic principle was to apply within the shortest time period a maximum effort against objectives in the densely populated Ruhr region, thereby assisting advancing Allied ground forces, and demonstrating to the enemy the overwhelming superiority and destructive force of the Allied Air Forces. In addition to the heavy bombers, the Tactical Air Forces were to attack targets of opportunity, such as airfields and transport systems, all within the locality of the Ruhr, adding concentration to the enormous demonstration of air power. The Allied fighter pilots' primary purpose was to escort the heavy bombers to and from the target area, but on the return journey they would be released to carry out this secondary objective of attacking targets of opportunity.

Operation Hurricane II was conceived as an extended bombing directive, to be employed over the coming weeks and months, beginning as soon as the first part of Hurricane was completed. This was more of a wide-spread coordinated operation involving the RAF and the USAAF Eighth and Fifteenth Air Forces, with the focus being on enemy oil plants and other priority targets such as airfields and transportation systems. There was considerable pressure to get RAF Bomber Command's Commander-in-Chief Sir Arthur Harris to allocate his destructive force to the bombing of oil installations. Results for September 1944 indicated that, as a result of the strategic bomber offensive, 25 per cent of the pre-attack oil was now available to the enemy, which resulted in heavily reduced operational capabilities to their land and air forces. The pressure had to be maintained, preventing the time to rebuild and repair. Without oil, the enemy war machine would grind to a quick halt. Harris, however, believed in other priorities, such as the bombing of other industrial targets and cities, and there would be continual tension with the Air Ministry over targeting.

The Hurricane objective for RAF Bomber Command was clear. To impress upon the German High Command the might and destructive power of the Allied Air Forces and the futility of continued resistance, and to destroy specific oil production plants and storage facilities, including the industrial/engineering sectors and major production plants. A third long-term aim and objective, not specific to the raids covered in this book, was to destroy the transportation systems and industrial establishments in certain key German cities, such as Duisburg, Brunswick and Cologne, and deny the enemy the opportunity to recover – forcing back the enemy rail heads and front-line transport systems.

On 13 October 1944 Sir Arthur Harris began finalizing the detail for Operation Hurricane I. It was exactly what he had hoped for and been waiting for, an example of the whirlwind bombing campaign he had set out in 1943. This carefully planned raid would require almost every operationally available bomber to be put into the air – a maximum-effort raid. The sheer scale of the operation and the intensity of the raids in such a short period of time had rarely been seen before. In less than twenty-four hours two heavy raids with approximately 1,000 heavy bombers in each, split into three waves, would visit Duisburg alone, without considering the diversionary raids to other targets or the USAAF raids planned to run concurrently. Such force would smash the industrial city. The might of the Allied bomber forces was clear.

The main target, Duisburg, was situated in the industrial heart of the Ruhr on the river Rhine. It was close to the advancing Allied armies and housed many of Germany's production and engineering plants. RAF Bomber Command, limited by aircraft range, weather and fighter escort capabilities, had difficulty operating effectively by day in winter much

beyond the distance of the Rhine. The Ruhr area contained the best targets of military return, such as a large number of first-priority oil targets.
Moreover, the population of workers in the area was estimated at five
million. If the raids destroyed morale, it was hoped a national collapse
would follow, with widespread repercussions throughout Germany. The
close proximity of the Allied armies in the area had already led to the
very brittle morale of the locals. Bombing on an unprecedented scale
would hopefully cause it to break. The industrial Ruhr stood out as the
best area to attack. The town selected for destruction was Duisburg.

There was, however, one considerable risk in attacking this area of
Germany in broad daylight. The Germans knew this location would be
of major interest and of high priority to the Allies, and they went to great
lengths to protect it. The Ruhr was one of the most heavily defended
parts of Germany, with thousands of heavy anti-aircraft guns. It was one
of the most feared targets for bomber crews. The Germans always
welcomed them with belts of deadly flak.

The cost of the operation, in terms of men and material, was given
serious consideration. It was likely to be far greater than if the same force
was used elsewhere in Germany. However, in mitigation, it was considered that the scale of the operation was likely to decrease the scale and
accuracy of the anti-aircraft fire as the attack progressed. The large
numbers of aircraft utilized would confuse and confound enemy defences.

Operation Hurricane extended to other targets beyond the 14 October
daylight raid on Duisburg: also included were Brunswick, Berlin,
Hamburg, Mannheim (railway centre), Düsseldorf (airfield) and Cologne,
and a second and third raid to Duisburg on the evening of 14/15 October. The smaller raids involving Mosquitoes to Berlin, Hamburg,
Mannheim and Düsseldorf were essentially designed as diversionary
targets, with the brunt of the force going to Duisburg and Brunswick.
The American Eighth Air Force also supported the operation with a raid
to Cologne during the day of 14 October.

In the densely populated Ruhr area, it was estimated that, in the time
frame of twenty-four hours, some 2,500 heavy Allied bombers could be
deployed in separate raids, and saturated bombing could be achieved
with an estimated 12,000 tons of bombs. To put this into perspective, the
RAF dropped fewer tonnes of bombs during the series of raids that would
devastate and 'firestorm' Hamburg in July 1943.

Early planning for this operation had started at the beginning of
October and details were finalized only days before it was put into action

on 14 October. The Royal Canadian Air Force No. 6 Group was also involved, contributing approximately one-quarter of the operational aircraft required for the raids and supplying just over 2,100 tons of bombs in the destruction of Duisburg.

The specific directive called for the operation to be initiated at the earliest opportunity and at a time when conditions would be favourable for visual bombing but not suitable for bombing the primary oil objectives in the remainder of Germany. Winter was fast approaching, and good visual bombing days were few and far between, which was one reason to place the targets very close together and so increase the chances of success. The operation would be executed only when exact weather conditions were expected over the target areas. The weather conditions were vital. Success hinged on effective damage through accurate bombing. The crews needed to see their targets. A strong wind would be preferable to dissipate industrial smoke and haze and reduce the effectiveness of any artificial smokescreens.

The most favourable conditions would be a wind from the north, allowing the bombers to approach and attack the target from the same direction, heading downwind. This route would minimize the opposition, as the bombers would not have to travel the length of the Ruhr defences. Along with a northerly wind, a cloudless sky was needed for the best chance of success.

To support the RAF, the USAAF would bomb targets in the Saarbrücken, Cologne, Karlsruhe or Stuttgart areas, chosen from a priority list of synthetic oil plants and sixteen Benzol chemical plants in the Ruhr, attacking visually or by blind marking. The air power and bombing were to be concentrated, including attacks on the transport systems and rail networks as close to the Ruhr as possible.

One of the reasons for carrying out an early bombing raid was to coincide with the German 'rush hour', thereby contributing to the huge disruption. To assist Operation Hurricane and compound the enemies' supply problems, further attacks were made on the Dortmund Ems and Mittelland canals, on the railway viaducts near Bielefeld and Paderborn and on the Sorpe dam.

The hope was that the heavy bombing would break morale and panic the Germans into evacuating the area. Momentum would be maintained following the raids of Operation Hurricane and increased where possible, with the Allied Air Forces directing further raids to the Ruhr area, with up to 25,000 tons of bombs dropped from blind bombing efforts in the subsequent three months. With the area bombed and ground troops moving in, forward Oboe and G.H. electronic target marking systems could be installed in captured territory, giving increased range and better marking for the Allied bombers, maximizing effectiveness.

Timing was crucial. 'H-hour', the opening of the attack on the morning of 14 October, was to be around 0840 hrs. The order of the RAF and USAAF attacks would be dependent upon the location of the targets and the direction and strength of the prevailing winds. Mistiming could lead to later bombers arriving over targets that were obscured by smoke from earlier raiders or smokescreens. The estimated time the RAF allocated for both targets was approximately 20 minutes, with that of the USAAF being a further 45 minutes—that is, from H-hour to H-hour plus 65 minutes. Reality proved to be a different matter, with bombers still arriving well after the allotted times.

The massed bombers streaming over Germany in broad daylight would face not only the brunt of the sophisticated array of anti-aircraft guns but also the Luftwaffe fighters. Daylight USAAF raids deep into Germany could still suffer huge losses, as the Luftwaffe desperately tried to defend its homeland. The bombers for the raid to the Ruhr were to be escorted by a large number of fighters, supplied by No. 11 Group of the RAF, the US Eighth Air Force and No. 4 Group of the US Ninth Air Force; these generally flew top cover up to an altitude of 30,000 feet, but with No. 11 Group in close escort.

Following H-hour plus 65 minutes, the US Eighth and Ninth Air Force fighters were to be released from their escort duties to carry out ground strafing attacks on transport and other targets of opportunity. The remainder of the escort would then stay with the bombers. Areas designated to the US Eighth Air Force, after the release of escort duties, were to the east of a line from Dortmund to Munster and Achmer, and north of latitude 51.20 N. The US Ninth Air Force was assigned to stay to the south of latitude 51.20 N. The fighter screen would also provide cover for the Eighth Air Force bombers that would be heading to attack Cologne and the marshalling yards. The tactical air forces of the Allied Expeditionary Air Force were to attack any transports trafficking in the Ruhr area at H-hour, both light and medium bombers and fighter bombers.

Despite the extraordinary numbers of bombers being deployed by the RAF, there was still the capacity for No. 5 Group to carry out a raid on

Brunswick on the night of 14/15 October 1944, with 232 Lancaster bombers deployed together with 8 Mosquito fighter bombers, although 7 Lancasters were forced to abort the mission. A further 319 aircraft were also deployed on other training missions and diversionary targets in support of the main raids.

Chapter 3

Wakey, Wakey Chaps

One of the bomber stations used for Operation Hurricane was RAF Wickenby, and the events that took place there on the morning of 14 October, from the aircrew briefing to the actual raid, are representative of the experiences of many of those who took part.

A battle order was posted on the board on Friday, 13 October, detailing who was to fly the raid to Duisburg. The crews knew they were to be up early the following day, so most retired early, some at approximately 2230 hrs, to their sleeping quarters in Nissen huts spread on the outskirts of the airfield.

Rumours were already rife as to what the target would be. The fuel load was known to the ground crews and the bomb load known to the armourers. Speculation was that a great number of bombers would be taking part.

Sergeant Ernest Peter Bone, based at RAF Wickenby as a mid-upper gunner with No. 626 Squadron, was one of six sergeants in his crew headed by Flight Lieutenant Lane. Their flight commander was Flight Lieutenant Reginald Major Aldus, who would be shot down piloting Lancaster NE163.

On the evening of Friday 13 October 1944 our names were found on the battle order, as it was called, for the next day. This was the culmination of two years of training that had begun, for me, in September 1942. A training programme throughout the Royal Air Force had discreetly omitted any references to the Geneva Convention, to which Britain was a signatory. It stipulated that civilians and their property were not regarded as military objectives. Being a reasonably intelligent young man who had some experience of being on the receiving end of bombs, I knew that in the area of bombing Germany's industrial cities, civilians and their property could not possibly remain untouched, any more than had been the case in Britain's industrial cities in the Blitz. I can't recall if I had any misgivings.

At precisely 0200 hrs on the morning of Saturday, 14 October 1944, the call came in for the crews to assemble. Staff ran around waking the crews for duty and informing them to get ready for the briefing and to attend the mess hall for breakfast, either porridge or corn flakes and bacon with one egg.

Flight Lieutenant Major Aldus, the commander of 'A' flight, No. 626 Squadron, began to rouse squadron members, shouting: 'Wakey, wakey chaps. Flying meal is at 0230. Transport at 0300, briefing to begin at 0330.'

The crews dressed speedily, with little or no time for washing, and many ran to the mess, in time for their meal. It was a pitch-black morning, and the low temperatures gave a crisp, fresh feel to the air.

At the mess hall, breakfast was served. The raid was only hours away. There was apprehension. Many sat at the table just looking at each other with little or nothing to say. The odd few cracked jokes and laughed nervously.

Not long after breakfast the roar of the motor trucks and buses could be heard as they pulled up outside the mess to transport the crews to their morning briefings. The airfield was a hive of activity. Some of the trucks had drop back tails with no steps and open roofs with the tubular frames. Alternatively there were buses. Most crewmen were silent on the short journey to the briefing room. Many knew what was to come, especially the 'veterans'. For others it was their first operational sortie. Some chose to cycle across the vast field on push-bikes and avoid the trucks altogether.

The trucks ground to a halt outside a large Nissen hut complex. The briefing room filled up as the men entered, some laughing and joking, and took their places in the rows of seats reserved for each crew. Outside at the aircraft, fuel trucks were busy finalizing loads and preparing the bombers for the coming operation. As more and more crews began to fill the small space in the briefing room, some pondered their fate and wondered what lay ahead. All waited in apprehensive anticipation for the black cloth to be pulled back from the map and reveal their destination – and the probabilities of their chances of life or death. Rumours circulated about the target based upon the fuel load.

No. 626 and No. 12 Squadrons were briefed together, each squadron sitting on one side of the Nissen hut, No. 626 on the right-hand side and No. 12 on the left, with the middle remaining free. Each row had seven seats, so as to accommodate an entire crew. A briefing prior to a raid was normally the only time the two squadrons came together, as, although they shared the same base at RAF Wickenby, their living quarters, messes and dispersal were separate.

The room was full of apprehension as the airmen talked and chattered among themselves, some laughing nervously at the jokes and comments. A senior officer took stage and barked 'Attention'. Everyone stood in silence. The station commander walked in and took his seat on the stage. Sergeant Ernest Bone recalls the morning:

We had an early night and were roused from our beds at 02:30 a.m. the next morning by our flight commander. After breakfast of bacon and eggs, the standard meal before and after every operation, we trooped into the briefing room to join dozens of other crews. Although all pilots, navigators and bomb-aimers had already had a mini-briefing and knew the target, they were sworn to secrecy. The arrival of the station commander was the signal for all of us to scramble to our feet. 'Be seated, gentleman.' The station commander ordered an airman to uncover the route map on the wall. The red tape wended its way south-east in a zigzag fashion and ended in the south-west corner of a big circle. 'Bloody hell, not the Ruhr again!' grumbled the more experienced crews. 'Ok chaps – simmer down,' said the adjutant sharply. Next up was the intelligence officer. This operation, he said, marked the resumption of the bombing offensive against Hitler's armament production after six months of concentration on transportation networks, supply bases and fuel depots in northern France, under the direction of the supreme commander of Allied Forces in Europe, General Eisenhower.

Operation Hurricane, as it was called in the Air Ministry directive, was to 'apply, within the shortest practical period, the maximum effort possible, to demonstrate to the enemy the overwhelming superiority of the Allied Air Forces'.

Many knew the dangers of flying into the Ruhr in broad daylight, knowing all too well that it was one of the most heavily defended areas in Germany. The officer stated: 'today's attack against Duisburg will be the greatest raid ever on a German city' and that approximately 1,100 aircraft would be taking part in the raid, which was expected to last around 30 minutes. The attack itself would be controlled by a 'Master Bomber', instructing the bomber stream over the R/T. His code name for this particular raid was 'Big Boy', with the bomber stream itself code-named 'Thunder.'

The crews were told they would have fighter support – six squadrons of American P51 Mustangs and ten squadrons of Spitfires, all flying top cover many thousands of feet above the stream. The raid would commence at 0845 hrs, when most of the population would be getting ready to leave their homes for work and the area would be busiest. The Path Finder Force (henceforth called Pathfinders) would open the attack with red target indicators dropped by Mosquitoes; then Pathfinder Lancaster bombers would provide back-up, carrying green target indicators. These would be dropped continuously throughout the attack to help mark the target for the main force crews. The intelligence officer told crews to bomb the red flares, but failing that to bomb the green ones; he repeated the instruction more than once for emphasis. Each bomber was given a height band to fly in the stream, and ordered to fly between the heights of 16,000 and 20,000 feet, with the fighter escort flying at between 30,000 and 35,000 feet.

The Meteorological Officer then took centre stage. The blanket of cloud that currently extended over England and northern France had been predicted, but it would disperse prior to the bomber stream reaching the target, leaving good visibility over the target area itself. The signals leader advised crews of the counter-measures that were going to be in force that day. Lancasters would be deployed from No. 101 Squadron, carrying a crew of eight instead of the normal seven, the extra being a German-speaking wireless operator whose job it was to transmit false instructions to German fighter crews. 'Window' (metallic foil strips) would also be used as a counter-measure, to jam enemy radar.

Sergeant Ernest Bone continues his account:

After the meteorological officer had indicated that the weather conditions would be fair to good, brief reports came from the Bombing, Signals and Gunnery leaders. Of course, of special interest to Frank and me was the knowledge that we would be escorted by our fighter aircraft, based in France for the first time in four years since the liberation of that country just two months earlier. Finally, we had 'Good Luck chaps' from the station commander, and we dispersed, chattering as we made our way to the crew room to don our flying suits and collect our parachutes. Then it was on to a crew bus to take us out to our aircraft. Both Wickenby squadrons, 12 and 626, were on this 'maximum effort' raid, and the airfield was in top gear as dawn broke. We were flying Charlie Two, piloted by a 34-ops man, Flight Lieutenant Hicks, while our skipper was doing the mandatory stint as a 'second dickey', as it was called, on a first op.

The briefing in total lasted about one hour, concluding just before 0500 hrs. After the briefing, the navigator discussed the route with the crew, with watches synchronized.

At 0500 hrs the crews made their way out of the briefing room, collected parachutes, Mae Wests, and other equipment, including their escape packs, flasks of coffee and chocolate. The WAAF staff at Wickenby handed out the parachutes with the well-known joke of the time: 'If the chute does not work, come back and see us.' Those on duty distributing parachutes to No. 626 Squadron appeared to be in a pleasant mood, with something good to say about each crew they dealt with. The airmen, dressed in their flying gear, were quieter, locked in their own thoughts of what lay ahead. The crews made their way into the cold morning, waiting for buses to take them to their aircraft, some smoking last cigarettes, some chatting. It was still dark as the crews reached the aircraft and met the ground crew, but first light was just beginning to show over the horizon. It was rather cloudy, with slight rain, but the forecast stated that it would become fair to good as the day wore on. The general wind direction was south-westerly, with a freshening speed of 25 knots and occasional gusts of up to 30 knots, veering to the west/south-west.

The aircrew made the necessary equipment and pre-flight checks. Many were nervous and anxious; the waiting was the worst part of the deadly game they were about to play. But many were also eager to get going and get on with the job. Gradually the Merlin engines sprang to life, and once all the checks had been made, permission was granted to move the heavily loaded bombers. Slowly, one by one, the Lancasters from both squadrons taxied out and joined the queue to prepare to depart. Engines crackled and spluttered, as the huge propellers drew the bombers to the runway. A flash from the green Aldis lamp gave each aircraft the all-clear to start the take-off. Throttles were adjusted to assist with the swing to starboard as speed gathered. The tail wheel began to rise at approximately 110 mph. If there was an emergency and more power was required, the throttles could be pushed through the 'gate', a thin wire in front of the throttles. A loss of power at this stage in the take-off with a heavily loaded bomber could be disastrous. On this particular raid, there were very few people to wave them off as they passed the control tower at Wickenby. One by one the bombers thundered down the runway, Merlins roaring. Steadily they rose and gradually disappeared into the cold winter-morning air.

Once airborne, the crews turned to port, with engines set to climb power, and the aircraft were soon disappearing into low-level cloud. As the bombers climbed away, the roar of the distant engines could be heard around the Lincolnshire countryside. At around 8,000 feet the aircraft began to burst through the cloud layer and into the clear, crisp sky above. Aircraft began to make their way to the point at which they would set course for the first leg of the journey. Each navigator flew his own course to the target and back, despite being part of the stream.

Flight Lieutenant Roy Yule, a No. 626 Squadron pilot, recalls the point when they joined the bomber stream:

There were lots of bombers surrounding us and we could see more of them bursting through the cloud below. The forecast wind must have been good, as I could see as the bomber stream formed, that we were right in the middle of it and stayed there.

Sergeant Ernest Bone remembers flying over the reassuring landmark of Lincoln Cathedral:

We set course at 0630 hours, the grey slate roof and the three sturdy towers of the 800-year-old cathedral seemingly wishing us Godspeed and a safe return as we left it behind in the morning mist. We were on our way, one of 519 Lancasters, 474 Halifaxes and 20 Mosquitoes carrying 3,574 tons of high explosives and 820 tons of incendiaries to Duisburg. It was a Saturday morning; as the intelligence officer remarked, it was market day. As the minutes passed, I saw more and more bombers joining the stream. It was an awesome sight.

Derek Waterman, DFC, No. 158 Squadron, recalls his experience of the Duisburg daylight raid in his Halifax, which was named 'Friday the 13th'.

Now our twenty-six aircraft, still close together, formed only a small part of a long procession. I didn't attempt to count the black specs which appeared to cover the entire sky – each with a sting of 10,000 lb… I could now see numerous squadrons of fighters circling some few thousand feet above us, but they appeared only as small dots and I was unable to identify them. It gave one a grand sense of security – they were there to protect us – the hazard of enemy fighters would be lessened considerably.
 Tommy was now flying thirty yards or so on my port beam – we kept together and climbed slowly towards the Dutch coast. Slowly gaining altitude made it necessary for me to increase the boost periodically. As the air became thinner with height, more power was needed to maintain a steady climb.

With the entire stream forming, stretching over many miles, the bombers climbed to their operational altitude of between 18,000 and 20,000 feet. It was becoming light. The flight appeared to be routine, and many may have felt safe being part of nearly 1,000 bombers all heading for the Ruhr. Some crews, maybe wiser, maybe more experienced, climbed higher, above the altitude advised for the stream. They knew what would be coming. There was fear every time they took off for a raid; there was always a real possibility that they might not come back. After all, they were heading towards one of the most heavily defended parts of the Reich. Even this late in the war, with this many bombers, no raid was 100 per cent safe, although the loss rate would prove to be less than those suffered in late 1943 and early 1944, where some rates reached more than 12 per cent.

On this particular morning, the route was rather a simple one, with very few dog-legs. Across the Suffolk countryside, out towards Bradwell Bay, not far from Orfordness, then out over the North Sea and hitting land north of Ostend, Belgium. Flying a short distance inland, they arrived just east of Bruges, and from here the bomber stream changed course, veering in a north-easterly direction towards Eindhoven. Near Eindhoven, the bombers turned slightly further eastwards and approached the target area, arriving to the north. It was here they began to turn south-east on to a track of approximately 130 degrees, to approach the target from the north-west. Bombers were bursting out of the cloud and forming in huge numbers into a compact stream stacked up in about five layers at 1,000 feet intervals, magnificent in the bright blue sky as the sun glinted off the Perspex. The stream stretched out over a number of miles. Crewmen usually did not talk among themselves. Chatter over the intercom was only for passing and acknowledging instructions or warnings. As they drew nearer the target, some of the Lancasters climbed higher hopefully to avoid the flak concentrations. Some Lancasters were seen to be well out on the extremities of the formation. Isolation could be deadly when flying over enemy territory without the protection of the bomber stream.

Despite the seemingly accurate wind forecast, most of the bombers ended up north of the approach point, some putting this down to the winds being much stronger than predicted. The run in to the target was free from fighter attack, and no enemy fighters were seen. The wide-spread cloud, as forecast, was not ideal, and, as crews drew closer to the Dutch coast, it obscured most of the ground. In fact it continued, with

10/10th cover, all the way to the target, with layers extending up to 15,000 feet at times. The Master Bomber would need to respond accordingly.

But after the Dutch border, and as they approached the target, the cloud began to break up a little, which enabled some crews to map read up the Rhine for the last few miles, although several crews would still fail to identify the target, owing to the remaining cloud. A number of crews would report that the weather was good en route, but the visibility was poor over the target area itself. But there was some improvement as time went on, and small breaks and gaps in the cloud layers gave some crews the chance to bomb anything they could see. Many of the operational record books for the squadrons state the same thing: 'Bombed through a break in the clouds' and 'Bombing was scattered, impossible to assess results owing to the cloud'. Some of the target was visible around 0850 hrs, and a number of crews state hitting the Thyssen works and the superstructure, as it was clear of cloud.

Once they had crossed the Dutch border, the feared flak batteries opened up. The flak came up in large, dense clusters. The defences quickly obtained the direction and height of the bomber force. The flak extended into a large corridor, which stretched from the approach area up to the target, over the target and on the route out of the target area. The pilots could see what lay ahead, knowing they were about to fly right into the barrage. The flak was predicted to be moderate to heavy, mainly in barrage form, and in the debriefing many crews reported the intensity of the flak over the target area itself.

Harry Irons, of Nos 9 and 158 Squadrons, flew sixty operations during the war on many different aircraft. He enlisted at the age of 16, lying about his age, and went on to serve two tours of duty without major incident or having to bail out. On the Duisburg raid, serving as a rear gunner, he was on board a Halifax which was flown by Flying Officer Brunton, with a take-off time of 0645 hrs. He recalls his experiences:

The raid was a daylight raid, and part of our bomb load that we were carrying was a 4,000-lb cookie, and a thousand incendiaries. While on the raid I never saw any German fighters, but there was plenty of flak, and when I say plenty, I mean plenty of flak! But to me it never looked as bad as what it did of a night time as during the day all you saw was black or white puffs of smoke whereas at night it burst with an orange and red flash. The main problem was when we hit the Dutch coast that morning, as it was then they began to unleash all the flak, giving us a warm-up when we went in and again when we came back out. There were hundreds of guns firing at us in box barrage form and we had to fly through it, and there was little we could do about it. I recall there were a number of near misses we had with flak, a number of shells burst close to us and rocked the aircraft causing us to be bounced about but luckily nothing hit us directly and we scraped through. We went home with a number of holes in our bomber that morning. It was rare to go home with nothing, but if one of those shells hit you, that was your lot. We were lucky.

There were others who recorded their experiences:

Sergeant Ernest Bone: *High above us I could see vapour trails behind little black dots: our fighter escort was on the job already. There was no opposition that day of any kind until we drew near to the target, where radar controlled anti-aircraft fire became intense. I saw a bomber go down in flames and huge explosions in the sky at our height of 17,000 feet. We had heard these 'scarecrows', as we called them, were shells timed to explode to simulate a bomber disintegrating. But we later learned that the explosions were in fact bombers blowing up before they had released their bombs.*

Harry Irons: *As we approached the target there was a stream of Lancasters and Halifaxes ahead of our own aircraft and as I looked to my port side from my turret, I saw the aircraft that had already bombed the target and were making their way back in a U turn. I then saw a Halifax that was on its own as I was watching the other aircraft, and instead of going on to bomb the target he cut across and attempted to rejoin the formation of bombers that were leaving the target area and making their way back out. Then I saw just three puffs of smoke, bang, bang and bang, and the last one just went right through the aircraft and it just blew up in the sky. Why he cut short and never went on his bombing run to follow the others I do not know; maybe he had engine trouble or something. I do not know, but he just blew up, and there was an explosion and he went down. It appeared the puffs of smoke followed him with the German guns singling him out.*

Derek Waterman, DFC: *The Dutch coast gradually became clear and Reg was checking his map carefully to give Wilf a pinpoint on crossing it. Our route did not take us over any large coastal towns. Experience told us that such places were heavily defended. Naturally it was impossible to miss some of the inland towns – one of these was Tilberg and the leaders of the stream were already being welcomed by clusters of black puffs.*

From a distance they looked surprisingly harmless, but as we neared the large town, I realized they could be and were desperately unpleasant. One or two bursts appeared rather too near to be healthy, so I made a slight climbing turn to the right to skirt the town. Tommy remained on the same course. I couldn't help thinking him rather foolish, it was definitely unnecessary and he was openly asking for trouble – trouble that could be avoided. Most of the stream in front of us had crept round to the right of the town's defences, just as we had ourselves. I watched Tommy until he emerged from the cloak of lingering black smoke puffs into the comparative safety of the clear blue sky on the other side of Tilberg.

We slowly turned to Port to regain our track. I couldn't reach Tommy again, as he must have been a few hundred yards ahead and had become lost from view and added to the forerunners of the stream. Other squadron aircraft were now mixed with us as we ambled onward towards the German border.

Wilf told me that the slight deviation from track had put us a minute behind schedule and asked me to increase speed. I explained that we were now at 20,000 feet and would climb the remaining 1,000 feet to bombing height then would increase air speed to 175mph.

At 21,000 feet, I levelled out and trimmed her to fly straight and level. The engines were behaving magnificently and the occasional word from Jock assured me that all instruments were showing fairly normal readings.

Another fifteen minutes to zero hour – soon we would reach our destination and my uneasy feeling had now returned – my clothes were moist with nervous perspiration. My jaws ached through chewing gum from the very moment I had entered the aircraft.

The attack on Duisburg was opened up at approximately 0840 hrs, H-hour. Mosquito Pathfinders had released red target indicators at H-hour minus 5 minutes, with other Pathfinders releasing red and yellows. The sky markers cascaded down in brilliant colour. Continued back-up marking was maintained using green target indicators, all quickly swallowed up by the cloud. Not long after the attack opened, the Master Bomber came over the VHF radio informing crews to bomb the red target indicators. Subsequently the order came to bomb any built-up area owing to the cloud. With the markers disappearing into cloud, the attack plan was breaking down. The Master Bomber was forced to issue a freehand order a short time later. Aircraft were scattering, desperately trying to find gaps in the cloud. Smoke would also begin to cause a problem as the fires grew below.

An extract from No. 425 Squadron records explains further:

A number of crews reported hearing the Master Bomber giving 'freehand' at approximately 0850 hrs, which was well repeated throughout the raid, and the crews selected various targets for bombing. This included built-up areas, a few crews bombing the built-up area for our approach point, but a number of the crews aimed at a built-up area in between the Rhine and the Marshalling yards, the No. 4 Group approach point, with few crews actually spotting any target indicators. The bomber stream were arriving from the north of track, and, upon freehand being issued, most of the crews identified the docks and the Rhine and turned south to bomb. A few scattered fires were seen, with smoke rising up to 2,000 to 3,000 feet with a large explosion being reported at 0853 hours. The weather over the target area was four- to eight-tenths of cloud, which was drifting, and rising tops were seen from 6,000 to 10,000 feet. Despite this poor cloud cover, some aircraft reported seeing yellow and green target indicators through gaps in the cloud and bombed on these.

The crews of two aircraft from No. 153 Squadron recorded their attacks over Duisburg:

PB633: *Bombed the target at 0846 hours from 17,000 feet on the estimated position of the target, having gained a visual from the river Rhine, as no markers were seen. There was smoke rising from the target area but the bombing scattered.*

PB636: *Dropped our bombs at 0847 hours from 18,400 feet on a built-up area, but bombing was scattered and spread over a large built-up area. No target indicators were seen, but numerous bomb bursts were observed with much black smoke.*

The crew of Lancaster ME648 of No. 166 Squadron reported: 'No markers seen, Master Bomber gave freehand, bombed from 18,500 feet on an unidentified built-up area.'

First-hand accounts record how the attack almost became a shambles because of the unexpected cloud cover, with bombers unable to find their targets. Many were simply following the instructions of the Master Bomber and releasing their payload anywhere a visual was gained. Others did endeavour to get their bombs on the target as best they could, with some going around on the bomb run twice. Flight Lieutenant Blenner, flying Lancaster LM726 of No. 626 Squadron, recalls: 'We arrived over the target at 0902 hours at a height of 17,000 feet on a heading of 100 degrees at 210 mph. There was 10/10ths cloud seen over the target and a considerable amount of smoke was seen coming up from three areas north of the main dock area. We made two runs before bombing to endeavour to get accurate bombing but were finally forced to estimate an overshoot of the river and docks.' Another example was reported by the crew of LM176 of No. 166 Squadron: 'Bombed at 0847 hours from

18,000 on the estimated position of the target from visual identification of the River Rhine. 10/10 cloud covered the target area although there were breaks on the run-up. No markers were seen. Cloud made it impossible to assess the target.'

Flight Lieutenant Roy Yule, flying Lancaster PA990 of No. 626 Squadron, and Syd Stewart, DFC, pilot of Lancaster PB112 of No. 15 Squadron, are among those who recalled their time over the target.

Flight Lieutenant Roy Yule: *Our Lancaster arrived over the target at 0850 hours at 17,000 feet on a heading of 130 degrees and doing 170 mph. We found that there was about 8/10ths cloud with tops that reached up to at least 9,000 feet. Visibility was good horizontally; there were built-up areas to the north-west of the aiming point, which were obscured by lots of smoke. No markers or target indicators were seen, and we were following the Master Bomber's instructions of freehand. Stan asked for the bomb doors to be opened, flak was exploding on either side of the aircraft, I then looked down to the side of my cockpit and through a gap in the clouds I saw a thread of silver beyond which spread the dark stain of an extensively built-up city. To the right, clouds of black smoke were billowing up, but Stan had spotted a huge built-up area through a gap in the clouds and directed me: 'Right, right, steady, steady – bombs away Roy, bomb doors closed!' I gave it a few seconds to give the camera a shot before banking the empty Lancaster hard over to port to follow the rest of the bomber stream out. Once crews had dropped their bomb load, they had to fly level for a set time to ensure any hang-ups were gone and to take the target photograph.*

Syd Stewart, DFC: *We were bombed up with 13,400 lb of bombs and loaded with 1,250 gallons of fuel for the trip. The raid to Duisburg was a daylight raid and there were bags of flak. The Master Bomber told us to bomb any built-up area that we could see. We even saw one chap blow up a bridge on the river Rhine when we were bombing.*

Ernest Bone: *We dropped our bombs and quickly turned for home. The attack was still in progress. The sky was peppered with black smoke puffs, some still ringed with red, others disintegrating in the wind. Smoke trails, earthward bound, told their own tale. I looked down at a fiery cauldron slowly receding behind the turret at the rear. I knew that Duisburg was a vital Ruhr port that also produced steel, had extensive rail yards, and coking, tar and Benzol plants. I also knew that, even as I gazed down, people were being blown to pieces and burnt beyond recognition, and that among them were certain to be women and children.*

Harry Irons: *Over the target area I saw breaks in the cloud, but there was an awful lot of cloud cover, although it did allow me to spot roads and houses through the small gaps. I recall our bomb-aimer just picking a target through the break in the cloud and bombing a built-up area, the aircraft lurching upwards as the load was delivered from the bomb bay to the target. I remember telling the pilot over the intercom to put the nose down and get the bloody hell out after the bomb load had gone! It was such a relief when those bombs went, as that was all we wanted to do. To get rid of those bombs, get out and get home.*

Derek Waterman, DFC: *Reg was now giving Wilf frequent pinpoints, which he plotted on his chart – the bomb sight was ready. I could see the Rhine winding its way through the large industrial towns of the Ruhr valley. One of these Reg identified: it was Duisburg. '0825', said Wilf, as he instructed me to alter course to 087 degrees. This was our bombing direction and theoretically should bring us over the target. The Pathfinders were now being fired at – the sky was gradually filling with black bursts, and it became difficult to distinguish the difference between the leading aircraft and the lethal puffs, most of which indicated spent 88 millimetre shells.*

'There are the first target indicators,' Reg shouted excitedly, as I observed massive red cascades bursting over the thickly built-up area forming the target.

Brian, the Wireless Operator, took command of the intercom and asked me to switch on the receiver to Channel D, the radio frequency for this particular mission. As the set warmed up, I was deafened by the atmospherics through the headphones and also the attempts by the Hun jamming. These attempts were usually unsuccessful, as somehow we always managed to receive the Master Bomber's instructions. We were now in the hands of Reg. He could see the target and it was his job to give me the necessary small alterations to course to bring us steadily up to the target. 'Hello Samson, hello Samson, this is Clever Boy. Bomb the north side of the red T.I's – bomb the north side of the red T.I.s.'

'Bomb doors open,' requested Reg, as we ran up with two minutes to go. I could now see stick after stick of bombs falling from the leading aircraft. A remarkably impressive sight – the town was already covered by thick volumes of grey smoke, which formed a background for the brilliant red flares still burning and marking the target, which by this time was more than obvious.

'OK Reg, bomb doors open.'

No longer were voices calm or steady; we now shouted, were extremely tensed and tempers were short.

'Five degrees starboard,' shouted Reg. 'OK, OK – keep her there – left, left, bit more, left, left, steady, steady.'

It was now a struggle to keep the aircraft on an even keel – the slip stream from

those in front tossed us about and made it extremely difficult to fly straight and level.
My legs ached as I used my entire strength to follow Reg's instructions. The flak was
now intense and I could smell the cordite, its unpleasantly pungent smell meant that
the bursts were dangerously close. A loud bang was followed by sounds like heavy hail
pounding a corrugated iron roof. I knew we had been hit by fragments – how badly, I
did not know; it might be serious and it might not; the aircraft responded to the controls,
that was the main thing. We would have to check up later.

'Bombs gone – keep her steady, we want a good photo. A red light flashed in the
cockpit, which meant that, as the bombs were released, the camera had automatically
gone into action and was taking a photo of the area over which our stick of bombs
were dropping. The fifteen seconds until a further two flashes of the red light appeared
indicating that the photo had been taken seemed like an hour. 'Bomb doors closed'. We
were now through the worst of the flak as I made a sharp diving turn to port, allowing
the speed to build up to 250 mph.

We had descended to 17,000 feet as I straightened out and turned onto a course that
Wilf had given me for our first leg on the homeward journey. I asked Jock to check the
bomb bays; by lifting small panels, he could see whether all the bombs had released
or not.

We were now out of range of the gun fire and could still see the rest of the stream
going in amidst a heavy curtain of flak. By now the target was almost completely covered
by smoke, which was forming into spirals and ascending over the whole town. It looked
like hell. I saw a Halifax just running up on the town receive a direct hit from a shell
and burst into a thousand pieces – I didn't see any parachutes. I didn't think it was
one of our squadron; they should have all bombed by now.

'All bombs have gone,' reported Jock, after I had asked Wilf to log the time and
position of the aircraft that was hit.

After bombing, the aircrew's main concern was to exit the target area and
get home in one piece. The stream veered to port in diving turns, with
many dropping their altitude down to 14,000 feet or below, exchanging
height for speed. But there was still flak. The danger was far from over.
Only when they had crossed the Dutch border did matters calm and the
flak cease. All was quiet with the exception of the air stream and roaring
engines propelling the Lancasters and Halifaxes homeward.

Derek Waterman continued the story:

I felt safer now; we were on our way home. We still could not determine where we had
been hit, but everything seemed ok, probably a few holes in the fuselage – I hoped. We
maintained height at 17,000 feet; our cruising speed should have been 175 but we flew

at 200 mph. Everyone hurried home. 'Everyone Ok?' I asked. Everyone was and very excited too. 'What about some rations, Jock – come on, you ruddy foreigner, give the driver some chocolate, I'm hungry.' Jock duly passed round a bar of chocolate cream, which, after unhooking my oxygen mask, I quickly consumed.

Oxygen always created an awful taste in my mouth and the chocolate tasted wonderful. On crossing the Dutch coast, I again put the nose down in a gradual descent endeavouring to be at the English coast at 10,000 feet, at which height we would fly up England. The sun was shining brightly – a heavenly morning – the sea looked bluer than ever before – the foam caused by the folding waves glistened like sequins on an evening gown. We were safe now – life seemed precious.

For the victims of the bombing, with the rumble of enemy aircraft engines in the distance, the sirens gave the all-clear. The people of Duisburg emerged from the shelters and were confronted with a scene from hell. Large portions of the city were burning, rubble was everywhere, factories and homes destroyed. Many people had been killed and injured. Water, gas, electricity and telephone lines had been smashed and put out of action. Much of the city had been cut off from outside intervention.

On this raid to Duisburg, BBC reporter Richard Dimbleby flew with Wing Commander Maurice Stockdale:

I think that not only in the smoke and rubble of Duisburg, but deeper in the heart of Germany there must be men charged with the defence of the Reich whose hearts tonight are filled with dread and despair. For the unbelievable thing has come to pass – the RAF has delivered its greatest single attack against a German industrial target since the start of the war. More than 1,000 heavy bombers, more than 4,500 tons of bombs, and it did it this morning in broad daylight.

At a quarter to nine this morning I was over the Rhine and Duisburg in a Lancaster bomber, one of the thousand and more four-engined bombers that filled the sky to the north and south-east. A year ago it would have been near suicide to appear over the Ruhr in daylight – a trip by night was something to remember for a long time. Today, as the broad stream of Lancasters and Halifaxes crossed the frontier of Germany, there was not an aircraft of the Luftwaffe to be seen in the sky, only the twisting and criss-crossing vapour trails of our own Spitfires and Mustangs protecting us far above and on the flanks.

The briefing officer had described Duisburg as the largest inland port in the world and an arsenal of the Reich when he addressed the aircrews. I saw Duisburg, the arsenal, just for a moment, in a hole in the patchy white clouds that lay over the Rhine and the Ruhr. I saw grey patchwork of houses and factories, roads, railways and the dirty dark waters of the great river curving its way through the inland port. Then target indicators and bombs, HE and incendiary, nearly 5,000 tons of them went shooting down; the German flak, of which there was a good deal, came shooting up.

Duisburg, the arsenal, disappeared under a filthy billowing brown bulge of smoke. I saw no fires from our Lancaster – there was far too much cloud for that – and I had a nervous eye on the chessboard of black bursting shells that had been superimposed on our fine clear piece of sky.

But I did see the heavy bombs, cookies going down into the brown smoke, and more clouds of it pushing their sullen way up from the ground. Duisburg lay underneath the shroud – and shroud, I think, is the right word.

In case it sounds rather easy, this smashing of German targets by day, let me say at once that the pilots who are going to do it from now are taking very great risks each time they set out on such an operation. The best they can hope for is a thick curtain of bursting shells through which to fly, and the sight – the sight we had this morning – of one or two of their companions twisting down to the ground in flames and smoke. But such hazards do not affect the plans of the Bomber Command, that astonishingly versatile organization that began the war with so little and by courage and perseverance has built up today's striking force.

As we flew home this morning, and saw a tight orderly formation of Flying Fortresses engaged on their Cologne operation passing us above the clouds, I could not help but realize that, together, Britain and America can now put into the morning or afternoon sky a mighty force of bombers that spells destruction and ruin for our enemies.

In the late morning of 14 October 1944, at numerous Bomber Command stations across the east of England, transports arrived to pick up the crews from dispersals and take them back for debriefing – quite a scene, with many high-ranking officers in attendance. Crews were taken to one side and asked about the raid and what they had seen. Most questions were directed at the pilot, bomb aimer and navigator, but other crew members could make clarifications.

Ernest Bone describes the news they were given on their return:

On our return to base, we found that our flight commander Flight Lieutenant Major Aldus and his crew were missing, and in fact, they never came back. Whatever feelings we had about it were quickly doused by the news that the morning attack had not been as accurate as hoped. Bomber Harris was annoyed, and therefore every crew would have to go back in the early hours of the next morning and do the job properly. A maximum effort was ordered the same night and we were included on the battle order to go back. We did!

A few hours later, just after lunchtime, crews were released. Many made their way to the mess for eggs and bacon. However, it soon became clear ops were on again, and a battle order was issued – once again a night raid with Duisburg as the target. The first attack had not been to a satisfactory standard. A return maximum-effort trip to the same target was ordered.

Many crews who had been detailed for the dawn raid were called upon again to fly the return mission. Most had been up since the early hours of the morning and spent the afternoon catching up on much needed sleep. For this return trip to Duisburg, two attacks were scheduled two hours apart, with 1,005 aircraft, including Mosquitoes, dispatched to try and finish the job. A city that was already burning was to receive a further 4,040 tons of high-explosive bombs and 500 tons of incendiaries. Crews were told that the night raid would wipe out what was left of Duisburg. A number of diversion raids were also planned. A small force of Mosquitoes would drop 'window' during a raid to Hamburg, attempting to confuse enemy radar and draw away night-fighters. Other diversion raids were detailed for Brunswick, Düsseldorf, Heligoland and Berlin.

Flight Lieutenant Roy Yule, a pilot based at RAF Wickenby with No. 626 Squadron, states that they felt 'cheated' not having any leisure or rest time before flying on another raid in such a short space of time – quite probably a common sentiment.

Chapter 4

Good God, Not Again

Many of the crews roused in the early evening of 14 October in preparation for the return night raid to Duisburg were taken by surprise. A number felt it was unfair. A repeat raid, with the same bomb and fuel loads. Pre-flight meals were taken at approximately 1830 hrs, with briefing commencing at 1930 hrs, leading up to departures beginning at 2200 hrs.

Upon entering the briefing room at RAF Wickenby, crews could be heard saying 'Christ' and 'Good God, not again!' as the maps revealed the same target for that night. No doubt comments and feelings among other aircrews at other bomber bases were similar. Taking the briefing at Wickenby was the same intelligence officer who had supplied the morning briefing. It was said that those at Command level were 'furious' with the poor results of the earlier raid. Another 1,000 bombers were going back tonight to do it again and finish the job. They would be going back again and again until it was completed properly. The main failure of the morning raid was as a result of the poor weather and cloud cover. However, this was not the only reason. Crews had not been bombing the target indicators, some bombing false markers and others not following the Master Bomber's instructions. The crews were, once again, taken to their aircraft. Word went around that the take-off had been delayed by up to an hour. Crews stood chatting, staring at the clear skies above or running through checks once again. For many it was the waiting around that was the worst. It was a time to ponder their fate: some were possibly hoping the operation would be scrubbed for another time, while for others it may have meant simply one more sortie towards their tour. The evening was very dark and clear, with no moon and a low temperature.

Flight Lieutenant Roy Yule, DFC, of No. 626 Squadron, recorded:

No one slept during the afternoon and after an early supper we reported for briefing. It was a surprise to learn that the target was Duisburg again. Before briefing commenced, Squadron Leader Shanley, our flight commander, had taken me aside and introduced me to Pilot Officer Marbaix, who was to be our navigator for tonight's mission. Pilot Officer Marbaix had just arrived on our squadron with his crew. He had completed nineteen operations on a previous tour but his captain, Flying Officer Charland, a Canadian, was inexperienced and was to fly as second pilot in the crew of Flying Officer Campbell, who had completed over twenty sorties. We were assured that the morning's raid had been a partial success and that in terms of losses it had been tremendous, as only thirteen Lancasters and one Halifax had been shot down. Tonight's raid, another thousand plus bombers, would wipe what was left of Duisburg off the map. This was the first time that two separate thousand-bomber raids had been mounted in such quick succession, and the ground crews were sorely pressed. Our own Lancaster Roger 2 had been taken out of service to get four new engines and we had been allocated O – Oboe 2. When we arrived at dispersal, refuelling had just completed, but bombing up had only just started.

Now, at nearly 2200 hrs, we were beginning to feel the effects of the long day, as we watched dispassionately our navigator chivvying the armourers to speed up their task of loading twelve 1,000-lb bombs into Oboe's bomb bay. Gus Marbaix was anxious to get started with his second tour and did not want us to miss the take-off deadline. We did not feel like it then, but we were to thank our lucky stars that this keen bastard had been detailed as our navigator that night.

Three of the squadron's Lancasters failed to get off before the deadline, but Oboe 2 was first off, which was entirely due to Gus's prodding. It was a dark night, and no other bombers could be seen as I turned onto the first course to Reading, although I could certainly feel their slipstreams. To foil the enemy radar system, the stream would fly at 1,000 feet most of the way across France and then climb up to 18,000 feet before reaching the battle lines. There were four legs to the target and four legs back, and before long I knew we had a good navigator. His crisp requests for courses and speeds gave me the feeling that here was a good man on top of his job. Mind you, courses and speeds had to be accurately adhered to by the pilot, and the navigator had repeats of the altimeter, airspeed indicator and compass facing him, so he could easily assess the pilot's reliability.

Derek Waterman, DFC, of No. 158 Squadron, recalls his experience of the night raid to Duisburg:

Again we waited for transport – the early morning procedure would be repeated. The rest of my crew, at this time all NCOs, had been collected separately from the sergeants' mess and it was not until I arrived at the briefing room that I saw them for the first time since we had departed at lunch time.

Various guesses had been made at the target, but I think it came as a surprise to most of us to see the red tapes still forming the same shape as they had earlier in the day and showing Duisburg to be the target again. I somehow felt easier – I thought of the chaos that the second air armada within fifteen hours would bring to the civil defence squads to say nothing of the misery of the wretched inhabitants of this unfortunate city. I didn't feel sorry for them, but felt that the end of the war was surely close. After all, they had bombed our cities with no mercy.

Briefing was effected similarly to the one previous – once again to form up with other squadrons to make a bombing force of 1,200 machines. The target was any part of industrial Duisburg that showed lack of attention from the morning's effort. Zero hour was 0230, our bombing time zero + 5.

At 2314 I waved chocks away and swung onto the perimeter track, the sides of which were shown by small lights placed at intervals of twenty to thirty yards on either side. I kept a safe distance behind Tommy's aircraft as we taxied slowly round to the west side of the field, his tail light making the outline of his rear gunner visible – a queer sight – ghostlike in his two flying suits and tight-fitting flying helmet.

A green flash from the Aldis lamp was our cue to line up on the runway. I opened up the motors and rolled her into position. A long narrowing avenue of lights made up the flare path which was to guide us on our take-off run into the dark night. As I gently opened up the throttles, the four engines roared responsively into action and once again took us rapidly down the lit path and lifted our twenty-seven-ton monster into the air. Once I had left the ground, the lights of the airfield formed their regular pattern below and gradually seemed to fade into the still dark night as we climbed steadily on our course seawards.

Soon I could see moving lights all around me: the green and red wing-tip lights of other aircraft formed a contrast to the ceiling of the stars above us, a wonderful sight. After we had crossed the English coast, the stars formed the only lights in the sky – all wing lights were switched off, and one wondered how so many aircraft could possibly maintain the route, without some of them colliding. Fortunately this rarely happened.

As the bombers approached the target, they were met with the all-too-familiar defences of the Ruhr: the moderate to heavy flak as experienced on the morning raid. This time they were accompanied by searchlights and prowling nightfighters. Some bombers became illuminated by fighter flares, dropped to guide the Luftwaffe pilots in to attack. Flak peppered the sky, the orange and red flashes glowing bright. Searchlights desperately scanned for prey. From as early as 1900 hrs German nightfighters were airborne, approximately eighty long-distance fighters, patrolling a huge line across Germany, running from Hamburg to Bremen, Siegen to Frankfurt, Wurzburg to Bayreuth and along to Bodensee. All aircraft were ordered to patrol at a height of 5,000–24,000 feet. There were no attacks reported in the early evening, but the first accounts began to filter in to the controllers at approximately 2330 hrs and lasted until 0010 hrs, in consequence of Mosquitoes attacking Hamburg between 2339 hours and 2350 hours from an altitude of 21,000–24,000 feet. Following their hit-and-run attacks, the Mosquitoes departed on a westerly and north-westerly heading. This was just one of the small distraction raids designed to draw away nightfighters ahead of the large raid to Duisburg. It worked. The fighter controller vectored many fighters to the Hamburg area, where 'window' was being used to fool the controller into seeing a large force, when in fact it comprised just a handful of bombers. The attacks caused little damage and were more of a nuisance raid, but they succeeded in drawing off fighters and probably saved the lives of many Bomber Command airmen.

Further alerts were given. Approximately another twenty Mosquitoes were picked up from 2350 hrs over the Mosel and Bad Kreuznach area and were followed on radar. They then began to unleash small attacks on the Mannheim railway centre and Ludwigshafen between the hours of 0010 and 0202 from an altitude of 18,000–21,000 feet. At the same time, a handful of Mosquitoes attacked the airbases at Biblis, Mainz Flinten and Düsseldorf. These aircraft then left on a westerly course out of the Ruhr, heading home. The first wave of the main force, approximately 675 four-engine bombers, began to arrive from the direction of Holland, following a slightly altered route from that of the morning raid, and were picked up on German radar at approximately 0115 hours. They were heading in the direction of the Rhine Gronau region, accompanied by approximately thirty-six Mosquitoes. Much of the city was still burning from the morning raid, lighting up the night sky and guiding the bombers to their target. Many crews did not need to navigate the last part of the route. The glow from the fires guided them in from well over 80 miles away. On the ground, many basic services were still in considerable disarray and non-operational in some areas. Pathfinder aircraft had been assigned to the raid, marking the target with red target indicators, backed up regularly by green target indicators.

The main bomber group then split up into two smaller groups, with one group, consisting of approximately 440 heavy bombers and

20 Mosquitoes, heading further south towards the direction of the Rhein– Westphalia industrial area. The main stream then attacked the area of Duisburg at 0124 to 0150 hrs from an altitude of 15,000 feet, departing on a westerly course out of the target area, their loads causing further damage, destruction and turmoil to the already burning town. More incendiary bombs poured down from the skies and hit buildings, splashing brilliant colours of white as the magnesium began to burn, soon changing into red and orange glows as the superstructure of buildings were set alight. Buildings were collapsing and transport systems and rail links thrown into further chaos. Within a matter of minutes the emergency services were again overwhelmed.

Some of the aircrews recalled the raid:

Derek Waterman, DFC: *Once again we crossed the Dutch coast. We were greeted with familiar star-like bursts, which abruptly trailed into puffs of grey smoke, which floated past one's wing tips with incredible rapidity. Again we were being fired upon. One or two searchlight beams added their doubtful beauty to the official welcome. I told Wilf, our navigator, I was altering course temporarily to starboard to evade the far-reaching beams of those dangerous lights. To be coned in perhaps half a dozen merging streams of lights was a nasty experience, a blinding one that made it extremely difficult to read the instruments on which one relied so desperately at night. We managed by this slight alteration of course to dodge their beams, and subsequently turned back on course allowing for our slight deviation.*

Far in the distance, a red glow appeared. I checked our position with Wilf, who informed me that we were 150 miles from Duisburg. Yes, it was the target, still burning furiously from the morning attack. As we flew on, the burning town portrayed by the glow became a lit carpet of flame against a dim horizon, gradually increasing in area until the winding Rhine showed its shape separating the two sections of the town.

Already the town was outlined by a ring of searchlights whose beams slowly waved up and down, and seemed to indicate helplessness in their feeble efforts to embrace the leading bombers that had already entered the target area. I felt very safe; gunfire was heavy but inaccurate. As we lined up on our bombing run, I looked down into a hell of burning ruins. For the first time I pitied the people below – for the first time I realized fully the misery and utter destruction that air bombardment could create.

My thoughts were quickly interrupted by Wilf, who gave me our bombing run course. Tonight we were going in on a heading of 065 degrees. I slowly banked and straight-ened out on the given course. The fires below turned night sky into day and one had little trouble in seeing the masses of aircraft slowly rolling in towards the blazing inferno, which only a little more than half a day ago would have been Duisburg, a large and important inland port. Tomorrow it would be a graveyard. The outgoing roads would be crowded with thousands of homeless people.

Reg asked me to turn onto 070. He had already picked out his target, a group of factories on the south side of the river. The flak was now a little more accurate but could not be compared with the intense barrage we had encountered during the morning's run over the same area and it in no way affected our run-up.

As we bombed, new fires were starting up in previously untouched patches of the town – the inferno grew larger and larger, and, as we turned and dived away from the target area having taken our photo, a large curtain of dark grey smoke ascended slowly over the town. Still the bombers were going in and still more fires were being started. Two aircraft went down in the target area, which I asked Wilf to log – I was sure they were bombers. I turned my head back into the cockpit; blazing aircraft falling from the sky were unpleasant sights.

Yet again 'Friday the 13th' was behaving magnificently. We flew on fast towards the coast. On either side, a few flak bursts appeared to be reminding us that we were not alone on our way westwards. A few scattered searchlights rose to the occasion to show there was no ill feeling.

Flight Lieutenant Yule: *Gus had navigated us dead on track and time, and the target appeared dead ahead. A Ruhr target was always heavily defended, and this one was no exception. The target indicators were dropping beautiful heavy blooms of red and green flares but above them was the deadly sparkle of unleashed flak. Stan then took over; bomb doors were open, left, left, steady, steady, bombs away. The Lancaster lurched upwards as over five tons of bombs left its belly.*

The bomb doors had hardly closed when a searchlight swung onto us. The cockpit was as bright as day. I turned the now empty Lancaster sharply to port and dived steeply. I had seen the deadly result of being coned during the Frankfurt raid and was desperate to avoid that. Our speed was now over 300 mph as I pulled hard starboard and left the beam behind. We had lost over 2,000 feet but were now in welcome darkness. Gus gave me a course of 285 degrees to steer as we regained lost altitude.

The crew of Lancaster NN718 of No. 300 Squadron: *We arrived over the primary target and attacked from 19,500 feet, releasing thirteen 1,000-lb general-purpose bombs and two 500-lb general-purpose bombs at 0143 hours in poor visibility, the target being identified by the concentration of red and green target indicators. The bombs were released in the estimated centre of these target indicators and the markers were well concentrated and appeared accurate in relation to the northern aiming point. The glow of many fires burning could be seen. However, heavy flak was bursting between 15,000 and 22,000 feet and two cones of about thirty searchlights on each side of the target were seen and attempting to cooperate with the anti-aircraft fire.*

Ernest Bone: *At 01:30 am we were over Duisburg again, our first night op. I recorded in my diary later: 'Duisburg 2. Took off at 1030 pm got over the target at 0139 hrs. Scarecrow went up just in front of us. Impossible to keep up the search over target. Whole sky lit up with flashes and flares. Bags of flak and searchlights, effective but few in number. Down below, Duisburg, an inferno. We weaved to avoid search-lights and turned for home. Got back at 0430 am. Interrogations, meal and bed. Very tired. First two ops done: day and a night. Slept until 2pm. In the evening wrote home.' We had been part of another 1,008 bombers to attack one city twice in less than 24 hours. Altogether, approximately 2,000 bombers had dropped nearly 9,000 tons of bombs on Duisburg, for the loss of 21 aircraft and crews. There must have been incredible scenes of destruction and carnage down there in the streets, as the fireman and civil defence workers did their best to cope with what have must seemed like Armageddon.*

The crew of KB776 of No. 419 Squadron: *Bombed at 0149 hours from 21,000 feet. The target was identified by red and green Wanganui flares, and we bombed the centre of the red and green target indicators and noted that the whole area was burning with concentrated fires around the centre of the target indicators. Best attack ever seen.*

The crew of KB722 of No. 419 Squadron: *Clear outside the target with two-tenths cloud with thin tops up to 14,000 feet. On the run-up to the target we saw red and green target indicators going down at 0126 hours, then Wanganui going down in red with yellow stars. The target was seen from a large distance and we bombed the centre of the glow on a cloud of green and red target indicators and saw that good fires had taken hold, with the glow seen for nearly 100 miles from the target. A very good concentration of bomb bursts was observed, and it looked like a very successful attack.*

The crew of ME746 of No. 166 Squadron: *Bombed at 0849 hrs from 18,000 ft on the aiming point. No markers seen, but a good deal of bombs fell on the northern part of the steelworks. Aircraft sustained damage to the starboard main plane from heavy flak.*

Flying Officer Legault and crew of No. 425 Squadron: *Overshot 1 second on the red and green target indicators, which were seen cascading down at 0125 hrs. Target was very well marked, sky marking also accurate. Numerous large fires were seen, also two explosions seen to starboard at 0140 hrs. Huge fires in the target area, which was seen on the homeward trip; excellent attack, best yet.*

Another key target for the Allied bombers was Brunswick (or Braunschweig), housing many war production plants: tanks, munitions, aircraft and precision instrument factories, together with a large railway centre and other research facilities. RAF Bomber Command's No. 5 Group sent 232 heavy bombers to the target on the night of 14/15 October 1944.

Brunswick had long featured as an RAF target, and through 1944 many attacks were launched in an attempt to put the military installations and factories out of action. To date they had not managed fully to complete the task. However, on the night of 14/15 October the RAF finally succeeded in blasting and burning most of the city and industrial targets to the ground. The attack by No. 5 Group was the worst raid on the town of the war, with a long-lasting effect on its landscape.

The stream of bombers began to near the target at approximately 0150 hrs on the morning of Sunday, 15 October. The air-raid sirens warned people to take shelter. The first aircraft to arrive were Pathfinder Mosquitoes, which marked the target with flares and brightly coloured target indicators. The main aiming point was the city's medieval cathedral. A red flare was to mark the main aiming point. Green flares were also to be used, the red being the Master Bomber's aiming point. The flares slowly floated down to the ground, burning for approximately ten minutes; they were replaced at regular intervals by the Mosquitoes.

Bombing was further assisted by the weather; any cloud on the way to the target had cleared, enabling good visual bombing of the target, with the assistance of the target indicators. The bombers equipped with 'cookies' unleashed their loads at 0220 hrs – huge blasts and shock waves tore buildings apart, destroyed walls and large superstructures, and blew out windows to make way for the incendiaries. The broken walls and smashed windows would allow plenty of ventilation for the fires that would come after.

The high explosives, followed by incendiary bombs, caused horrendous damage. The fires spread very quickly as the incendiary bombs rained down. The brilliant white of the exploding bombs rapidly turned to bright red as the wooden structures and the timbers of the historic town were set on fire. Soon the entire city was ablaze, with emergency services overwhelmed. House after house and building after building were set alight, burning ferociously. Factories and warehouses were engulfed in flames, as the bombers continued to pour their loads into the city centre. The red and orange glow from the fires lit the way for miles around.

Buildings were collapsing and crashing to the ground. Brunswick was in chaos.

The situation was made worse by the type of buildings in the town. Many were constructed of wood and stone, dating back as far as medieval times. This, combined with the typical structure of narrow streets, made easy work for the fires. The heart of the blaze took hold at the city epicentre, the cathedral and the historic town. Rescue crews and emergency services were hampered by the intensity of the flames and embers. Roads were almost impassable, owing to unexploded incendiaries and bombs littering the streets. Many water mains had been blown open at the start of the raid, and fires, aggravated by fierce winds, could not be controlled. The town was utterly devastated. By 0247 hrs the bombers were turning for home. In just twenty-seven minutes the city had been annihilated.

The attack went very well for the RAF, with a total of just one aircraft, a Lancaster, ME595, lost over the target area to anti-aircraft fire. However, another bomber was lost without trace en route to Heligoland, seen to be diving into the sea in flames. This aircraft was part of over a 100 aircraft on a training exercise. Everything appeared to be in the Allies' favour for this particular raid: excellent target marking by the Mosquitoes, clear weather and accurate bombing. The objective was met with an extremely low loss rate.

A brief report was compiled by the German authorities regarding the attacks on Brunswick, but, as many of the services were in disarray, it was difficult to surmise the full extent of the damage done. They record the warning sirens sounding around 0120 hrs local time, with the attack beginning not long after. The report heads the summary with 'Extensive and horrific attack on Braunschweig' and estimates that it received approximately 650 high-explosive bombs, 200,000 incendiaries and 10,000 liquid accelerant bombs, which all contributed to most of the city being burnt to the ground. One interesting point to note is that, even though the city's historic cathedral was the main aiming point, it remained untouched by the fire or bombs and was still standing after the raid was complete. Industries and factories such as the Wilke Works shipbuilders, Niag armoured vehicles works, Bussing NAG and the Bussing Aircraft Engine Works were heavily damaged. There was extensive collateral damage, with hundreds of buildings destroyed and many more in various states of ruin.

Hamburg also received hits between the hours of 2320 and 0100, after it was targeted by approximately fifteen Mosquitoes, according to German reports, but the damage was minimal. Approximately forty-two explosive bombs were delivered, including five shipping mines. The North German Decorative Stone works was the only factory that was hit, and that was slight, although areas that included Einbeck, Hohenfelde, Wilhelmsburg, Niedergeorgswerder in the docks received damage to a small number of dwellings. There was no disruption to traffic or any services. There were six civilian casualties, with a further seventy-five injured.

As the last of the Brunswick bombers were heading home, a third group of approximately 330 heavy bombers began to arrive over the Dutch border, lumbering towards their target, arriving from the direction of Amsterdam and Zwolle, heading in an easterly direction before veering south to their main target – Duisburg again. The bomber stream was detected at approximately 0310, dropping their bombs on the already blazing and ruined city of Duisburg from 0320 to 0330 hours from an altitude of 15,000 feet. The aircraft were clear of the area from 0400 hrs, with nightfighters still trying to pursue the last of the bombers. A handful of other bombers and aircraft were picked up on German radar, but they did not play a significant part other than attempting to divert German resources and aircraft away from the main streams and confusing the controllers.

The weather contributed to the success of the night raids, rather than being the hindrance it had been to the morning raid. Much clearer conditions prevailed, with only zero to three-tenths cloud at approximately 1,000 feet over the Duisburg and Brunswick areas. Visibility was reported as more than 10 kilometres. But it meant that the German nightfighters were not hampered by weather either and were airborne in force to greet the intruders. Generally the conditions for bombing were excellent. Crews were able to see the objectives and target indicators clearly and reported the target could be seen ablaze up to some 80 miles away, with the glow lighting the night sky from even further.

Roy Yule, DFC: *Oboe's wheels touched the ground just after 0400 hrs. At the debriefing Gus kept looking round for his skipper, but ominously all the other Lancasters had landed except the one flown by Flying Officer Campbell. By the time we had breakfast and got back to our hut we had been twenty-eight hours without sleep and had been in the air for more than ten and a half hours. Later that day it was confirmed that Flying Officer Campbell and crew, along with Gus Marbaix's pilot, Flying Officer Charland, had all been killed over Duisburg. Rather than returning to the OTU with a headless crew, Gus asked me if he could stay as our navigator. I felt like jumping into the air and shouting 'yippee' but constrained myself to: 'We'd be delighted to have you Gus.'*

Slightly fewer aircraft were lost on the night raids to Duisburg and Brunswick compared to the daylight raids, perhaps because of the cover of darkness, but also no doubt as a result of the defences being smashed during the morning raids. Other aircraft were damaged and some were written off and crashed back at their bases. Overall these were a fraction of the force dispatched, and the losses were more than acceptable for Bomber Command. A number of the flak batteries had been destroyed earlier, with many of those manning the guns killed or wounded. Nevertheless the remaining flak batteries were active and still packing a punch. Searchlights were operating but it appeared not to great effect. Many crews in fact reported them being of small or no effect at all.

Despite their considerable efforts, the German nightfighter units achieved little. It appeared the diversion raids to towns north and east such as Hamburg, and the large amounts of window used, had confused the fighter controller into thinking the main target was actually Hamburg. Many fighters were sent away from the area of Duisburg and the central Ruhr area.

The aftermath of the night attacks left the city of Brunswick in ruins, with 90 per cent of the old city destroyed, and the industrial sector of Duisburg was desolate. Many industrial buildings were destroyed. Numerous crews reported the night attacks had been productive – a combination of good weather and accurate marking. It was far more successful than the first daylight raid. The cumulative effects of all the raids to Duisburg were simply devastating. Almost half of the largest and most important industrial targets had been hit, with vital machinery and production lines smashed. Many were temporarily put out of action, some destroyed completely. Large sections of the transport network and rail utilities would remain silent, with no movement possible. Public services were ruined and out of action, including the Thyssen gas and water works, and two gas-driven power plants. In addition to those killed, many thousands were left homeless. A further 4,040 tons of high-explosive bombs and a further 500 tons of incendiaries had been dropped onto Duisburg alone – a 'whirlwind' attack.

For RAF Bomber Command, the raids encompassing Operation Hurricane I had been a complete success in terms of acceptable losses sustained and the destruction caused. The RAF had met its objectives, delivering a mighty blow to the enemy. But in one respect the operation could be viewed as a failure: it apparently did not affect enemy morale. There was no break in morale, no mass panic and not nearly as many enemy casualties when compared to other raids such as that against Hamburg in 1943. Considering the amount of heavy bombers dispatched to the target area, and the strength of the Ruhr defences, the RAF Bomber Command casualties were extremely low. Less than 1 per cent of the bombers failed to return – a more than acceptable loss rate for the RAF.

The raids on the town are still considered by the Germans today as the worst raids on Duisburg of the entire war. Although Duisburg had been subject to previous air attacks, this operation was the most devastating in terms of damage caused, casualties and tonnage of bombs dropped. It is marked in the town's history and still remembered by many as one of their darkest moments. After the war almost the entire town had to be rebuilt. Nearly every cemetery in the area has the graves of those killed during the three heavy raids.

Chapter 5

The Destruction of Duisburg

At the time, the industrial city of Duisburg, located in the western lowlands of the Ruhr area adjacent to the river Rhine, was one of the largest river ports in Europe, if not the largest. It produced heavy machinery, and housed many industrial works, such as Benzol plants, oil-processing plants and factories producing other war materials. Its docks and rail yards were vital communication centres. Today the city is still an important industrial centre, especially steel production.

As a major logistical centre, with production plants for steel, iron, chemicals and coal mines, the city was a prominent target and was attacked numerous times. The attacks of 14 and 15 October 1944 were the heaviest raids on the city, with a total of 2,589 sorties flown and approximately 9,000 tons of bombs dropped in a period of less than twenty-four hours – a record amount of bombs never exceeded in the war over such a short period. The town and surrounding areas were hit hard and industrial plants suffered huge amounts of damage with some areas being completely demolished. This city was truly reaping the seeds of Sir Arthur Harris's 'whirlwind'.

A total of 3,574 tons of high-explosive bombs were dropped on to the target in the first raid and on top of this a further 820 tons of incendiaries. Bombing took place between 0838 and 0911 hrs and was rather scattered, owing to the conditions over the target, although it did appear to be concentrated around the docks itself. Many fires and explosions were observed, with a considerable amount of smoke over the target towards the final part of the attack. This seriously hindered accurate Allied interpretation of the results of the raid.

Damage was widespread, and was particularly severe in the built-up areas within and to the east of the Thyssen Steel Works, north and west of Ruhrort, Beeck, Lar and Stockum. Severe damage was also caused to the industrial plants to both the north and the south of the main docks. Most of this was because the poor weather caused many bombers to drop their bomb loads on the areas that happened to be visible through the breaks in the cloud.

Many barges and boats were also destroyed and sunk in the docks, which caused blockages to transport movements. As crews were turning for home, smoke from the burning steel works and industrial areas was reaching heights of up to 6,000 feet, with thick blankets of heavy smoke covering a wide area. Many raging fires were visible through the gaps in the clouds and smoke. Flying Officer McKinnon and the crew of No. 425 Squadron recall the results:

Target visually identified by a canal, cloud 6/10 tops at 8,000 to 10,000 feet. Attack scattered to fairly well concentrated, bombed on master bomber's instructions, who gave freehand at 0840. Saw explosions and fire with red and black smoke up to 6,000 ft. Results not observed due to cloud. A fair attack although bombing well scattered.

The following report describes the extent of damage to the Duisburg sector, particularly the main district's railway and transport systems. It was compiled by the German authorities on 15 October 1944, following the three heavy raids. It has to be appreciated that this German report is somewhat incomplete, figures may not be exact, and there is no 'Final Report' because of the intensity of the raids and the disruption caused to the civil services.

Ruhort 'Hafen neu' (New Harbour Station)

The railway buildings and the offices were hit by bombs and partially de-molished, together with the train drivers' workshops. The main railway lines, which exited to Oberhausen west, were destroyed, and the railway junction at Mathilde, together with the Duisburg railroad and Central Styrum, were useless, as they had been completely blocked. The station warehouses numbers one and two were wrecked, with three operatives killed. The port railway and Kaiserhafen station number three, as well as the north and south harbour areas, were obstructed owing to bomb damage. Six dud bombs that failed to explode were found in the harbour basin C sector.

Duisburg Ruhrort (Ruhr Place)

Extensive devastation was caused through direct bomb hits. Operations and connections to Meiderich and the new harbour station were impossible, as tracks had been destroyed owing to bomb damage.

Sterkrade

Numerous incendiary bombs fell, which resulted in many fires, including on a munitions train, although several were extinguished.

Hamborn

This area received extensive railroad track damage from the bombing, with all operations being suspended, as movement was impossible. The waiting room for the third-class passengers and the station master's flat were partially burnt down and destroyed.

Walsum

The station buildings at the railway yard were severely wrecked by bombs and fire, with track number 2 in Walsum being interrupted. The tracks between Walsum and Hamborn were also damaged and interrupted, making transport difficult.

Duisburg Meiderich North

This station was completely destroyed, as parts of an Allied bomber came crashing through the roof; it also received a direct bomb hit, which caused one train shed to be demolished completely.

Osterfeld South

The railway tracks between Hamburg-Nenamel, Sterkrade and Oberhausen Central Station were completely blocked, because of bomb damage.

Oberhausen Central Station

This railway station received many multiple hits from bombs, and the railroad tracks were damaged. The platform run-offs were damaged, with the railroad tracks from the Central Station to Osterfeld South and Sterkrade to Oberhausen Central Station being completely blocked by damage and debris. The new staff kitchen was also severely damaged. The canal bridge near to Oberhausen also received a hit, and post 18 was destroyed by it.

Oberhausen West

Many bomb hits were received to this area, with the added problem of dud bombs that failed to explode. Multiple strikes were noted on the long-distance and highland tracks near the junction of the Ruhr valley and at 1.4 kilometres distance along the stretch to the Mathilde railway junction. The railway connections to the Thyssen Hutte 3 were destroyed, while the service to Hamborn was made impossible. Three furnaces at the Thyssen Hutte were also hit.

Duisburg-Beeck

The railway bridge after the Baerl junction was damaged and unusable for a number of days following the bombing.

Central Station, Duisburg

Railway tracks to and from the central Duisburg railroad station to the Ruhr Place and Oberhausen were damaged by bombing, which in turn also destroyed a number of railway wagons on the tracks.

Eppinghofen Centre

The main block was hit by incendiary bombs, which caused multiple fires; these were quickly extinguished, but vital cables were destroyed.

Wadau

This area received bomb damage, and many tracks and buildings were damaged. Explosive bombs were found that failed to detonate on the run-off tracks on this line.

RA Works at Duisburg

Direct hits from bombs were received on the works; as a result, access to and from the works was blocked and the carpentry works were severely wrecked.

Essen Central Station

The area was hit by incendiary bombs, and numerous fires were ignited. Many railway wagons were set alight, but these were extinguished immediately. The P block at point D2146 was hit by incendiary bombs, causing one railway wagon to be destroyed and a further seven to be damaged, with one passenger being injured.

Steele Central Station
Only glass damage was observed here, with many windows being blown through, because of pressure-waves from nearby bombs. Steele South Station and the reception buildings were also hit by incendiary bombs; the cable cupboard was burnt out. All fires were quickly extinguished.

Kazernenberg North
Railroad tracks nine to eighteen were completely destroyed by bombing.

Duisburg main line railway station and surrounding area
Numerous explosive and incendiary devices hit this station and its surrounding lines, causing large amounts of damage. The Central Station itself was burnt to the ground, and there was severe bomb damage to the station buildings on the east side of the station. The urgent deliveries warehouse was completely destroyed, as well as the works kitchen buildings, together with the goods transfer hall next door, which was hit with both explosive bombs and incendiary bombs. The main deliveries warehouse was destroyed; however, the dispatch warehouse fared a little better, although it was severely damaged and partially demolished.

The platforms themselves were hit. The roofing over numbers five and six was smashed by bombs, with the service platform at number six being completely burnt out. A number of the fires resulting from incendiary bombs in the waiting rooms by the platforms were extinguished, although the neighbouring officers' office was damaged by air pressure alone, and further bomb hits were recorded on the tracks by the platforms.

Clearing operations and fire extinguishing were completely suspended for some time as bombs were continuing to fall and explode, and this included the rescue of the service personnel who were trapped and possibly killed at Heide Straße in their accommodation.

Matters were made worse by the water storage pool in the vicinity of the transfer hall being bombed and completely emptied. The reports from the city were that there were severe surface fires and very severe bomb damage. A fire engine belonging to Duisburg main line station was also destroyed in the process, although no station personnel were reported as being lost. The fire crews struggled to deal with the overwhelming number of fires being generated and were thinly spread all over the area of the town and the nearby surroundings.

Numerous railway tracks had to be closed and shut off because of the large number of bomb hits and dormant unexploded bombs that lay nearby. Neighbouring areas reported having to close lines, listed below as extracted from German reports.

Reich Rail Services: Munster
The stretch of railway running between Osnabrück and Lohne was closed between Westerhausen and Twistringen owing to bomb damage.

Reich Rail Services: Cologne
All the railway services in and around Cologne had to be suspended, and transport was maintained by the use of cable cars.

Reich Rail Services: Hanover
Rail damage was reported in the region of Brunswick; however, at the time of writing the reports, the extent of the destruction was not yet known.

In addition to the above there is another summarized general report detailing the chaos caused by the raids of 14 and 15 October – documented in German records for Duisburg and its surrounding areas. It provides a further example of the sheer scale of the damage caused on the raids:

The exact number of victims of the three attacks on Duisburg is unknown, but it is estimated that more than 3,000 people were killed as a result. Many of the deaths from the night attacks are thought to be attributed to the failure of the general alarms, a number failing to go off after having been destroyed in the first strike. The night raids are thought to have killed more than 1,000 people, although early figures were estimated between 484 and 640 people dead. Approximately 95 of these people alone suffocated to death at a shelter located at No. 31 Schöppenstedter Straße.

Duisburg town
Bombers were over Duisburg between 0848 and 0903 hrs, with approximately 2,000 general-purpose bombs, 40,000 incendiaries and 1,100 high-explosive bombs dropped. Substantial damage to 2,000 homes was confirmed, with a further 528 destroyed or burnt out. It was established that 92 persons were dead, together with a further 220 persons injured. Commercial and utility sectors, including the docks and ports, were hit, a countless number of warehouses, stores and docks were substantially

damaged, with 25 barges and ships sunk. The transport system, which included rail and road networks, was seriously disrupted along with the steel works, which now lay silent, together with severe damage to residential utility buildings. Many supplies were disrupted.

Oberhausen

Bombers were present and recorded overhead between 0842 and 0915 hrs, with an estimated 700 general-purpose bombs, 35 mines, 10,500 incendiaries and 800 high-explosive bombs being dropped on the town. The main rail and road networks were left severely damaged, with the main rail links to Wesel, Mulheim and Gelsenkirchen disrupted and destroyed. However, no new industrial damage, other than the transport system, was reported. It was confirmed that a total of 21 houses were destroyed in the area, with approximately 2,300 homes damaged, and other buildings also severely damaged; 16 people were reported killed, with a further 21 injured.

Molheim/Ruhr

Bombers were present overhead between 0842 and 0915 hrs, with 455 general-purpose bombs and approximately 1,500 incendiary bombs dropped within this area alone, causing substantial damage to the industrial works. A great deal of havoc was caused to the Deutsch Eisenworks and Deutsch Rohrenworks, although no loss in production resulted; the ammunition work hall also suffered hits, together with the munitions storage magazines. The road and rail networks were severely disrupted, especially the links between Gleis and Gebauscheden. This resulted in 12 houses being completely destroyed and 230 damaged or burnt out; a total of 21 people were killed, with a further 64 injured.

Dinslaken

This town is situated north-west of the main target area, and bombers were overhead between the hours of 0845 and 0930 hrs, with the town receiving no less than 100 general-purpose bombs, 2,000 incendiary bombs and 180 high-explosive bombs. Two main factories in the town, which included the rolling mill works and the tubing works, received hits, causing damage but no loss of production, while a number of civic buildings were also struck. A four-engine bomber came crashing through the roof of the rolling mill at Thyssen Strasse. The rail networks were disrupted, and the main railway station was damaged. In total, 8 houses were completely destroyed and 250 more damaged; 26 people were killed, 23 of whom were in an air-raid shelter in Hiesfeld, taking refuge from the bombing, with 21 injured.

Moers

Bombers were reported overhead between 0858 and 0918 hrs, with hits received from 52 general-purpose bombs and 100 incendiary bombs. There was no industrial damage reported in this sector. Only a small number of dwellings were hit, with 2 houses destroyed and a further 85 damaged; 11 people were reported injured, with no loss of life reported in this district.

Reinhausen

Aircraft flew overhead the area between 0850 and 0912 hrs, with hits being received from 35 general-purpose bombs, which destroyed 8 houses and left 60 more damaged, and injured 5 people. Railways here were also damaged, with the main lines between the areas of Duisburg Moers and Krefeld being disrupted because of bomb damage and unexploded bombs.

Camp Lintfort

Aircraft bombed this town between 0845 and 0855 hrs, with it receiving approximately 7 mines, 17 general-purpose bombs, 3,700 incendiaries and 300 high-explosives, which caused heavy damage to the carpentries works facility and light damage to the welding factory, together with a small amount of damage to the ammonia factories. Despite this damage by the bombs, no loss of production was reported. In residential areas, 7 houses were reported as being completely destroyed, together with a further 12 damaged; 4 people were killed.

Düsseldorf

In this district no industrial damage was received to factories, although the Düsseldorf road and rail networks to the nearby town of Duisburg was severely disrupted and damaged, with lines broken. There was also substantial damage to the signal tower at Düsseldorf. In total, 30 houses were struck with none completely destroyed; 4 people received injuries but no deaths were recorded.

Essen

Essen received hits between 0848 and 0906 hrs, resulting in the metalworks being substantially damaged and several ammunition storage facilities being destroyed, with 17 houses demolished or uninhabitable and 980 houses being damaged. This resulted in 2 persons dead and a further 22 injured. In total, approximately 2 mines, 300 high-explosive bombs, 5,500 incendiaries and 82 general-purpose bombs were dropped on the district.

Bottrop

Bottrop escaped with no damage to any industrial targets or transport systems, but instead to residential areas, with 6 houses destroyed and 210 houses struck, which resulted in 15 people wounded although no deaths were recorded. Bombers dropped bombs between the times of 0846 and 0912 hrs; these comprised 35 general-purpose bombs, 65 high-explosive bombs and 400 incendiary bombs.

Krefeld

The weaving mill works were heavily damaged by the bombing, and the factory works were laid silent afterwards. No transport systems were effected, but residential areas reported 110 houses hit and 6 completely destroyed or burnt out. Bombs were received on this district between the hours of 0847 and 0911 and consisted of 47 high-explosive bombs. This resulted in 15 people losing their lives and a further 21 being injured.

München-Gladbach

Bombing was noted here between the hours of 0902 and 0910 with only eight high-explosive bombs being dropped, which devastated the weaving mill works causing it to cease production and lie silent. In total, 21 persons were killed, with a further 12 injured, while 3 houses were destroyed and 20 damaged. No damage was caused to any nearby transport systems.

PART TWO · THE LOSSES

Chapter 6

The Search for the Missing

When airmen failed to return from raids, and were reported as missing, the RAF began to liaise with other countries and agencies, initiating enquiries to locate the whereabouts of the missing airmen and finally put to rest those who had lost their lives. This was carried out in conjunction with the Imperial War Graves Commission, which registered graves and dealt with the formalities once the men had been located. These enquiries lasted many years after the war and in some cases well into the 1950s, although not all airmen were located, and a number of still have no known graves. The investigations were conducted by the RAF's specialist investigation units, 'Missing Research and Enquiry Teams'. Many were airmen themselves and had volunteered for the detachment and posting. Information was sometimes scarce, and several of the airmen who failed to return were listed as 'Missing, Believed Killed' unless other sourced information was received via the International Red Cross Committee (IRCC) or through other sources such as the Germans or Resistance workers.

The Missing Research Section of the Air Ministry, formed in 1941, was in charge of attempting to locate airmen who were missing from air operations. A major problem confronting the enquiry teams dealing with the missing airmen from Duisburg on 14/15 October 1944 was the severity of the raids. The local civil defence and the police force were in considerable turmoil. It was many days later before the civil authorities were able to take stock of their situation. These facts help us to understand why the German records, both civil and military, which in many cases were found to be very useful and accurate, were for this period almost useless and confusing. It was revealed that far more aircraft were actually reported as crashed than had done so. The Germans recorded almost every piece of aircraft wreckage as a crashed aircraft, which added to the confusion, and they attached details of a crew to it, making it complicated to decipher and reveal who was actually unaccounted for.

Most of the missing were eventually located and dealt with. But, with regards to five particular missing aircrews, their story is rather difficult to solve. Many of these, with the exception of the KB780 crew, and a small number of individuals, are still missing today, their whereabouts unknown. Those crews that had been located were eliminated from the list of the missing, leaving just these five remaining crews: those from aircraft (serial numbers) ND805, KB780, LL774, ME748 and LM165. Most of the case documents held by the Germans included many names from these five crews, but they were hopelessly mixed up. However, in none of the documents were any crew names mentioned from LL774. Careful investigations were carried out by the Missing Research Enquiry Service teams, and LL774 failed to show up anywhere; only the other four aircraft were mentioned in any reports. This indicated strongly to the investigating officers that, although LL774 was reported missing from the Duisburg night raid, it had not crashed anywhere near Duisburg and certainly not in the target area. Possibly it came down en route to the target or on the route home – very likely in the sea. This particular case was considered closed by the Air Ministry, and neither the crew of LL774, nor the aircraft, has ever been found. Focus and attention were then given to the remaining four crews. Their story, together with the accounts of the other crashed aircraft, is told in the remainder of this book.

At this point, a general note on the recovery teams in the west Ruhr area is necessary fully to understand why perhaps some airmen were never located. From previous investigations and enquiries it was ascertained that there were two recovery teams working in the west Ruhr area during October 1944. One was from the airfield at Düsseldorf – Lohausen – and the other from the airfield at Mulheim – Essen. As a general rule all bodies recovered from aircraft crashes were taken to the north cemetery on Danizger Straße in Düsseldorf for burial. However, just before these raids to Duisburg, the cemetery at Düsseldorf was declared closed for further burials except for bodies actually found in Düsseldorf. So thereafter bodies that were recovered were sent to various cemeteries scattered over the countryside and were no longer concentrated – a problem confronting the MRES enquiry teams with regards to the missing airmen from the Duisburg raids.

All cemeteries in the western area of the Ruhr were checked and rechecked by a number of search teams for the missing crews many times over a period of years. All unidentified bodies in these cemeteries, with certain exceptions, were looked at again, and all doubtful cases exhumed and examined. The exceptions were made in cases of large mass graves containing hundreds or thousands of people from forced labour gangs or locals who had died during the war. It was obviously an impossible task to try and deal with these mass graves, even though it is not inconceivable that the bodies of missing aircrew found their way into some of these graves. The search teams also tried to locate the workers of the recovery units, who without doubt would have been able to identify where they had actually buried these airmen. A great deal of research was conducted in an effort to trace these members, but unfortunately no real successes were reported and eventually investigations ceased. At some point, probably in 1950 or 1951, the Air Ministry was advised of a report that search teams had found some members of the recovery teams, and German recovery teams stated that the responsibility for the work was in the hands of senior NCOs, who passed the reports to a higher authority through their airfield commanders. All of the German officers were then spoken to and interrogated at the airfields at Düsseldorf and Mulheim, but unfortunately none could provide any answers. They did recall signing and sending off many reports in connection with the Royal Air Force burials but could not provide definitive answers, other than that the normal procedure was to bury the airmen in the Düsseldorf cemetery. They did not recall any particular crews or cases either. In addition, officers would use anybody available to go to the scene of a crash and recover the crew. There were no particular personnel assigned to the job.

The task of locating the airmen who failed to return from the attacks on Duisburg was very difficult and painstaking. Locating the graves was only the beginning of the problem. The gruesome task of exhuming the graves and identifying the individuals was a further unpleasant obstacle. Many airmen were also found to be listed as buried in one particular cemetery, only to be positively identified by means of exhumation in another cemetery.

In most of the investigation team records, the actual crash sites were listed vaguely, as the main goal was to determine the location of the crew and not that of the crash site. In some of the reports it is noted that identifying wreckage of a particular aircraft was found on scene, and, where known, map references were noted. These areas were thoroughly searched after the war, and many enquiries were made, as it was well known that in several instances the fallen airmen were buried near to the place where they were found by the Germans. Once the airmen had been located and positively identified by the RAF investigation units, they were then moved to main Commonwealth War Graves Commission cemeteries. Many were laid to rest in individual graves, side by side with their deceased crew mates. Others were interred in collective graves, where mixed remains were discovered. It was felt that the fallen should not be left to lie in isolated cemeteries throughout Germany, but should rest together in special military cemeteries.

The Germans established a system for documenting the crashes of Allied and German aircrews, known as *Totenlisten* (Death List). Where identification could be made and names and other details noted, the information, whenever possible, would be sent to IRRC. This information was then forwarded to the Air Ministry, which would pass it on to the families and next of kin. Normally only very basic information was enclosed. An example of one report received by the IRCC reads: 'A further telegram from the IRCC quoting German information states that Flying Officer Campbell and Flying Officer Charland were killed on the 15 October 1944. Their burial particulars are not stated.' Sometimes the information was not recorded correctly and mistakes took place.

Some airmen's names did not appear on the *Totenlisten*, and the body's identity was simply recorded as 'unknown'. As such, no details were forwarded to the IRCC, and various airmen were still recorded as missing until the MRES teams were able to complete their investigations. The Germans also recorded the details regarding crashes on what were known as KU or KE reports. If a loss of the aircraft occurred over German territory, a German Kampf Flugzeuge document was prepared by the Luftwaffe. This concerned the location of the aircraft wreckage and the fate of the crew, with details of the crash if known, including the time of loss and burial details of the airman. However, these details were often confused and mixed up, so could not always be relied upon to provide accurate information.

Chapter 7

RAF Bomber Command Losses

This section of the book lists and details losses of aircraft in flight and in the target area. Heavy bomber losses on the diversion raids, with the exception of Brunswick, and write-offs such as damaged aircraft reaching base after the attack, have not been included.

No. 12 Squadron		
Lancaster NF928 PH-S		
Pilot	Flight Lieutenant Ray Lloyd Clearwater	KIA (RCAF)
Flight engineer	Sergeant William Arthur Berry	KIA
Bomb aimer	Flight Sergeant Robert Clark	KIA
Navigator	Flying Officer Henry James Watts	KIA
Mid-upper gunner	Sergeant Richard Wolsey	KIA
Rear gunner	Sergeant George Fearnley Walton	KIA
Wireless operator	Flight Sergeant Allan Selwyn Price	KIA

No. 12 squadron lost a total of three Lancasters in the morning raid of 14 October. NF928 was a relatively new aircraft when it was lost – in fact just over a month old. At the time of its crash the aircraft was approaching the target from the west-north-west with the rest of the bomber stream on a course of approximately 130 degrees true, although each bomber flew its own course to the target and did not just follow the stream. It would have been at the start of the bomb run, if it was not already on it. It is not known if the bomb doors were open or not; however, if the aircraft had commenced the bomb run, it is highly likely that the bomb doors would have been open, with the bomb aimer supplying commands to the pilot.

NF928 was then fatally hit, falling victim to the flak, and was lost at approximately 0846 hrs about 2km south-east of Dinslaken, with the wreckage falling down into a small village named Hiesfeld, known also as Hiesfelder Bruch, which is located on the outskirts of Dinslaken and Sterkrade Holten. German records recalled a '4-motored aircraft' disintegrating in mid-air, and the German report for the loss of this bomber states that the aircraft was 100 per cent destroyed. The No. 4 Flak Division claimed this bomber, and it is presumed that it caught fire first rather than just exploding straightaway. There is a very real possibility that this crew were preparing to bail out and exit the aircraft, as the exhumation reports for some of the crew members, including the rear gunner, state that parts of parachute were found with the crew's normal harness. The only person actually to wear a parachute in flight would have been the pilot; the other members wore a harness but not a parachute, so each would have had to leave his station to locate his parachute and clip it on to the harness in preparation to bail out. An eyewitness recalls finding a dead airman in the village with his unopened parachute.

Flying Officer Frank Augusta, the pilot of Halifax MZ453 who was flying close to an unknown Lancaster, witnessed what happened to that aircraft when it was hit. There is no concrete evidence to prove that this bomber was NF928, but the times and the area match up, together with the fact that a large portion of the aircraft broke up.

Flying Officer Frank Augusta recalls:

On the way to the target area, there was lots of flak, black bursts as well as white bursts, which appeared to contain phosphorus, as this could be seen from the result of the explosion. These were called scarecrows, and we were told by the RAF that they were harmless and we could fly through them, but in fact they were exploding bombers and were not anti-aircraft shells fired by the Germans.

The Master Bomber instructed 'freehand', and Flying Officer Augusta's bomb aimer spotted a break in the clouds a number of miles from the aircraft in the target area and saw what he thought was an industrial target by the river. He then instructed his pilot to fly towards this and prepare for the bomb run, when the mid-upper gunner alerted the pilot that a Lancaster and another Halifax had spotted the same target in the break in the clouds and so the three of them joined up in loose formation at about 100 yards apart from each other. The pilot then looked round and saw that both were level with his own aircraft at the same altitude. He continues:

Flying level at approximately 18,500 feet not long after the three bombers joined up together, the unknown Lancaster then received a direct hit from a flak shell with such force that it caused extensive damage to the fuel tanks in the starboard wing which immediately caught fire. A short time later, the Lancaster with the wing now ablaze, was seen to explode in a fireball. This explosion resulted with the tearing off of the starboard wing from the fuselage at the point where it joined the starboard inner engine, which in turn caused it to pitch up and roll over onto its back where it then went upside down, and quickly disappeared into the clouds below, engulfed in flames. We dropped our bombs and a few minutes later we ourselves were hit.

The pilot's account of what he saw would coincide with eyewitness reports from the ground, which stated the aircraft broke up in flight as it came down, scattering wreckage over a small area. Another point to support this fact is that the crew of the Halifax MZ453 completed their attack at 0848 hrs, two minutes after NF928 crashed, as given by the German records. The times would suggest it could have been the same Lancaster. But, of course, there could easily be some discrepancy here.

The main crash site itself of NF928 is quite small, although some wreckage fell over an area of a few kilometres, with parts of the aircraft in neighbouring streets and fields, together with remains of airmen. The original building on which part of the wreckage came down still exists, but has since been rebuilt; the premises even now contains shops, as they did back in wartime.

Some of the main parts of the wreckage, possibly still containing bombs, fell on the chemist's at No. 257 Sterkrader Straße, and twenty-three civilians were killed in the air-raid shelter situated in the basement below. This was witnessed by a Mr Alfred Semmler, who was just 9 years old at the time. Eyewitness Fritz Van Laak describes the morning raid and the destruction of his family business in Hiesfeld. Some members of his family were also killed when the aircraft wreckage and the bombs hit the chemist's.

On the morning of 14 October 1944 the sirens began around 0800 hrs but this was the short alarm and a little time later this was followed by the main alarm. To the north-west could be heard the noise of the hostile bombers approaching, together with the thundering roar of the air defence cannons. In the city of Dinslaken, incendiary bombs fell and some of these set the drug store alight together with the nearby vocational school. An enemy aircraft was also shot down by the flak and crashed here in Hiesfeld. Before it had got rid of its bomb load, it smashed into the town, with debris falling down all around the area. An entire line of houses, including the chemist and the butcher's shop, was hit by falling debris and incendiary bombs, which caused fires to start. Bright colours burst from the fires in the area. In the cellar of the chemist were twenty-three persons, who were all killed, having burnt to death after taking shelter upon hearing the air-raid sirens. They could not be rescued in time.

Large parts of the wreckage also fell into a nearby field, not far from the town centre, where a Mr and Mrs Schawitzke, recovered two bodies from the field using a wheelbarrow. They saw parts of an aircraft lying in the fields beside their home, although they did not witness the actual crash.

Another eyewitness was Mr Wilhelm Grube; a flak battery operator who was busy at the time attempting to shoot the bombers down. He noticed an aircraft falling from the sky in flames that then crashed in the centre of Hiesfeld. Later the same day he visited the crash site and also noticed a propeller lying in the front garden of a house about 2 kilometres away. He saw a dead airman, with his unopened parachute nearby, lying close to the site at Hiesfelder Straße (known nowadays as Karl Heinz Klingen Straße), not very far from his flak battery.

The bodies of some of the airmen were located at the main scene of the crash, but it is not known if they were found in the wreckage or not. It is, however, likely that they would have been contained in the fuselage of the aircraft or very near to it. Other bodies were found in a nearby field and one was found in a road.

The crew of NF928 were originally buried in a small communal grave in a small wooded area just outside the main boundary of a German cemetery called Waldfriedhof (Forest Cemetery). This is located on the outskirts of Hiesfeld, in Dinslaken itself, on Willy Brandt Straße. The cemetery is still in existence today, but is now known, not as Dinslaken Waldfriedhof, but as Park Friedhof. The communal trench in this cemetery contained a total of seventeen RAF airmen, as the bodies of two other crews from the same raid were buried there, as well as two other airmen not involved with the same raid but who died on 19 March 1945 and 10 April 1944. A cross depicting 'seventeen unknown RAF' was above the grave site, but it was to emerge that there were eighteen airmen buried there.

The bodies interred at Waldfriedhof were reburied at the Reichswald Forest Cemetery in Kleve in June 1947. It appears they had been exhumed for identification purposes on two previous occasions, by an American exhumation unit on 11 April 1946, and then again on 17 July 1946. They had to be exhumed again on 6 June 1947 prior to being moved to their eventual resting place for final concentration. Once the

plot numbers and final grave registrations had been confirmed and the
bodies reinterred complete with headstones, the next of kin were supplied
with letters giving the details. Some of the aircrew were quickly named,
but in some cases they were not identified until much later on, and so
they were still classified as missing rather than killed. The bodies had
been found because they were all in the same trench, but if there was no
evidence found on the early exhumations to suggest who they were,
assumptions could not just be made. More thorough investigations had
to take place before they could be formally identified, and the airmen were
exhumed a number of times in the process. According to the German
records, the trench that included the crew of NF928 held in total
seventeen airmen, but in fact it was discovered that the mixed grave
actually held eighteen airmen, none of whom had been buried in coffins.
The bodies had simply been covered with cloth sheeting, and the remains
of two of the crews had been mixed up, which was why a collective
trench had been used. The graves were exhumed by the No. 4 MRES
team, No. 39 Graves Registration Unit (GRU), with the witnessing officer
being Flight Lieutenant Keen.

Buried in the first grave was the body of an airman from another crew,
with no connection to the crew of NF928. This was Flying Officer
J. MacMillan of Lancaster NE163, who was named by his identification
disc.

The second grave to be examined was that of the pilot, Flight Lieutenant Ray Clearwater, who was identified by means of his identity disc
on the second exhumation; however, his tunic was located in another
grave, and this bore the rank of flight lieutenant and a pilot's brevet.
Scraps of an officer's shirt were found in the grave with him, and on him.
Clearwater had not been identified immediately after the crash, nor for
some years afterwards, and it was not until the exhumation teams began
enquiries after the war that he was formally named. His mother received
numerous letters from the Air Ministry stating her son was still missing,
even after the remainder of his crew had been identified. Clearwater was
still wearing his parachute harness together with its locking device,
numbered Mo83254, his Mae West, and white silk flying gloves. A lighter
was also found on his person. His white flying sweater was also intact.

The third grave to be opened up was that of Sergeant Richard Wolsey,
service number 1402906. He was identified on the first exhumation by
his identity disc, and this was supported on a second exhumation when
part of his shirt and tunic was found with an air gunner's brevet and rank

of sergeant. He also had on his electrically heated flying suit, under which he had a standard issue white flying sweater and flying boots. Parts of a Mae West survival vest were also located. His height and build could not be determined, although he had long wavy dark hair.

Interred in the fourth grave were the remains of Flight Sergeant Robert Clark, 1564949, the bomb aimer. Identification was by means of his clothing, as no further means of recognition were available, because of the general state of the deceased airman and the fact that he had been badly burnt. He wore his electrically heated flying suit, white sweater and his Mae West survival vest.

The fifth grave contained the body of the flight engineer, Sergeant William Arthur Berry, 1868459. His name and number on his identity disc and clothing meant he was identified positively on the first exhumation, even though there were unfortunately no further means of identification as his remains were badly burnt. Other items on his person included his parachute harness with locking device numbered M067730, Mae West survival vest, white flying sweater, oxygen mask and intercom and white flying gloves.

The sixth grave was a little larger and contained the bodies of more than one airman. The remains had been mixed, which was why a shared grave had been recommended, but this led to problems with identification. Two skulls were located in the grave, but also three blouses, one of which belonged to the pilot, Flight Lieutenant Ray Clearwater, as mentioned above. Another blouse had a navigator's brevet and the last a flying officer's rank and 'S' brevet. Small scraps of officers' shirts were also found. The navigator's brevet belonged to Flying Officer Henry James Watts, 153578. On the first exhumation the body of a badly burnt and broken flying officer with a navigator's brevet was located and was identified as Henry Watts, but there was also a flying officer with a wireless operator brevet on his clothing. Further identification proved problematic because of the effects of fire, although parts of the airman's Mae West, parachute-locking device numbered M238244 and white flying sweater were found. This was a little difficult, because of the nineteen airmen still listed as missing two were flying officers and both were wireless operators: Flying Officer R. E. Blake (RAF) from Lancaster NE163 and Flying Officer J. Lindsey (RCAF) from NG190. Flying Officer J. Lindsey was then located in a grave in Walsum in the district of Aldenrade and was positively identified there, which meant that only one wireless operator was left of the same rank; hence the body buried in the Dinslaken cemetery had to be that of Flying Officer R. E. Blake. It was recommended that a joint grave be listed for Flying Officer R. E. Blake and Flying Officer Henry James Watts, as mixed remains were discovered in the same grave with no means of separating them positively.

In the seventh grave was the body of Flight Sergeant Allen Selwyn Price, service number 1273886. On the first exhumation an officer's shirt was found with an 'S' brevet. On the next exhumation of this body, part of a service number was located on the neck collar of the shirt, which was 13881, but the number was believed to have been misread, and, as a brevet was found bearing the rank, it was enough evidence to list this as the body of Allen Price. He too was found with a parachute on and dressed in his electrically heated flying suit, under which he had his white flying sweater and shirt. It is likely that this airman was in the process of bailing out, given that he was found to have his parachute strapped on.

The last grave to be opened was that of the tail gunner, Sergeant George Fearnley Walton. On both occasions of exhumation he was identified by his identity disc. He was also found wearing his Mae West, the surviving parts of his parachute and an oxygen mask, and he was dressed in his electrically heated flying suit, under which he had his pyjamas on. George was found in possession of a lighter and a set of keys. The remains of his parachute would indicate that he too was in the process of trying to bail out.

These exhumations represented only part of the graves in the long trench at the cemetery. The graves numbered nine to fifteen contained the bodies of the crew of Lancaster JB297, while the sixteenth and seventeenth graves revealed the remains of two airmen who were not connected with the October raids.

The pilot of Lancaster NF928 was Flight Lieutenant Ray Clearwater. His story is typical of that of thousands of other airmen of the time. He was the son of John Wesley and Catherine J. Clearwater, who resided in Welwyn, Manitoba, on a farm that was owned and run by the family. It was a large family, with three brothers and five sisters. Ray, who was born on 7 September 1912, was the youngest boy; his older brothers were Robert Clinton Clearwater and Wesley Calvin Clearwater.

Ray left school at the age of 17 to work in farming, before enlisting in the Royal Canadian Air Force on 17 June 1941 in Regina, Saskatchewan. He would be killed just under five years later on active service overseas.

At his age of 28 he was older than most of the airmen being recruited at that time, but with the war gearing up large numbers of aircrew were needed, with many men being enlisted to fill the ever-increasing number of gaps. Having been born and raised on a farm, Ray would naturally have moved into agriculture, and when his father died in a farming accident in October 1935 Ray took over the farm and supported his mother. So by the time of his enlistment he had just over six years' experience running the family farm. His background on enlistment was listed as mixed tractor farming. Many of the aircrew recruited from the prairie western provinces of Canada at around this time period came from this type of agricultural background.

Ray was of a medium build, standing at 6 foot and 1 inch tall, with a confident and sincere manner. His speech was slow, but he had a self-assured and easy approach to things. When he applied to the RCAF, he expressed a desire to become a pilot and then to move into commercial flying. He was listed as 'above average material' overall by the inter-viewing officer, who recommended him as a pilot who should develop well into the position but without a commissioned rank. Ray was declared fit for active service with no medical issues, although he had to have a second medical on 16 May 1941, as the first medical had shown a tendency for slightly high blood pressure. However, this was put down to nervousness at the re-examination. Ray had a habit of smoking 15 cigar-ettes per day and consuming 1 bottle of beer a week. His hobbies included baseball, hockey and hunting.

On graduating from flight school, Ray had a short period of leave and then embarked for the UK, leaving Halifax in Nova Scotia on 8 January 1942 and arriving in the UK on 20 January 1942. He was received into the No. 3 Personnel Reception Centre in Bournemouth, where he was posted to the No. 1 Flight Instruction School at RAF Church Lawford in Warwickshire. Here he was sent on a flight instructors' course, and once he had passed that he was sent to No. 14 Advanced Flying Unit, which was based at RAF Ossington, Nottinghamshire, as a flight instructor on Oxford twin-engined aircraft.

It was while practising night flying on 16 May 1942 with No. 14 Advanced Flying Unit that Ray was involved in a flying accident that hospitalized him for a number of months, as his injuries meant he need-ed to have part of his face and feet reconstructed by plastic surgery. Sergeant Clearwater was flying an Oxford Air Speed Mk 1, call sign BG183, as a second pilot, with Pilot Officer G. Milne as first pilot, when the aircraft crashed on take-off at the end of the runway at 0255 hours and ploughed into a field. Both men received injuries. It was later discovered that the pilot had failed to carry out the cockpit drill, and the take-off was conducted with the flaps fully down. At the time of the incident Ray's recollections of the crash were hazy; he recalled only that the instruments were reading as they should, with no horizon on the very dark night, and that he had seen the flare path on his left, indicating he had turned crosswind into the circuit. He had no recollection of anything being wrong or of the crash itself.

Both men were trapped in the wreckage for some time. The pilot sustained only slight injuries, including a broken nose, but Ray had suffered shock, concussion with impaired vision and facial injuries, including lacerations to the right side of his face and a broken jaw. He was initially admitted to hospital locally, but was then moved to Ely, where he received months of treatment, including plastic surgery on his face at the Maxillo facial unit at the East Grinstead Military Hospital by Dr Albert Ross Tilley.

Not wanting to stay as an instructor and with war raging, Ray requested active flying duties, and on 29 February 1944 he was assigned to No. 83 OTU (Operational Training Unit). Here he met his fellow crew mates and began training on bombers, with initial instruction on Wellingtons. Following further training, the crew were assigned to No. 12 Squadron for operations.

The mid-upper gunner of NF928 was Sergeant Richard Wolsey. (*Author note:* In the course of research I discovered he was my grandfather's cousin.) He was one of two sons of Elsie and George Gustave Wolsey, who lived in Balham, London. Richard was born on 27 December 1920 in Holborn, and he lived with his mother, father and only brother for the duration of his childhood and early adulthood. He enlisted with the RAF on 29 March 1941, and served just 3 years and 200 days until his death on Saturday, 14 October 1944, while flying on air operations over Germany. Qualified service was less than this: just 3 years and 163 days.

Richard passed his medical with no problems. He stood 5 foot 10^1/$_2$ inches tall, with black hair and brown eyes; for identification purposes, he cited a number of scars on his left knuckles and a mole under his left armpit.

He was already qualified in civilian life as an electrician's mate grade 2, so initially enlisted within the RAF for ground duties as an electrician rather than flying duties and progressed through the RAF serving in this trade. But on 30 August 1943 he volunteered for active service as an air gunner and began gunnery training. He became a full air gunner with the rank of sergeant on 25 January 1944. Following further service, training with Advanced Flying Units and an Operational Unit, and obtaining the good conduct badge with gleaming character references throughout, he joined No. 12 Squadron with the rest of his crew on 9 August 1944. He served there until the date of his death just over three months later.

The rear gunner of Lancaster NF928 was Sergeant George Fearnley Walton, who was born in Poplar East Ham on 12 June 1908. As the senior member of the crew, he was seen as the 'father' figure. He came from a large family, being the eldest of seven children of his father George and mother Elizabeth; he had four younger brothers and two sisters.

George lived with his wife, Edith Ellen Walton, and his daughter Doreen, who at the time of his death was only 2 years old. He was the only member of the crew to be married. He had left home at the early age of 14 years and became an apprentice electrician. He worked first at the Battersea Power Station, but then in 1934 at the Metropolitan Vickers plant. He married his wife, Edith Sherwell, in 1935. In 1936 he changed employers again and worked for London Transport as a bus conductor, because he was offered a higher salary, and he stayed there until 1941, when he received his call-up to the RAF. He had enlisted in the RAF volunteer reserve a year previously.

After basic training, he served as an armourer, and was posted to various locations around the country, until he finally volunteered for active flying duties. He began his training as an air gunner in mid-1943, although it was a year before he saw action.

No. 12 Squadron

Lancaster ME788 PH-Q

Pilot	Flying Officer C. H. Henry	Survived
Flight engineer	Sergeant F. H. Hesketh	Survived
Bomb aimer	Flying Officer N. L. V. Chesson	Survived
Navigator	Sergeant G. C. Haywood	Survived
Mid-upper gunner	Flight Sergeant E. O. Martin	Survived
Rear gunner	Sergeant E. W. Kendall	Survived
Wireless operator	Flight Sergeant J. K. Penrose	Survived

LANCASTER ME788 WAS nicknamed the 'Queen of the Chase', a name chosen by Flying Officer Peter Thompson and his crew of No. 12 Squadron in the summer of 1944. On 14 October that year, when it became airborne at 0640 hrs from Wickenby, fully laden with bombs destined for Duisburg, it was piloted by Flying Officer C. H. Henry. However, it never reached its planned destination, but instead now rests on the bottom of the North Sea, after an incident on board. Just after take-off, as the bomber was climbing at just 300 feet, on the outbound leg en route to Ely, the port outer Merlin engine caught fire and burst into flames.

The pilot tried to feather the propeller to reduce the drag, but, when this was unsuccessful and the fire was spreading on to the main plane and wing, he took the decision to fly out to sea, so as to jettison the bomb load, and then either ditch or land, depending on the state of the fire. The wireless operator was instructed by the pilot to transmit a 'mayday' call at 0645 hrs. The broadcast continued until the wireless operator had to leave his position and take up the ditching position, near the main spar in the fuselage.

By this time the aircraft was over the sea and close to 1,000 feet in altitude. The bomb load was jettisoned successfully, although the 4,000 lb cookie exploded when it hit the water, which severely rocked the aircraft. The wind at the surface was estimated to be about 40 to 45 mph and the sea was running rough, although with little or no swell. About 5 miles north-east of Mablethorpe, at approx 0710 hrs, the aircraft ditched onto the surface of the sea at approximately 95 mph with flaps set to 25 degrees. When the aircraft hit the sea, the fuselage broke in two just behind the mid upper turret.

The life raft was inflated and the crew exited the aircraft very quickly, as it began to fill up with water. Within twenty seconds the aircraft had disappeared below the waves and had sunk. By this time six of the crew were in the raft, while the captain was still in the water, holding the raft lifeline. The rear gunner then cut the line free. Red signals from the markers pack were used at ten-minute intervals, and the crew then spotted a light signal from the shoreline stating 'help coming'. At 0832 hrs, nearly two hours after take-off, the crew were rescued by H.S.L. (High Speed Launch) 2578 of No. 22 A.S.R. (Air Sea Rescue). None of the crew was seasick, but three succumbed aboard the H.S.L.– perhaps from the effects of rum. It is not known whether the aircraft has ever been found on the sea bed or dived upon.

No. 12 Squadron

Lancaster LL909 PH-Y

Pilot	Flying Officer Theodore Sorenson	KIA
Flight engineer	Sergeant Crawford Fernie	KIA
Bomb aimer	Flying Officer Richard Walter Randall	POW
Navigator	Flying Officer Harold Spencer Gartrell	KIA (RCAF)
Mid-upper gunner	Sergeant Stanley R. Smith	POW
Rear gunner	Sergeant D. R. Smith	KIA
Wireless operator	Sergeant Ross Allen	POW

This Lancaster was one of 450 aircraft ordered from Sir W. G. Armstrong Whitworth and Co. at the beginning of April 1942. LL909 was delivered to No. 12 Squadron in April 1944. It was one of three Lancasters lost on the Duisburg morning raid.

LL909 was dispatched from RAF Wickenby, becoming airborne at 0645 hrs. The flight was uneventful until the aircraft reached the target area. It flew through the initial flak barrages as it approached the target area and then pressed on to begin its bombing run. The aircraft was seen over the target by a number of crews, but it did not emerge on the other side of the target area and was never seen again, lost in the confusion and concentration of all that was going on.

Bomb doors would have been open at this point and the deadly load vulnerable. This was the most hazardous point of the operation, when the bomber was flying straight and level. It is thought that the bombs were dropped and that the trouble began when the aircraft was hit by anti-aircraft fire. It is believed this caused fires on board, probably in the wings, and that the fuel tanks ignited, causing the bomber to explode and break up. Only three of the crew managed to exit the stricken bomber before it was too late. Two of the crewmen were incarcerated in hospital because of the extent of the injuries they received while escaping from the aircraft.

One of those was Sergeant Ross Allen, the wireless operator. He was caught in ground fire from German troops as he came down on his para-chute, landing on a railway line near to the crash site. He received two bullet injuries upon landing, one to his leg and one to his rear. Ross sadly passed away from cancer at the age of 55 years in 1977. For many years he suffered nightmares, as he was convinced he had taken someone else's parachute when the time came to leave the aircraft.

When LL909 was hit, the command to jump was issued by the pilot, Flying Officer Sorenson, once it was clear that the aircraft was beyond saving. The first to exit was Stanley R. Smith, second was Ross Allen, and third was Richard Walter Randall, although he was blown out of the aircraft. He was the last one to survive the ordeal. Unfortunately no one else managed to escape from the aircraft in time. Leaving the aircraft was made much more difficult as the main escape hatch in the nose of the aircraft could not be opened, which effectively trapped the majority of the crew inside, leaving only the rear exit door. This was a considerable distance to reach from the front in an aircraft that was plunging from the sky out of control. It is likely that, by the time the situation was realised, escape from the front of the aircraft was not an option, as the forces would have prevented adequate movement rearwards. It can be assumed that the remaining crew members were trapped as the bomber became increasingly uncontrollable. They could also have been suffering from the effects of lack of oxygen, as this would have been disconnected to allow them to move through the aircraft. Eventually their time ran out, and the aircraft exploded violently, believed to be due to the petrol tanks igniting.

The three survivors of the crew were kept in German POW camps and hospitals for the remainder of the war and released to the UK following the end of the war in 1945. After repatriation, Flying Officer Richard Walter Randall was debriefed, and gave an account of what took place on board and after he left the aircraft.

On the order to abandon the aircraft I put on my parachute, disconnected my oxygen and intercom. I then proceeded to the forward escape hatch, which was beneath me. I could not open it and to make matters worse the flight engineer had moved down from his station into the nose of the aircraft with me, coming from behind me, and sat on my feet. By the time I got out from under him and in the nose of the aircraft I was too stupid, from the lack of oxygen, to even move. Apparently the flight engineer was in a similar condition, because he sat down and looked at me and I sat and looked at him even though we both knew in our minds we should be trying to get out.

Then there was a terrific explosion and I went out through the nose of the aircraft. I was unconscious most of the way down and when I came to I was hanging upside down. The harness had been cut through at the shoulders and it was only the long straps that were holding me. My Mae West had been cut through as well and was hanging down around my knees. My flying boots were missing and I felt myself slipping from the harness so I crossed my feet to prevent this. My parachute was a tangled mess and I was falling very fast. On the last part of my descent I can remember seeing two other parachutes, fully opened and coming down. I hit some telephone wires upon landing, which broke my fall and was then knocked unconscious again and woke up in the street.

I was picked up by civilians, who told me that five other comrades were captured two streets away. I do not know if they were living or dead or even if they were from the same crew. I was taken to a Catholic hospital, where some days later I was informed by a doctor there that three other lads had been found. One was dead when found and the other two died from injuries in another hospital in Sterkrade. Both those reports are rumour and I cannot be sure whether the boys mentioned were from my crew.

It can be deduced from the bomb-aimer's report that the other two crew members, Stanley Smith and Ross Allen, left their stations and made their way to the rear of the aircraft and exited through the rear door, as the front hatch could not be opened. The other airmen on board were probably in the process of making their way to the exits. Presumably the navigator and pilot would have been trapped in the front of the aircraft, which was blocked by the flight engineer and bomb aimer in the nose. Perhaps they realized this and were either moving to the back of the aircraft or were delirious from the lack of oxygen and so also made little attempt to move.

This Lancaster crashed between Hamborn and Oberhausen-Sterkrade. German reports state that a British Lancaster crashed at 0848 hours, 3.5 kilometres north of Hamborn, with parts also found at a place named Mattler Busch, which is a small woodland located south-west of Holten. The main bulk of the wreckage came down very close to this area, on to a house in Cornelissen Straße, adjacent to where the hospital is today. The aircraft crashed in the rear garden of a house, destroying it completely, as noted in the German reports. This particular bomber was also claimed by the No. 4 Flak Division.

In March 2010 I went to the area. Visiting the site one afternoon, I found an elderly female living at the house next door to the crash site, who recalled the crash, and confirmed that the aircraft had come down in her current neighbour's rear garden, destroying the house. She advised me that the neighbour living opposite her house, a Mr Schafter, would possibly know more, as his mother had lived in the same street at the time of the crash. Mr Schafer was a flak gunner in the area of Sterkrade and an anti-aircraft helper at a flak battery. He recalls how he saw the incident.

We were firing our 88mm guns at the aircraft that were coming overhead from the flak station. Shell after shell was being sent up and as the bombers came over from the north, they had their bomb doors open and were dropping their bombs. Bombs were falling down all over the area. The aircraft were heading for Duisburg. The morning was sunny and the weather was good early on. While firing my flak gun, I saw a British Lancaster bomber coming down; it was tumbling and spinning down, although the wings were still attached, but I don't think it was burning until it got closer to the ground, when there were fire and smoke coming from it. I heard the crash, as it was not far away from our flak station. In the afternoon I came to the crash site, as my mother lived in a house nearby, and I saw the wreckage of the bomber. Its wings had been taken away, but there were machine guns and other parts still there. My mother was very angry, as the Germans came and took the bodies away on a cart, but were seen to just throw them onto the carts without care. My mother said, they are not animals, they are human people. One of the Germans said to my mother, 'be careful, there are bad people listening, the Gestapo may come for you'. My mother left the scene and went quickly away back to her house.

Four unknown dead airman were recovered from the crash site by cart, leaving three airmen who had bailed out to be accounted for as prisoners of war. The dead airmen were removed by the Germans and taken for burial to a small Jewish cemetery in Holten, which is located along a road named Sieges Straße. Interestingly, the German council states that the last burials in this cemetery were in 1930, yet the recovery reports for the bodies state that it was from this cemetery that the airmen were recovered. Access to the cemetery is by a small side road, named Venn Straße. From this a small walkway leads up to the gate of the cemetery. The exact area and plot inside the cemetery could not be located, although it is thought it could have been either at the very front to one side or at the very rear.

The Germans carried out the burial of the airmen on the same day and placed them in a collective grave, together with the dead airmen of Lancaster PD319, which also crashed in the same vicinity.

The entire collective grave of eleven airmen, four from LL909 and the remainder from Lancaster PD319, were exhumed by the Americans on 3 May 1945 and removed to Margraten United States military cemetery in Holland. All exhumed bodies were then reinterred after this move into nine graves, as the American reports stated that the remains constituted only those of nine airmen. However, later exhumations proved there were actually eleven. When burial took place in Holland, following the initial exhumation at Holten, the Americans were able to identify only three airmen from the two crews of LL909 and PD319. Flying Officer T. Sorenson was the only crewman of LL909 to have been fully identified during the first exhumation.

When the final graves were registered, following investigations and enquiries by the No. 4 MRES team, the airmen were moved again for the last time. Sorenson, Fernie and Gartrell were individually identified and buried in their own marked graves in Nederweert Cemetery. These three airmen rest in Row B, Plot 4, in grave nos 11, 12 and 13. The only member of the crew of LL909 not to be buried in this cemetery is Sergeant D. R. Smith, who rests in a collective grave in Venray War Cemetery with the seven crew members of Lancaster PD319. He rests in Plot 7, Row A, collective plot graves numbered 1 to 6. The other two airmen from PD319 rest in the same plot and row but in graves numbered 7 and 8 respectively, next to their comrades. It is likely that he was not removed because of the difficulty of separating the remains. The Air Ministry decided to accept the remains in the shared grave at Margraten as the missing airmen from both LL909 and PD319, following identification of a number of them. A request was made at the time by the investigating officer to have the crew of LL909 buried together in the same cemetery, but the Air Ministry denied the request for unknown reasons. The remaining crew members of LL909 were therefore interred in graves in Nederweert Cemetery, Limburg, Netherlands, and Sergeant D. R. Smith in a collective grave in Venray cemetery. The airmen were all moved from Margraten cemetery, as the Americans were relocating all their bodies back to the USA because there was a shortage of space in this cemetery.

As was typical of many crews from that time, the crew had nicknames for each other. Theodore Sorenson was referred to in the correspondence as 'Ted', Harold Gartrell as 'Hal', Richard William Randall as 'Dick' and Crawford Fernie as 'Jock'.

Flying Officer Harold Spencer Gartrell was the Lancaster's navigator. He was one of three sons of Edward and Alice Mary Gartrell, born on 26 May 1915 in Colmonton, Alberta. He was one of the older members of the crew. Both of Harold's parents were of British citizenship, as they had been born in the UK, but the family lived together at Robson Street, Vancouver.

Harold was well educated in public school and carried on his schooling all the way through to technical school, which he attended in his home town from 1928. He had chosen to undertake courses in accountancy, bookkeeping and business, with the accountancy course being completed in his spare time. From 1935, at the age of 20, he took employment with a local wood producing company as a bank clerk and store keeper, but he was only there until 1937, as the company ceased trading and closed down. For the next three years he worked for a mining company, looking after the books and payments as a bookkeeper, and from there he enlisted with the RCAF on 18 May 1940. Initially he enrolled for ground duties rather than flying duties, as he wished to carry on in his profession as an office accountant clerk, having already gained four years' experience in this field.

Flying Officer Richard Walter Randall, the bomb aimer, was another of the older members of the crew at 27 years. He had been a farm machine manager prior to enlisting in the RCAF and resided in Saskatoon, Canada. He was one of the lucky crewmen who managed to escape, despite being blown out of the aircraft. He was captured near Sterkrade, Oberhausen, just after landing, although he had been injured upon hitting the ground and left unable to walk properly. He spent the entire time from capture until 3 April 1945 in St Josef's Hospital. As described in his earlier account, he fell at a high descent rate because of his tangled parachute, and this probably caused most of his injuries. The hospital was located in the town of Sterkrade on Mulheimer Straße and still exists today. While in hospital Richard also contracted diphtheria, a respiratory tract infection, and suffered with this for approximately eight days until it was properly treated. He also stated that he did not know what had happened to the rest of his crew.

Sergeant Ross Allen, the wireless operator, had been a clerk prior to volunteering his services to the RAF on 13 October 1941. Almost three years to the day he was to be shot down and captured. He jumped out via the rear exit door and was captured as soon as he landed over mainland Duisburg. He was transported to Krefeld on the same day and then on to Düsseldorf and remained there until he was sent to Oberursel on 9 November. There he was subjected to solitary confinement and interrogation interviews. This ordeal, however, did not end here as he was forwarded on to another transit camp located at Wetzlar, arriving here on 16 November and staying until 23 November. Arriving at Stalag Luft VII on the 29 November he stayed here until forced to march to Luckenwalde, where he was imprisoned again in Stalag Luft IIIA until the camp was liberated on 22 April 1945. Although his possessions were taken from him when he was captured after bailing out, while at Krefeld, a Luftwaffe officer also took his personal watch from him.

Sergeant Stanley Ronald Smith, the mid-upper gunner, who had been a typewriter mechanic before enlisting, was also captured just after he had landed by parachute in the Duisburg area. He was wounded when he was found and was then sent to hospital in Obermasfeld on 1 November. He stayed there until 19 January 1945, when he was moved to a transit camp located in Meiningen. It was there that he was interrogated. Stanley was at Meiningen for just over a month before being sent to the prison camp Stalag Luft III, which was to be his home until 3 April, when he was marched to his final destination, Stalag Luft VII.

No. 115 Squadron

Lancaster HK599 KO-K

Pilot	Flying Officer Rhodes Dempster Lister	POW
Flight engineer	Sergeant Peter Herbert Frederick Hughes	KIA
Bomb aimer	Flying Officer Harry Thomas Ford	KIA
Navigator	Flying Officer Ronald Brown	KIA
Mid-upper gunner	Sergeant Robert Hamilton	KIA
Rear gunner	Sergeant Raymond Eayres	KIA
Wireless operator	Flight Sergeant Justin Francis Loughnan	KIA (RAAF)

No. 115 Squadron lost two heavy bombers during the raid of 14 October 1944. Lancaster HK599 was airborne at 0710 hrs from RAF Witchford and crashed just under two hours later at 0905 hrs, together with Lancaster ND805 of the same squadron. At the time HK599 had just 128 hours on the airframe.

Witnesses knew that Lancaster HK599 was hit by anti-aircraft fire, but initially it was seen only to catch fire. However, a short time later it was seen again, falling out of control, and it then started a spiral descent, before entering a full spin and exploding into a number of parts. The flaming pieces fell to earth and crashed at Volksgarten, Osterfeld, a district of Oberhausen. Volksgarten (or People's Garden) is located approximately 1.2 kilometres north of Osterfeld and is a modest wooded area similar to a small woodland or nature park. The German reports state that the aircraft was approximately 95 per cent destroyed when it was discovered and that a claim was put forward for the aircraft's demise by the No. 4 Flak Division.

When the aircraft was hit and began to fall, any chance of escape would have been extremely difficult, especially when the aircraft started to pick up speed as it entered the spiral descent and then a spin. The gravitational forces would have prevented crews from moving easily and reaching their parachutes and exits. It is likely that the bomb load exploded or the remaining fuel in the tanks ignited, causing the aircraft to be ripped apart. Six of the crew were killed, but one crewman, Flying Officer Rhodes Dempster Lister, escaped with injuries, having parachuted down after the explosion. It is most probable that he was blown out of the aircraft.

All of the deceased crew members are now buried together in the Reichswald Forest Cemetery, after having originally been laid to rest by the Germans in a small cemetery in Osterfeld. This particular cemetery is known locally as the New Osterfeld Cemetery and is located on the western side of the district of Oberhausen. All six airmen were exhumed from this cemetery in August 1947 and reinterred in the Reichswald Forest Cemetery, Kleve. They rest alongside their squadron comrades from Lancaster ND805.

Flying Officer Lister had been a baker before the war, living in west Yorkshire. He had volunteered for active service with the RAF on 23 February 1942. After the incident over Germany, he was confined to hospital for a number of weeks. While in German custody, Rhodes was questioned at the interrogation centre in Oberursel, 13 kilometres northeast of Frankfurt. This was one of the main transit camps, and almost all Allied aircrew passed through here prior to being sent on to their main prison camp. While at the camp, prisoners were kept in solitary confinement. Rhodes was then transferred from the hospital to Stalag Luft III, located in Sagan, on 9 November 1944, where he remained until 28 January 1945. On 4 February he entered Stalag Luft IIIA in Luckenwalde, where he remained until April, when the camp was liberated by the Russians.

The wireless operator was an Australian, Justin Francis Loughnan. He had been born on 3 September 1919, the son of Francis Joseph and Mary Josephine Loughnan, who resided in Glen Iris, Victoria, Australia. Justin was 5 foot 10 inches tall, with black hair, a dark complexion and brown eyes. He enlisted in the RAAF on 1 August 1940 at the No. 1 recruiting centre in Melbourne at the age of 20, as a general clerk. He was then remustered for aircrew and began training on 3 January 1943. Justin was sent to the No. 1 Initial Training School to complete basic training, but three months later, in March, he was sent to the Wireless Air Gunners'

School for a wireless operators' course and then on to an Air Gunnery School on 23 August 1943.

No. 115 Squadron

Lancaster ND805 A4-J

Pilot	Flying Officer David Mayson Price	KIA (RCAF)
Flight engineer	Sergeant Frank Martin French	POW
Bomb aimer	Flying Officer Clyde George Redden	KIA (RCAF)
Navigator	Flying Officer Roy Stevenson Johnston	POW (RCAF)
Mid-upper gunner	Pilot Officer Douglas Stewart Haggis	KIA (RCAF)
Rear gunner	Pilot Officer Dale McGowan Hamilton	KIA (RCAF)
Wireless operator	Sergeant Joseph Charles Brunning	KIA

At 0700 hrs Lancaster ND805 lumbered down the runway, and with a full bomb load at full power, its Rolls-Royce Merlin engines gradually pulled it skywards. On the way to the target area, it was hit by anti-aircraft fire, which caused it to explode over the target area, and it was seen to crash on to the slag heap and smelting house of the German iron works located on Hamborner Straße, Meiderich, Duisburg. German records stated that it was next to a railway bridge. Today the main smelting house and slag heap have been demolished and removed, but the grass hill, railway bridge and land where the smelting house once stood are still there. Nearby stands a new shopping park.

The Lancaster came down very close to an anti-aircraft battery position and was witnessed to explode in the air, before catching fire again when the wreckage came to rest on the slag heap and smelting house. Smaller parts of the aircraft smashed through the factory roof. After the war, post-war investigation teams visited the crash site, and the aircraft was positively identified by one of its engines at the scene of the crash. The aircraft wreckage was known to be a Lancaster at the time of the crash by the Germans even recording the fuselage markings as ND805.

ND805 was seen to crash at approximately 0845 hrs on 14 October 1944, with this time being recorded in the German records. Initial information regarding the loss of the crew was forwarded to the RAF from the IRRC, and it noted that a Lancaster had crashed, with six unknown airmen killed and two more captured. However, the German report recorded five unknown dead airmen at the scene, one a little further away than the others, but also stated that two further crew members were missing. It was assumed they had been completely burnt inside the wreckage, but we now know that these two airmen were captured and remained as POWs. The Germans documented that, when the wreckage was investigated and the fire had been extinguished, four or five burnt crew members had been removed from the wreckage by an Air Force recovery team.

According to the investigating officers, this team visited either the same day or the day following the crash. No identification of the airmen was possible, and they were removed for burial. The German report, KE 9826, stated that some of the crew were buried in the Garrison E cemetery at Beeck, located near Duisburg, although no grave positions were mentioned. Another airman was buried in an isolated plot near the scene of the crash. After much investigation, he was later identified as Pilot Officer Dale Hamilton. He had fallen through a roof of an upper-floor office building. Unfortunately the remainder of the missing airmen of this crew were never identified in any cemetery and are still listed as missing, commemorated today on the vast Runnymede Memorial, Surrey.

A year after the crash, on 6 October 1945, a statement was taken by an investigating RAF officer from a worker at the factory, Egldlus Radermacher. An exact, and therefore difficult to read, translation, was filed with the original report.

Egldlus Radermacher
Duisburg – Meiderich, Bugel Strasse 13a.
　　On Saturday 14 October 1944, during the morning hours of between 9 and 10 a.m. during an air raid, a four-motored aeroplane fell burning down on Schlackenburg Huttenbetrieb (Melting House) Meiderich. According to the existing prescriptions an announcement of the crashed aircraft was delivered from Workluftschutz-leiter (Leader of air raid precautions of the works) Mr Garbeck, to the Flak command Schlackenburg of the works by a messenger.
　　During a walk around about the works later between 12 and 13 hrs with a Workluftschutz-leiter (Leader of air raid precautions of the works) by the statement and damage we found the place of the crash of the airplane guarded by a soldier of

the flak. The near admittance was forbidden. In the neighbourhood of the aeroplane's
ruins there were found two corpses. Where these two bodies have gone to, is not known
to me.

Duisburg-Meiderich, 6 October 1945
Signed Egldlus Radermacher

The officer in charge of this particular investigation, concerning the whereabouts of this crew, was Flight Lieutenant S. W. Gould of the No. 8 MRES unit. He returned to Duisburg–Meiderich on 23 October 1945 in an attempt to get further information on the crew and burial locations, as initial investigations were unclear and further evidence was required. As well as trying to locate the whereabouts of the crew, he also needed to clarify the confusion surrounding the airman who had fallen through the upper-floor office roof of the factory. There was little evidence to suggest exactly who this airman was, despite the presence of an identification disc. There was also no forthcoming information regarding the whereabouts of the other crew members. The main obstacle requiring clarification was the wording of the German report. This stated that the identification disc on the airman who came through the roof had been found in the 'neighbourhood' of the body and, because of this wording, clarity was needed to ascertain whether this meant in the surrounding locality or further away in the general area.

Flight Lieutenant S. W. Gould visited the crash site on Hamborner Straße and was escorted around the location by Herr Garbeck, who took the investigating officer into the room where the body of an airman had been found at the time of the crash, having fallen through the roof. He supplied a diagram, but he knew little else. At the end of November 1944 Flight Lieutenant Gould spoke to Herr Ischebeck and Herr Theil, who were on the board of directors of the 'Deutsche Eisenwerke', Werke Huttenbetrieb, and they showed him around and discussed the case.

It was discovered that, as well as an identification disc, the airman's tunic, badly broken wrist watch, unopened parachute and a wrist bracelet had been removed from him when he was found, although the tunic bore no identification badges whatsoever. The items were handed over to the German Kommandantur after the burial, and these had been locked away in an office cupboard for safe keeping. Sadly they were stolen from there after a few days, so the items were not available for the investigating officer to see. The wrist bracelet was of particular interest to the officer, as it had been inscribed with 'Mater' (Mum), on the back, and on the front with 'Royal Can Air Force' in a blue stone, together with Yak Hamilton. From this evidence and the identification disc bearing his name, it was believed that this airman was Pilot Officer Dale Hamilton, but further evidence was required. So the airman was recorded as unknown, as the disc had not been located on his body and identity could not be certain. The airman was recovered from the office room and buried at an isolated spot in a bomb crater within the grounds of the factory, not far from the crash site, but not with the remainder of the crew. It is not known why.

The matter was cleared up once the investigating officer spoke to Herr Garbeck and it was confirmed that the disc had been located within 3 feet of the airman. It was also confirmed with the family of this airman that his mother had indeed given him a wrist bracelet with the inscriptions as described above. This was enough to satisfy the Air Ministry that this airman was indeed Pilot Officer Dale Hamilton. The other crew members had been found within the main wreckage itself, approximately three-quarters of a mile away, which also further supported the suggestion that the identity disc near this particular airman was Pilot Officer Hamilton's. The fact that the aircraft was seen to explode in the air prior to it hitting the ground and that this airman was three-quarters of a mile away and he had fallen through the roof of the office at the factory would strongly suggest that he was thrown out of the aircraft while trying to escape by parachute – especially as two of his comrades had had time to attach their parachutes and make their escape before it exploded. The director of the factory stated that this airman's parachute had failed to open and he had fallen to his death.

It is also likely that the other crew members who did not make it out in time were also trying to abandon the aircraft. However, it cannot be ruled out that there could have been a problem with the airman's parachute itself and it had failed to deploy properly, which would suggest that he could actually have exited the aircraft before it blew up. The other four airmen who were killed were found together at the main scene of the crash, which would indicate that sadly they had run out of time and were still in their aircraft when it exploded.

It was confirmed that the crew were not buried for five days following the crash. Pilot Officer Hamilton was left in the factory garage until he was buried on 19 October 1944 by Russian prisoners of war; they removed all of his overclothes. The reason given for this delay was that the bombing raid had completely destroyed the town. It was the view of the company director that the airman and the crew should have been buried by the soldiers of the anti-aircraft guns, but they themselves had twenty-one dead bodies to deal with, together with many more wounded soldiers, among them their commander and deputy commander. The directors promised to make further enquiries, but it appears little else came to light. Why the crew were not buried together is unknown. It is possible that this particular airman was buried alone because he was discovered some three-quarters of a mile away from the rest, or perhaps he was found sometime later, after the burial of the other airmen had taken place.

The fate of the other missing airmen remains unknown. Witnesses who were interviewed on the spot and had dealings with the flak barracks could not bring any light to the case. The reason it appears they were never located is that there was only one individual who knew the exact burial location of these airmen. His name was Herr Resseng, a worker at the factory, and at the time of initial enquiries in October 1945 he had left the area and was unavailable, but was back approximately ten days later. Flight Lieutenant Gould returned to the area in November to make further enquiries with the directors and Herr Garbeck, but un-fortunately, even though Herr Garbeck was spoken to again, he could not give further information apart from advising the officer to speak to Herr Resseng. Flight Lieutenant Gould's enquiries proved unsuccessful again, as Herr Resseng could not be located and did not return. He had disappeared completely after he had been involved in some trouble with the works.

Out of the crew of seven, five were killed, and two managed to escape by parachute to become prisoners of war. Only one of the crew has a known grave. This was Pilot Officer Hamilton, located in an isolated grave in Duisburg near to the site by post-war investigators and who was identified by his identity disc and wrist bracelet.

A letter dated 9 September 1949 addressed to the commanding officer of the No. 20 MRES unit states there is no trace of the other missing air-men and nothing could be located. When the RAF investigation teams visited Beeck, no trace of any British airmen was found. On many an occasion airmen were listed in German reports as being buried in one cemetery, only to be found in another; and it is well known that, when MRES teams went through the cemeteries of Duisburg, the number of unidentifiable airmen they found appalled them. Normally crews were found buried near to their crash site rather than spread over an area. But sometimes airmen were recovered with no identification at all and buried as 'unknown' in the Commonwealth War Graves Commission cemeteries, and later commemorated on memorials.

This particular case was not helped by the fact that the worker who knew the exact location could not be located. There must have been enough remains for the Germans to list four individual bodies at the time of the crash, as a captured summary of records states that there were four or five unknown airmen discovered at the time of the crash and all of them had been badly burnt. It is likely that these airmen were found in a cemetery but were left as 'unknowns', as identification would have been problematic.

Very thorough investigations into the loss of this crew took place, but eventually in 1951 these enquiries ceased, as no further results could be obtained. All personnel in the works who could have had anything to do with this air crash were closely interrogated, including Herr Thomas, the liaison officer between the works and the military authorities during the war, and numerous employees of all grades. All enquiries resulted in the information that the bodies had been taken away by the military recovery team. Almost every responsible former member of the flak battery, all the officers and most of the NCOs were interrogated, but unfortunately none of them had any idea where the recovery team had taken the bodies. The one German report that stated the bodies were buried in Duisburg–Beeck was thoroughly followed up and all 'unknown' airmen in the cemeteries in the area were carefully checked, with the doubtful cases exhumed, all with no result. The Air Ministry had no choice but to record the missing airmen from this crew as having no known graves, and today they are commemorated on the Runnymede Memorial to the missing.

One of the survivors of ND805 A4-J was Sergeant French, who had been an aircraft woodworker and resided in the area of Norfolk before his enlistment in the RAF on 4 June 1942. It is believed he was injured on his landing, as he was wounded when captured. He was taken into custody and sent to Stalag Luft VII, located in Bankau, Silesia, arriving there on 12 November 1944. This was temporarily to be his home, until he was marched with many other prisoners to Stalag Luft IIIA, Luckenwalde, south of Berlin, on 16 January 1945. He remained there from his arrival on 9 February 1945 until he was liberated on 22 April 1945.

The second POW from this crew was Canadian Flying Officer Roy

Stevenson Johnston. Prior to the war Roy was working as a general clerk before he volunteered for the RCAF on 8 December 1941 at the age of 20. He was another one of the lucky crew members to escape and take to his parachute. He was slightly wounded on landing and was captured shortly after. Roy was relieved of his possessions and sent for interrogation to the Dulag Luft transit camp near Frankfurt, where he spent the next eleven days subjected to solitary confinement and interviews. Following this, he arrived at the Stalag Luft III prison camp on 8 November 1944 and remained there until 25 January 1945, when he was marched with other prisoners to Stalag Luft IIIA, Luckenwalde. He was released the same day as his comrade Sergeant French.

Pilot Officer Dale McGowan Hamilton of the RCAF, born 20 March 1924 in Lethbridge, Alberta, was an air gunner on the bomber and was one of four siblings, having one brother and two sisters. He was the son of Allan Ross Hamilton and Bertha Marie Longpre and resided with them at Cedar St, New Westminster, British Columbia. Dale was brought up with his family and attended Christopher Lake School for both his primary and secondary education between 1930 and 1940. He left school at the age of 16 to take up employment with the Alaska Pine Company, New Westminster, where his duties included marking lumber. Dale stayed with the firm for two years, when he left to join another lumber company. It appears he disliked working nights, and following his new appointment his main duty was that of a tallyman. This position appeared short-lived, however, and sometime in the same year he moved yet again to a ship salvage company to begin an apprenticeship as a pipe fitter. On 1 March 1943, at the age of 19 years, he enlisted with the RCAF at a recruitment station in Vancouver.

The pilot of ND805 was Flying Officer David Mayson Price. He was born on 28 February 1921 in Ottawa, Ontario, the only son of Frederick Llewellyn Price and Jane Mayson, who were both of Canadian citizenship. His father was involved in a civil service occupation, being a chief examiner auditor. The family resided at 30 Glendale Avenue, Ottawa, Ontario. David spent much of his younger years in good education, attending a senior matriculation course between 1934 and 1939 and going on from there to university, attending the Queens University at Kingston, Ontario, from 1939 to 1942. David had previous military experience, as he served from 1939 with the military as a 2nd lieutenant in artillery while at Queens University. He applied for a position with the RCAF in late 1941 and was accepted for a placement upon finishing his university course. He enlisted with the RCAF on 4 May 1942 for flying duties, with the preference of becoming a pilot.

The mid-upper gunner on ND805 was 20-year-old Douglas Stewart Haggis (R201481), one of seven brothers and sisters born to Albert E. Haggis and Frances Vinney Haggis of Josephine Avenue, Windsor, Ontario. He was born on 9 August 1924, in Coniston, Ontario. Douglas was educated at the Prince of Wales School from 1931 to 1939 and then attended Windsor Walkerville Vocational School, where he chose to study a course in welding and electricity, which he completed in 1941. His main job after graduating from school was that of a butcher with Wing Brooks in Windsor, Ontario, but he was there for only a short period from January 1941 to sometime in 1942, after which he left to enlist with the RCAF. He applied to join the RCAF at No. 8 recruiting centre, Windsor, finally enlisting on 9 February 1943. He applied for flying duties, but did not specify a particular occupation. He told the interviewing officer that he preferred to serve in whatever category his services could best be used.

The bomb aimer on this Lancaster was Clyde George Redden (R153151), born on 7 November 1922. He was one of five siblings (he had three sisters and one brother) born to George Alexander Redden and Annie Teressa Walker of Nova Scotia Hospital, Dartmouth. It appears from the address given in his records that his parents must have resided in hospital accommodation, but he was born in New Ross, Lunnenburg Co., Nova Scotia, on a farm. Clyde spent his early primary education at St Joseph's Orphanage School, moving through grade one to grade eight from 1928 to 1936. He then left to attend St Ann's College for high school from 1936 to 1939, reaching grade ten. From there he chose to further his education, reaching grade eleven at St Andrews School, where he finished his course in 1940.

After graduating from school at the age of 17, Clyde Redden took up work in 1940 as a labourer with Acadia Construction Company, which was only temporary employment, as it appeared that work had dried up sometime after he joined the company. It was not until 1941 that he sought work as a machine trimming cutter with Claytons and Sons, but he left the company after just four months to take up an appointment more to his liking with Clark Ruse Aircraft Company as a labourer. Again, after only one month, the work dried up, and it appeared he was unemployed. On 14 March 1942 Clyde enlisted with the RCAF in Halifax, Nova Scotia, applying for pilot or observer, but ultimately ended

up as a bomb aimer, destined to lose his life serving with Bomber
Command in Europe in October 1944.

No. 550 Squadron

Lancaster NG133 BQ-F2

Pilot	Flying Officer Alec Abrams	POW (RCAF)
Flight engineer	Sergeant Kenneth William Nettleton	KIA
Bomb aimer	Flight Sergeant Raynold Frank Veness	KIA
Navigator	Flight Sergeant John William Brown	KIA (RCAF)
Mid-upper gunner	Sergeant Albert Percy Soper	KIA
Rear gunner	Sergeant Kenneth William Salton	KIA
Wireless operator	Flight Sergeant Philip Leonard Brooker	KIA

Lancaster NG133, part of 'C' flight, became airborne at 0639 hrs and crashed just over two and a half hours later, with the loss of six of the crew. The pilot, Flying Officer Alec Abrams, was lucky enough to be thrown clear when the bomber blew up after being hit by anti-aircraft fire, and became a prisoner of war. The remainder of the crew lost their lives and are buried at the Reichswald Forest War Cemetery at Kleve. The case was eventually closed in September 1948, after the deceased crew had finally been laid to rest in Kleve. The crew were experienced and well into their first tour and on their eighteenth sortie.

On the approach to the target, NG133 encountered extremely heavy flak and was hit by anti-aircraft fire. The bomber exploded a short time later. The wreckage fell from the sky and came crashing down into the garden of a house in Gest Straße at Ort Baerl, approximately 6 kilometres north-north-west of Moers. The pilot was extremely fortunate, as he was thrown clear of the aircraft and managed to operate his parachute and land safely, whereupon he was quickly captured by the Germans. The aircraft was claimed by the No. 4 Flak Division and, according to the German reports, it crashed at 0846 hrs and was completely destroyed.

However, the time given on other reports was much later.

The aircraft was hit by anti-aircraft fire, and we can assume it did not explode immediately. The airmen were found at the crash site with un-opened and half-opened parachutes, which means that the order must have been given by Flying Officer Abrams to abandon the stricken and presumably burning Lancaster. Crew members would probably have struggled through the cramped and possibly smoke-filled Lancaster to get to their parachutes, clip them on, and then make their way to the nearest exit, but unfortunately they did not get out in time. The aircraft was probably losing altitude and more than likely burning, so it must have been only a short time later that it exploded.

After this aircraft had been reported missing, no information was received for several weeks, and each airman was listed as missing. Eventually a telegram was forwarded through the IRRC quoting German information, which stated: '14/10/44. Lancaster six dead. 1171961 Soper A.B. Five unknown. No reclassification of unknown as there were seven members in this crew.'

From this it can be assumed that, following the crash, the Germans were able to make a positive identification of only one airman. This informa-tion was also recorded on the *Totenlisten* ('Death List') and on the German death cards. Some time later another telegram was received, with information about the pilot: 'Flying Officer J87651 Alec Abrams and Pilot Officer 178897 Douglas Deleney have been captured.'

RAF investigation teams made an enquiry into this Lancaster and the location of its crew after the war. The No. 4 MRES unit was assigned to the task, with Flight Lieutenant F. Adams, No. 22 section, in charge of this particular case.

Flight Lieutenant Adams visited the area of Moers, Germany, in the late summer of August 1946 to make his enquiries and began by search-ing four local villages in an attempt to locate houses into which an air-craft was known to have crashed. After much probing he eventually located a woman by the name of Mrs Gilbers, who resided in Gest Straße in Baerl. She confirmed that on 14 October 1944, between approximately 0915 hrs and 0950 hrs, an aeroplane had crashed into her garden. Although it was apparently without a bomb load on board, it had never-theless badly damaged her house. She told the officer that, like everyone else on that morning, she had sought refuge in the air-raid shelter at the time of the heavy attack, which was said to be heading to Duisburg, and so she did not actually witness the crash. Flight Lieutenant Adams could not locate any eyewitnesses at all, despite asking many of the local population in the village, as it appeared everybody had taken shelter. He also made numerous enquiries with the population about souvenirs, and bits and pieces of the wreckage, but again without success. No one witnessed any airmen coming down by parachute either.

The damage to the occupant's house was extensive. It had been partly destroyed by fire, which, according to Mrs Gilbers, was thought to have been started by the petrol spilling out of the aircraft's fuel tanks and pouring into the rooms. She did, however, tell the officer that the fire did not last long and was soon extinguished. The bodies of three of the crew, each with a partly opened parachute, were located inside the house itself, and two more were on the grass next to the house. Another was thought to have been inside the wreckage of the aircraft. However, another eye-witness states that one airman was seen in the local school yard along the road to the rear of the house. It is, therefore, unclear exactly where the sixth body was located, although it is likely to have been in the school yard, as Mrs Gilbers only assumed the other airman was inside the wreckage itself. Mrs Gilbers mentioned that all the bodies of the airmen were taken away to the local cemetery at Lohmannsheide. The wreckage was cleared by the German army and local police units, who then arranged for the removal and burial of the crew.

Following this interview with the home owner, Flight Lieutenant Adams made his way to the cemetery, on Kastell Straße, at Lohmann-sheide, a short distance away from the crash site itself. Here he questioned Mr Stermann, the cemetery keeper at the time, regarding the airmen from this particular crash. Mr Stermann stated that he recalled the bodies of a number of airmen being brought into the cemetery by a special German unit named Bergungskommando, a unit that had long since been disbanded at the time of enquiries in 1946. He also claimed that the bodies were brought in from a crash site at a house in Baerl and they were all buried as 'unknowns' in a communal grave in field 4a, a field in the cemetery used for enemy Air Force dead. The only other information that Mr Stermann and his staff could give regarding the identity of the crew, was that they had been brought into the cemetery at the same time as another crew, who were also buried as unknowns. He had heard of only two aircraft crashes in the area from the date in question.

Flight Lieutenant Fyfe of the investigation team then arranged an exhumation of the graves numbered 53 to 63 inclusive, and also grave no. 65. All airmen had a cross showing 'English Flyer'.

Nothing could be located on the bodies that would give an indication of the individual identities of these airmen, although it was confirmed they were from the crew of Lancaster NG133, probably by a process of elimination, as the other graves were known to contain the crew of KB800, and these two aircraft were the only two to have come down in that area. It was found from the records that grave no. 64 contained the body of an Italian, who was not affiliated with either crew, and so arrangements were made with the cemetery keeper for the Italian body to be moved into grave no. 65 and for the British airman to be moved into grave no. 64, so as to keep them all together. This then made a row of six graves numbered 59 to 64 inclusively for the crew of NG133, with the graves numbered 53 to 58 for the crew of KB800. The final exhumation for the crew of NG133 was carried out by Captain Cockburn and Flight Lieutenant Keen on 25 June 1947 and revealed the full extent of the explosion, crash and fire.

Grave 59 revealed only a small number of badly burnt remains. No clothing at all was located on the body, and no particulars could be determined. Sadly this airman remained unidentifiable.

Grave 60 contained the badly shattered body of an airman. The height and build of the individual could not be determined, and the only clothing present were small parts of a Mae West survival vest and an electrically heated flying suit. The airman was not identified.

Grave 61 contained the remains of a flyer. Only parts of the airman were present and these were badly burnt, so again identification could not be determined. However, a number of other items were located on his body, including parts of his woollen flying jumper, shirt, Mae West survival vest and his electrically heated flying suit.

Grave 62 revealed very little in terms of any remains, and again sadly no identification could be established. The only items of clothing found were scraps of a shirt and civilian clothing, together with shattered parts of a Mae West survival vest. Nothing else was left.

Grave 63 bore only a very small number of remains, which were burnt. The height and build of the body, as in the other graves exhumed, could not be determined, and again no positive identification could be obtained from the exhumation. Only scraps of clothing existed.

Grave 64 also contained very little in terms of any remains; what was there was again burnt. No details of who lay here could be identified. Only a black tie and parts of a white flying sweater were visible.

The investigating officer then arranged for a fence to be placed around the graves in order to make it a 'comrades' grave'. A large wooden cross was then erected at the site bearing the name, numbers and ranks of the airmen, including also the date of death. These airmen were recommended for a joint collective grave when the time came to relocate them to their final resting place in the Reichswald Forest Cemetery, Kleve as individual identity was just not possible.

The funeral for these airmen was carried out on 20 October 1944, almost a week following their deaths. No one can account for the delay, although the main reason is likely to have been the major disruption caused by the intensive bombing. Many services were in a dire situation. It appears from the records that this crew were exhumed on more than one occasion and that each time the investigating teams found nothing further to identify each member individually.

While I visited Germany with two friends and tried to locate the crash site, I had only the name of the road, which was a long residential street. However, luck was on our side, as we stopped an elderly lady walking down the road, who told us that her mother, now in her nineties, was still living in the road and remembered the crash site. A quick telephone call to her revealed the exact two houses into which the bomber had crashed: nos 32 and 34 Gest Straße. So we were quickly shown the area by the eyewitness's daughter, who then introduced us to another resident, who filled in the details. She recalled the heavy bombing, and hearing the crash and explosion while taking refuge in the air-raid shelter. She remembers leaving the shelter, which was located at her house, after the sirens had finished, and coming face to face with the burning wreckage of an aircraft opposite her house. Debris fell into the two houses, and an engine was found further up the street. The airmen were discovered in and around the wreckage of the aircraft, although one was found at the village school in Schul Straße, the road behind Gest Straße. He was lying in the yard, presumably after he had fallen out of the aircraft just before it hit the ground. The eyewitness explained that the bomber was thought to be heading in the direction of Duisburg and came from behind the houses. Today the houses are new builds, like most of the houses in the street, but the school is still there.

Flying Officer Alec Abrams was thrown clear from the escaping aircraft and captured by the Germans after landing by parachute. He was incarcerated in various POW camps. Initially he was taken to Stalag 6J, a hospital located at Düsseldorf, and he remained there until 7 November, being treated for the wounds he had incurred from the explosion and his exit from the aircraft. On 9 November Alec arrived at Dulag Luft, a holding camp, before he was sent to Stalag Luft III in Sagan, Silesia. His stay there was short, as at the end of January 1945 he joined the forced march to Stalag Luft IIIA, Luckenwalde. It was from there that he was liberated on 22 April 1945.

The navigator on NG133 was Flight Sergeant John William Brown, J92163, of Toronto, Ontario. He was born a Canadian on 23 August 1922, despite the fact that his parents did not originate from Canada. His father, John Brown, had been born in Ireland and his mother, Ellen, in London, but both had obtained Canadian citizenship. He was their only child. After finishing his higher matriculation at the Jarvis Institute in Toronto in 1940, John was employed as a clerical clerk with an electric power company. On 4 September 1942, at the age of 20 and with no previous military experience, he enlisted with the RCAF, expressing a wish to carry out flying duties although he did not state a preference as to what he wanted to do. He was listed as wanting to return to his previous employer on discharge. John came across as alert, with a quick response and a real desire to fly. According to the medical examination, he had an average physique with a stocky build and a weight of 142lbs he had a fair complexion, blue eyes and fair hair. John qualified as a navigator, earning himself the navigator's badge on 17 September 1943, with both performance and character rated as very good. Initially he held the rank of sergeant, and his final promotion, on 17 July 1944, was to flight sergeant.

No. 550 Squadron

Lancaster PD319 BQ-G

Pilot	Flying Officer Harry Dodds	KIA
Flight engineer	Pilot Officer Arthur Reginald Brown	KIA
Bomb aimer	Flying Officer Henry Black	KIA
Navigator	Flying Officer Douglas John Kenneth White	KIA
Mid-upper gunner	Sergeant Harold Lewis	KIA
Rear gunner	Sergeant Albert Laidlaw	KIA
Wireless operator	Flight Sergeant Clarence Walter Beckingham	KIA (RAAF)

The crew of Lancaster PD319 boarded their bomber at North Killingholme airfield, Lincolnshire, 8 miles north-west of Grimsby, before dawn and began their normal routine in preparation for the mission. The aircraft's wheels left the ground for the last time, its four Merlin engines thundering skyward, at approximately 0647 hrs.

Flying Officer Dodds's original crew arrived at the squadron on 13 August 1944, and flew their first operation on 28 August. The original crew consisted of Dodds, flight engineer Sergeant J. W. Brown, bomb-aimer Flight Sergeant R. J. Moran, DFC, navigator Flying Officer L. O. Browning, mid-upper gunner Flight Sergeant H. Lewis, rear gunner Sergeant A. Laidlaw, and wireless operator Flight Sergeant C. W. Beckingham. From their arrival at the squadron, the original crew flew together for a total of seven operational sorties, but then changes began, most likely because of sickness or leave. Flight Sergeant Horlor was drafted in to replace Flight Sergeant Beckingham for two sorties, beginning with the raid to Neuss on the night of 23/24 September 1944. Flight Sergeant Beckingham, however, returned to the crew for the tenth and final mission to Duisburg, and the two sergeants, R. J. Moran and J. W.

Brown, were replaced by Flying Officer D. J. K. White and Flying
Officer H. Black respectively. Flying Officer Black and Flying Officer
White were never meant to be on this fateful raid to Duisburg. Shortly
before the flight, the navigator and bomb aimer of PD319 had
presumably gone sick, and Dodds's crew were subsequently two men
short for the trip. Flying Officer White was either chosen or volunteered
to fly and as he had worked closely with the bomb aimer Henry Black,
he was also taken along for the sortie. And so their fate was sealed.

As the heavily laden Lancaster lumbered towards the target area from
the north-west, it soon ran into trouble and became a victim of the No. 4
Flak Division. For whatever reason, this crew was unable to get out of
the stricken Lancaster when it was fatally hit by anti-aircraft fire over the
target area, and all were killed in the subsequent crash. It is thought that
the aircraft exploded, as the German report mentions that this aircraft
had 'crashed in the air', a comment that appeared on reports of other
aircraft that are known to have exploded in the air. The report also notes
that the bomber was 100 per cent destroyed.

According to German records, the Lancaster crashed at approximately
0848 hrs, with wreckage coming down into August Thyssen Straße,
Wehofen, in the vicinity of Dinslaken, leaving seven dead airmen for the
Germans to remove from the remnants. August Thyssen Straße is located
on the outskirts south-west of Sterkrade Holten and south of Barmingholten. It is known that other wreckage was spread further afield, as a
debris line was located to the north-east of the crash site and many parts
were found in the forests. But the crash site was given as this street, so it
is likely that the fuselage and crew were recovered from there. Evidence
to support this explosion comes from a piece from the rear of a fuselage
clearly showing the number '319'. This was found by a forest worker and
has been donated to a museum at North Killingholme.

In March 2010 I visited the area and went first to August Thyssen
Straße. The road itself is a normal residential street, a few hundred yards
in length, with rows of houses on each side, mainly derelict and many
appear unused. Despite the small number of habitants, there are a small
local supermarket and a church approximately halfway down the street.
The properties were originally built to house the local coalminers and
their families, many of whom have moved on. I spoke to a number of
elderly locals, but none could give specific details of the crash. Several
had been in air-raid shelters at the time of the bombing or had moved
here after the war. So I was unable to pinpoint the exact position of the

crash and knew only that the wreckage came down somewhere in the street, as stated by the German records.

The bodies were removed from the wreckage and the crash site and were buried the same day at a small Jewish cemetery in Sieges Straße, near the junction of Venn Straße, Holten. They were interred in the same communal trench as the four members of Lancaster LL909, which had crashed at the same time, just a few kilometres to the south-east. The cemetery is close to both the crash sites, which is probably why this cemetery was chosen (although in some circumstances aircrews were located at a considerable distance from the crash sites). The bodies had not been buried in coffins, but presumably just wrapped in sheeting, like so many of their comrades. The consequent deterioration of clothing and bodies, added to the severity of damage from impacts and fire, increased the problems of identification.

I went from the crash site to visit the cemetery, which still exists, though may no longer be in use. The front entrance was locked and access denied, but a recent wreath just inside the entrance was a sign that the cemetery was still tended. The cemetery is so small that the entire area could be seen from the gated entrance. Without records, there was no way of knowing where in the cemetery the airmen were interred, though probable sites were at the very far corner or to one side at the front near the entrance. The German army would probably have enlisted locals or POWs to assist with the removal of the wreckage and deceased airmen.

The graves at this cemetery were exhumed on 3 May 1945, initially by the American investigation teams. Only two of the seven members of the Lancaster PD319 crew were identifiable: Sergeant Laidlaw and Sergeant Lewis. But, with two of the seven crew members identified, the Air Ministry decided to accept that the remaining five bodies were the missing airmen of Lancaster PD319. Following identification of Flying Officer Sorenson, the pilot of Lancaster LL909, it was also decided at an early stage to accept that the other three were airmen of his crew. Of the crew of Lancaster LL909, only Sorenson was identifiable upon the first exhumation; however, it eventually transpired that the rest of the airmen from LL909 were buried in this cemetery in the same trench, mixed with the crew of PD319. The remains of both crews were then taken away by the Americans to an American cemetery at Margraten. The five remaining unidentifiable airmen from Lancaster PD319, Flying Officer Dodds, Pilot Officer Brown, Flying Officer Black, Flying Officer White and Flight Sergeant Beckingham, were buried together in a communal grave. The two identifiable airmen, both air gunners, Sergeant Lewis and Sergeant Laidlaw, were buried together in their own marked graves, but laid to rest together in a line with the other members of the crew.

The seven crew members of PD319 and the four crew remains from Lancaster LL909, initially buried in Margraten American military cemetery at Limburg, Holland, were later moved again when their graves were registered for the last time. The seven airmen of PD319 were transferred to Venray cemetery in Holland following investigations by the No. 4 MRES team. The remaining unidentifiable mixed remains of Sergeant D. R. Smith of LL909 also rest in this cemetery in the same communal grave as the seven crew of PD319, no doubt because they were unable to be positively separated. Flying Officer Sorenson, Sergeant Fernie and Flying Officer Gartrell, the other three deceased crew members of Lancaster LL909, rest in the Nederweert Cemetery in separate graves, but are buried side by side. Venray War Cemetery contains 692 Commonwealth burials of the Second World War, 30 of them unidentified, and one Polish burial; Nederweert Cemetery contains over 350 war casualties.

Flying Officer Henry Black, the bomb aimer, came from a military background. His father, also named Henry Black, had been killed at the Battle of Aubers Ridge in 1915. Henry was born on 13 June 1911 and lived and grew up in St Andrews, Scotland. In 1932 he joined the Kirkcaldy Police Force in Fife, and served as a police officer until he enlisted with the RAFVR on 12 January 1942, starting off with the rank of leading aircraftman 2nd class. Henry was posted to Edinburgh and after prelimenary training was sent to No. 1 Initial Training Wing. Before his posting to Canada on 13 January 1943, Henry received a commission as pilot officer on probation to the General Duties Branch of the RAFVR. Following arrival in Canada, he spent two months with the No. 32 Elementary Flying Training School and then three weeks with the No. 38 Flying Training School. He was also taught navigation and attended courses at the Air Observers' School while overseas in Canada.

Flight Sergeant Clarence Walter Beckingham, the wireless operator, was born in Bexley, New South Wales, Australia, on 22 October 1923. Clarence was the son of Charles William and Sarah Hadley Beckingham. He was brought up in this area, living at 110 The Boulevard, Dulwich Hill, with his family, and attended Dulwich Hill Commercial Superior School from 1927 until 1938. Following school he undertook an apprenticeship with Claude R. Odgen in Sydney as a woodworking machinist. Although under an apprenticeship, Clarence still attended college part time at the Sydney Technical College from February 1941 onwards. During his second year he decided to enlist in the RAAF. An application was made on 8 October 1941 and, because Clarence was still under the age of 18, his father had to complete the certificate stating that he was in agreement with his son joining the RAAF for active duties home and abroad. On 22 May 1942, at the age of 18, Clarence took himself to the No. 2 Recruiting Centre in Sydney and took his oath to serve his sovereign Lord and King. He chose to enlist for full flying duties and undertook (and passed) his medical examination the very same day. The terms of his enlistment meant that he was to serve for the duration of the war plus an additional twelve months.

Clarence was remustered for aircrew training on 13 July 1942, and at the end of August was sent to Calgary, Canada, to complete his training as a wireless operator and air gunner. He went first to No. 2 Wireless School in Calgary, with his training beginning on 10 October 1942. He was then sent to No. 2 Air Gunners' School in Saskatchewan and following this was posted to No. 22 OTU, where his training was put to practical use under crew conditions. Throughout his training his conduct was considered 'very good', and he would receive his WAG badge on 11 March 1944. Clarence stayed in Canada until October 1943, when, having embarked on a ship from the USA, he came to the UK, arriving on 16 October 1943, just under a year before his death. He was sent first to No. 6 Advanced Flying Unit to polish his skills, then, following brief postings with No. 18 OTU at Finningley and No. 11 Base at RAF Lindholme, where conversion to the four-engined heavy bombers took place, he was posted to No. 550 Squadron on 13 August 1944.

No. 300 Squadron

Lancaster NF959, BH-R

Pilot	W/O Stanislaw Sarachman	KIA (PAF)
Flight engineer	Flight Sergeant Czeslaw Marona	KIA (PAF)
Bomb aimer	Flying Officer Henryk Swiniarski	KIA (PAF)
Navigator	Flight Lieutenant Zbigniew Osuchowski	KIA (PAF)
Mid-upper gunner	Flight Sergeant Stanislaw Swiecicki-Stecki	KIA (PAF)
Rear gunner	W/O Waclaw Brulinski	POW (PAF)
Wireless operator	W/O Joseph Perun	KIA (PAF)

No. 300 Squadron lost only one bomber in Operation Hurricane, on the raid to Duisburg on the morning of 14 October; the crew were all Polish nationals, and all but one were killed.

Lancaster NF959 was one of 400 Lancaster Mk 1s ordered from Sir W. G. Armstrong Whitworth Aircraft Company under the contract number 239/SAS/C4/C. It was manufactured at Whitley, in Coventry. The Lancaster was delivered to the Polish No. 300 Squadron, which served in the UK from March 1944 to January 1947, based at RAF Faldingworth in Lincolnshire. NF959 was received at the base from the factory on 21 August 1944, and had accumulated only fifty-eight hours of flying time when it was shot down.

On the morning of 14 October 1944 this aircrew were briefed, together with other crews, to attack the industrial city of Duisburg, with bombers becoming airborne from 0630 hrs and NF959 leaving the runway at 0640 hrs. The aircraft failed to return and exploded with the loss of all of its crew bar one, who became a prisoner of war. As the aircraft made its way towards the target from the north-west, it was hit by flak, which caused the aircraft to explode a short time later. The claim was made by the No. 4 Flak Division. The pitiful remnants and debris from this aircraft fell to earth engulfed in flames, possibly throwing clear the rear gunner Warrant Officer W. Brulinski. It is not known whether he bailed out or was thrown clear by the resulting explosion. The aircraft was probably on the bomb run, with the bomb bay doors open. Records show that the 4,000lb cookie that the aircraft was carrying was hit, causing the bomber to blow up at approximately 19,000 feet. It is likely that the bomber had caught fire and then exploded, as the rear gunner had attached his parachute, suggesting there must have been time for the order to abandon the aircraft. The wreckage was scattered, and the Germans actually listed two crash reports for the aircraft.

The sites for the crash included Walsumer Mark (Oberhausen), Kirchellen and Walsum, with the first being the most probable, as wreckage was found scattered near to a hill in the vicinity of Walsum district. However, the German reports also list the crash sites as 1 kilometre west of Kirchellen with a crash time of 0850 hrs, and also south of Grafenmühle, 5 kilometres north-west of Bottrop, with a crash time of 0848 hrs. A hill very close to the village of Grafenmühle, used for storing the remnants of local coal mine deposits, is not far from where the airmen were found, and it was in this vicinity that parts of wreckage were located by the enquiry teams after the war. The deceased crew members were eventually located after an extensive search by the RAF enquiry teams in the main cemetery at Kirchellen.

Post-war investigators took some time in locating the airmen and the wreckage, with initial investigations being made in the areas of Dinslaken, Walsum, Veorde, Mollen, Lohnen, Orsoy and Aldenrade. Initially no trace could be found, but another two crews were found in the process. Enquiries were made with eyewitnesses and the local police stations, but no one could supply details of a crash in the Walsum area. Eventually the crew were located in a communal trench at Kirchellen Cemetery, 41 Allee Straße, Bottrop, 11 miles north-west of Essen. This is the original cemetery in Kirchellen, located in the north-west area of the town. No new burials are placed here now – most are in the new cemetery, a few minutes' walk away. The bodies were in plot A, row 7, graves 14–18, row 6, grave 7, and row 7, graves 1–4. The crew were exhumed and removed from this cemetery in May 1947 and reinterred in the Reichswald Forest Cemetery at Kleve.

Very little is known about this crew, with the only details coming from the airmen's record sheets. W/O Waclaw Brulinski, service number

704290, was the NF959 rear gunner. He was the only survivor of the crew when the bomber exploded, and escaped using his parachute, but was captured upon landing. Having been taken prisoner, he was transferred to Dulag Luft and interrogated before being transferred to a prisoner of war camp. Brulinski survived his time in captivity interred in camp L7; his POW number was 1057. He died in 1968.

The flight engineer, Flight Sergeant Czeslaw Marona, 780079, a Polish national, was born on 7 September 1912. He worked as a mechanic before enlisting with the RAF on 18 December 1939. He was part of the volunteer reserve and was posted to RAF Eastchurch to complete basic drill training before being moved to No. 18 OTU on 26 January 1940. Towards the end of that year he completed training at No. 12 OTU at RAF Benson and was then assigned to No. 301 Squadron. Marona qualified as a flight engineer, being awarded his service badge on 19 May 1943. He joined No. 300 Squadron on 2 June 1943 and remained there until his death.

Flying Officer Henryk Swiniarski, service number 70427, was born on 18 November 1920, the son of Franciszek Swiniarski. He worked as a technician before joining the Polish Air Force, but, for reasons unknown, he was discharged. He then joined the RAF on 11 September 1942, and trained and qualified as a bomb aimer. He was promoted to sergeant on 23 August 1943.

The wireless operator, W/O Joseph Perun, 783189, joined the RAF on 5 August 1940 at the height of the Battle of Britain. He was born in Poland on 2 May 1918 and had been a butcher. He spent a number of months training at the Polish Depot Signals School in Blackpool from 26 October 1941 and then trained as an air gunner at No. 7 Air Gunners' School, moving to No. 18 OTU on 17 March 1942. He arrived at No. 300 Squadron on 3 July 1944 and was killed just under four months later.

The pilot, W/O Stanislaw Sarachman, was born on 23 May 1917, and joined the RAF, with the intention to fly as a pilot, on 5 August 1940, having previously been a clerk. He arrived with No. 300 Squadron on 29 May 1944, after training on bombers with No. 6 and No. 18 OTUs. He was promoted to flight sergeant on 1 May 1943, and to W/O on 15 July 1944, just three months before his death.

No. 419 Squadron

Lancaster KB800 VR-C

Pilot	Flying Officer Arthur McAllister Roy	POW
Flight engineer	Pilot Officer George Adams	KIA
Bomb aimer	Flying Officer Jules Napoleon Robert Therreault	KIA (RCAF)
Navigator	Pilot Officer Harold Sigal	KIA (RCAF)
Mid-upper gunner	Pilot Officer Robert Henry Bowen,	KIA (RCAF)
Rear gunner	Pilot Officer Robert Gordon Manwell	KIA (RCAF)
Wireless operator	Pilot Officer Lucien Charles Le Vasseur	KIA (RCAF)

This aircraft was one of 300 Lancaster Mk. Xs ordered from Victory Aircraft of Canada. The batch of aircraft were all manufactured in Ontario, Canada, and flown over to the UK. Lancaster KB800 was delivered to No. 419 Squadron, brand new from the factory on 29 September 1944 and this Squadron was based at Middleton St George airfield. It had gained only twenty-eight hours of flight time when it was shot down.

On the morning of 14 October 1944, the entire No. 419 Squadron was to bomb the city of Duisburg. KB800 was airborne at 0615 hrs, with an expected home arrival time of approximately 1115 hrs. It was the only bomber from the squadron that failed to return from the operation. The pilot that morning, Flying Officer Arthur McAllister Roy, was on his twentieth operation and became a prisoner of war, having been thrown clear of the aircraft when it exploded. The remainder of the crew are now buried at the Reichswald Forest Cemetery. This was an experienced crew. For all but one of the crew members, the raid was their nineteenth or twentieth operation. For the wireless operator, W/O Le Vasseur, it was his twenty-sixth operation. He was replacing the wireless operator who was regularly used by the crew, W/O Nicolas Walter Karpassiti, DFC (20 July 1945), who was unavailable to fly. W/O Karpassiti was in fact a spare and would fill in with various crews when required, but he had flown with Flying Officer Roy's crew on a number of occasions. He had taken sick leave and while away had also spent time with his partner. It was not until he returned a week later that he found out that attempts had been made to contact him, as he was required for the raid.

On the morning of 14 October 1944 KB800 was making its way through the flak-filled skies over the Ruhr, approaching the target on its bombing run, when disaster struck. A flak shell exploded close to the aircraft in front, but as far as anyone was aware did no damage. But a very short time later a second flak shell exploded, just off the starboard wing tip, causing a piece of the wing to be blown off and also punching a large hole through the starboard aileron. The fuel tank was damaged, causing fuel to flow over the wing, and the two starboard engines caught fire. With part of the wing missing, fuel now ablaze and the aileron damaged, the aircraft began to shudder violently and appeared to be stalling, before dropping into a spiral dive to starboard. A short time later the aircraft exploded in flight.

As the pilot was thrown clear he was knocked unconscious, but he came to at approximately 6,000 feet, and was able to pull the ripcord on the parachute. He had no recollection of hitting the gound, but he was swiftly captured by anti-aircraft gunners and became a prisoner of war, the only crew member to survive. When questioned, the flak gunners confirmed they had seen the aircraft blow up, but had seen nothing of the rest of the crew. When this aircraft exploded, the bomb load was still on board and the bomb doors were open, so debris from the aircraft was scattered over a wide area north-west of the target.

KB800 was hit at approximately 0845 hrs and crashed a short time later on a family-run farm at Hoher Weg, near Replelen, 4 kilometres north-north-west of Moers. Post-war investigators conducted a thorough search of the area in an attempt to trace missing aircrew. An extensive search was made to ascertain the position of the crash site, carried out by the RAF's MRES unit, led by Flight Lieutenant P. Adams, who made numerous enquiries with the local population. A number of key people were located and the investigation was pieced together.

The Germans stated in their report that the aircraft had been on fire when it crashed, with 95 per cent of the aircraft being destroyed. The claim went to the No. 4 Flak Division. The investigation by the RAF states that a police master by the name of D. Fuhnderich, who worked in the area of Repelen, clearly remembered the crash of this particular aircraft. He was up and about for the first time following an operation on his neck and saw this aircraft in flames when it was still very high up in the sky. He stated he saw no flak and thus presumed it had been shot down by fighters.

He watched the bomber descend rapidly and hit the ground. It crashed into a barn on the farm at Hoher Weg, owned by Frau Huffen. A barrel-shaped bomb, presumably the 4,000lb cookie, was observed leaving the aircraft before it crashed and was seen to hit the ground and explode some 200 yards further south of the crash site. He saw no parachutes fall to earth. Frau Huffen, along with her children, were not at the farm at the time, but were staying in the countryside, presumably to escape the bombing. But her mother, Frau Biermann, was at the scene and remembered the incident, although she did not actually see the crash, as she was in an air-raid shelter at the time of impact. It was she who confirmed the time and date of the crash to investigators. Another eyewitness, a Dutch labourer called Mr Smith who was based at Repelen-Bornheir, recalled seeing one of the crewmen descending by parachute. This would have been the pilot, Flying Officer A. M. Roy. This eyewitness recalled this date and confirmed it was 14 October; he had been attacked and beaten up by the Germans himself and so remembered the date clearly. Everyone spoken to by the investigators recalled that the area was sealed off immediately after the crash by the German flak soldiers, with no one allowed near the site.

The area of the crash site today is still a farm, and it is run and owned by Mr Huffen, who also manages a guest house at the location with a restaurant. After speaking to Mr Huffen on the telephone, I was given permission to visit and enter his land in an attempt to locate parts of the aircraft. I arrived at the area with two friends on a crisp and cold morning in November 2009. After a brief interview with Mr Huffen, another farmer, who runs the farm opposite the crash site, was invited to join us. This farmer took us to a field where, as a child, he witnessed an airman fall down from the wreckage. He described the body falling from the sky with no parachute, hitting the ground violently and bouncing, before coming to rest by the roadside. The boy inspected the airman and found that he was intact, with his full flying kit on. He also described hearing the almighty crash when the Lancaster hit the ground and recalled that the explosion sent shock waves through the air and blew all of the windows out of the buildings.

The boy's father had attended the crash site after the incident in order to help the authorities in moving the bodies after the fire had been extinguished. The airmen had been removed by wheelbarrow, some unrecognizable, as they had been severely burnt in the fire. The only airman not to be burnt was the one who had fallen clear and landed in the field without a parachute.

With the landowner's permission, I walked over the site. Many small parts were found, including items from the cockpit, Plexiglas and fuselage, as well as many balls of molten and melted aluminium. A large part of a propeller blade was also recovered, together with engine parts. The deceased crew were not interred until 20 October 1944. No one can account for this delay, but the investigating officer did discover that the Germans had left the bodies in the cemetery grounds for a number of days awaiting the 'authorities' to attend to identify them, before a burial. The date of burial was confirmed by Mr Sterman Jun of Lohmannsheide Waldfriedhof, a cemetery keeper although not the person in charge at the time of the burial. It was also confirmed to the investigators that the crew were brought into the cemetery as 'unknowns', presumably because the Germans had not been able to confirm their identity at the crash site. But this contradicts the cemetery records, which are still available today, as they clearly show the names of the airmen for the date of burial given. However, it is possible that these names were updated once the RAF teams had confirmed the identities following exhumation. A special unit named 'Bergungs-Trupp', which had been disbanded at the time of the 14 August 1946 report, brought the crew in. All the crew were buried in Lohmannsheide cemetery, in grave numbers 53–58. Two of the bodies were interred together in a communal grave as the remains could not be distinguished. Later they were exhumed to be identified and removed to the Reichswald Forest Cemetery. In charge of the investigation were Flight Lieutenant Fyfe and Flight Lieutenant Adams of the No. 4 MREU. These officers also investigated the Lancaster NG133 crash, located a short distance away.

The first body to be exhumed by the team was in grave No. 53. This turned out to be a negative result, as it was impossible to identify the airman. Scraps of a shirt were the only remains other than the body.

The body in the second grave, No. 54, was positively named by identification discs on its first exhumation as Pilot Officer Bowen of the RCAF. A laundry mark X026 was also found and, though rather indistinct, it was presumed to be '626', the last three numbers of his personal service number (R60626).

Grave No. 55 was like the first, with no positive identification other than the remains of the deceased airman.

Grave No. 56 also proved to be elusive, as there was no positive identity of the body itself; however, there was a laundry mark that read X154, very similar to the one found on Pilot Officer Bowen. This is thought to be the last few digits of the service number of R260154, making this the body of Pilot Officer Manwell.

There was a positive identification in grave No. 57, the body was named as Pilot Officer G. Adams. A tab on his flying suit that read '1592117 Adams G.' allowed identification. Note that the number written here is his full service number. So identification was by both name and airman service number.

The last grave to be opened, No. 58, again offered no positive identification other than parts and shreds of a shirt, but a body was present.

The team now used a process of elimination to pinpoint the bodies although complete identification never happened for two of the crew. The pilot had been blown clear of the aircraft, so he was eliminated from the equation. Three other airmen had been positively identified, but more scrutiny was needed to establish the bodies in graves 53, 55 and 58. The remaining three airmen to be accounted for were one officer (Flying Officer Therrault) and two at the time non-commissioned officers (Pilot Officer Sigal and Pilot Officer Le Vasseur).

Graves No. 53 and No. 58 both contained shirts, and it was therefore assumed that these two were Pilot Officer Sigal and Pilot Officer Le Vasseur. The remaining body, in grave No. 55, therefore had to be Flying Officer Therrault, and upon further investigation the body was found to be bearing a commissioned officer's rank.

These findings resulted in Pilot Officer Sigal and Pilot Officer Le Vasseur being buried together in a joint communal grave, as the difference between the two could not be established. Flying Officer Therrault was buried under his own identity in his own grave. Following exhumation, the investigating officer had the graves fenced in a comrades' grave and a large wooden cross placed between grave numbers 55 and 56, inscribed with all of the airmen's names, ranks, service numbers and the date of death of all the airmen. The airmen were finally interred in the Reichswald Forest Cemetery, Kleve, towards the end of 1948, but Pilot Officer Sigal and Pilot Officer Le Vasseur had to be re-exhumed and moved into a collective grave, as initially they were buried in separate graves in the Reichswald cemetery, and the mistake had been overlooked initially. It was not until pictures of the graves were received by the Air Ministry that the error was noticed. They were reinterred together in 1949. The crew are now buried side by side in plot 34, row A, in graves one to six.

The pilot, Flying Officer Arthur McAllister Roy, was seen descending on his parachute and was captured soon after landing uninjured. Relieved of any possessions, he was taken into custody and transported to Dulag Luft transit camp, Wetzlar, arriving on the following day, 15 October. Here he was put through long interrogation interviews with the German officers and subjected to starvation and solitary confinement. On 22 October he was then sent to Stalag Luft III prison camp at Sagan, reaching there just three days later. His stay was short lived, arriving at Stalag Luft IIIA, Luckenwalde, on 2 February. He was there for just over two months, before being liberated by the Allied forces. Arthur was a student prior to joining the RCAF in 1942 and was raised in Winnipeg, Manitoba.

Pilot Officer Robert Gordon Manwell (J92365) was the rear gunner on the Lancaster. He was born on 26 November 1924, the son of Harold Wilfred and Emma Alice Manwell, both Canadian citizens who resided in Portage du Fort in the province of Quebec. Robert was one of eleven offspring, and had seven brothers and three sisters. He left the public school in 1940 and chose to work rather than embarking on higher education. He had various occupations, including working as a labourer with the Canadian National Railways, a machine apprentice with Sudbury Mining and Technical School, and a machine operator with the Canadian General Electric Company, and it was this that he left to enlist in active service. He enrolled with the RCAF in a recruiting office in Toronto, Ontario, on 28 May 1943, with the hope of enlisting for aircrew flying duties within the service, although no preference was given as to which duty at the time of enlistment. Robert expressed an interest in returning to his previous occupation of a machine operator after the war. He sailed through his medical examination with ease and was recommended for aircrew. He was 5 feet 3$^{1}/_{2}$ inches, with perfect 20/20 vision, blue eyes, dark brown hair and a ruddy complexion and generally enjoying swimming and hiking for his hobbies. Robert was in service for only a short time before being shot down and killed, in all serving just over fifteen months. He qualified as an air gunner and was awarded the

1 NF928: Rear row, L to R – U/K ground crew, Sgt William Berry, Flt/Lt Ray Clearwater, Sgt Robert Clark, Flt/Sgt Allan Price, F/O Henry Watts. Front row, L to R – U/K ground crew, Sgt Richard Wolsey, Sgt George Walton, U/K ground crew. RAF Wickenby 1944. *Courtesy of Gary White*

2 Six of the crew of NF928 standing outside their Nissen hut at RAF Wickenby, late 1944. Rear row left to right – Sgt Wolsey, F/O Watts, Flt/Lt Clearwater. Front row left to right – Sgt Walton, Flt/Sgt Price, Sgt Berry. *Author's private collection*

3 NF928: Sgt George Fearnley Walton. *Courtesy of Gary White*

4 NF928: Sgt Richard Wolsey. *Author's private collection*

5 NF928: Flt/Lt Ray Clearwater. *Courtesy of Bob Richardson and family*

1 The crew of Lancaster ME788 with the captain of the Air Sea Rescue unit who rescued them from their ordeal in the North Sea. *Photo courtesy of the RAF Wickenby Museum*

2 LL909: F/O Harold Spencer Gartrell. *National Archives of Canada*

3 LL909: Sgt Crawford Fernie. *Courtesy of Mrs Chris Broughton*

4 LL909: Sgt Ross Allen. *Courtesy of Mrs Chris Broughton*

5 ND805: P/O Dale Hamilton. *National Archives of Canada*

6 ND805: Flt/Sgt Douglas Haggis. *National Archives of Canada*

7 ND805: F/O David Mayson Price. *Courtesy of David Archer*

8 HK599: Sgt Peter Hughes. *Courtesy of Vincent Hughes*

9 The crew and ground crew pose by NG133. The aircrew are at the rear, left to right, starting second in – F/Sgt Raynold Frank Veness, one of the gunners (unknown which one), F/O Alec Abrams, one of the air gunners, Sgt Kenneth William Nettleton, F/Sgt John William Brown, F/Sgt Philip Leonard Brooker. *Courtesy of the cousin of the flight engineer, Mr Robin Dansie*

1 PD319: Sgt Albert Laidlaw.
Courtesy of Peter and Evelyn Miller.

2 PD319: Flt/Sgt Clarence
Beckingham together with his
girlfriend Audrey James. *Courtesy
of Chris and Christine Cole, Australia*

3 The crew of W/O Tapsell.
This was F/O Black
and F/O White's (of PD319)
original crew.
F/O Black is on the far left,
F/O White is the second in from
the left, both rear row. It is
unknown who the five men are
in the front row, probably
ground crew. *Courtesy of No. 550
Squadron association and Norval Black*

4 NF959: Rear Gunner F/Sgt Waclaw Brulinski.

5 NF959: Navigator F/Lt. Zbigniew Osuchowski.

6 NF959: Bomb Aimer F/O Henryk Swiniarski. *All pictures are courtesy of Thomas Rajkowski, Germany*

1 KB800: P/O Harold Sigal.
National Archives of Canada

2 KB800: P/O Robert Gordon
Manwell. *National Archives of Canada*

3 KB800: P/O Lucien Charles Le
Vasseur. *National Archives of Canada*

4 KB800: F/O Robert Jules
Napoleon Therreault. *National
Archives of Canada*

5 KB800: P/O Robert Henry
Bowen. *National Archives of Canada*

6 NE163: Flt/Lt Reginald Major
Aldus, training in Winnipeg.
Courtesy of Chris Bill

7 NE163: Crew of NE163. Taken
in August 1944, Yorkshire.
F/O Thurston Culshaw, (far left,
front row). F/O John Mervyn
MacMillan, (middle front row)
F/O Ronald Ernest Blake, (far
right, front row). Sgt Harry
Jeffries, (far left, rear row).
Sgt Joseph Marks, (second in from
the left, rear row). F/Lt Reginald
Major Aldus, (third in from the
left, rear row). Sgt Vernon
Sheppard, (far right, rear row).
Courtesy of Patricia Jeffries and family

8 NE163: Thurston Culshaw. *Courtesy of Chris Grande*

1 LM596: F/O John Allan Orr, **DFC.** *Courtesy of David Stapleton and Tom Bint*

2 LM596: F/O James Commodore **Campbell.** *National Archives of Canada*

3 LM596: F/O Robert Albert **Charland.** *National Archives of Canada*

4 LM596: P/O Roland Marcel **Joseph Champagne.** *Courtesy of Wickenby Museum*

5 LM596: F/O Ross Cuthbert **Clouston.** *National Archives of Canada*

6 LM596: P/O William Frederick **Palmer.** *National Archives of Canada*

7 Six of the crew of KB780. Believed rear row, left to right: P/O Walter Henry Killner, Flt/Lt William Janney, F/O Archie Verdun Batty. Front row, left to right believed to be: P/O Paul Riviere Jones, P/O Albert McFeetors, P/O Francis John Harrison. *Courtesy of Ray McFeetors.*

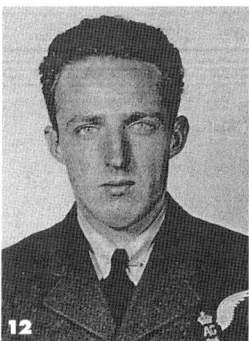

8 KB780: P/O Walter Henry Killner. *Courtesy of Amette Facer and Barbara Stokes*

9 KB780: P/O Albert McFeetors. *Courtesy of Ray McFeetors*

10 KB780: F/O Archie Verdun Batty. *National Archives of Canada*

11 KB780: Sgt Leonard Brotherhood. *Courtesy of Andrew Leech*

12 KB780: P/O Paul Riviere Jones. *National Archives of Canada*

13 KB780: F/Lt William Harold Janney. *National Archives of Canada*

1 NG190: F/Sgt William Greene.
National Archives of Canada

2 PD224: F/O Andrew McNeill.
National Archives of Canada

3 PD224: F/O Bryn Evans Roberts.
National Archives of Canada

4 PD224: F/O Edward Roger
Lambert. *National Archives of Canada*

5 PD224: F/Sgt Leonard Schaff.
National Archives of Canada

6 Lancaster LL956, Q – Queenie
Left to right: F/Sgt Roy Strachan
RCAF, Sgt Jack Soule RAF,
F/Sgt Lloyd Hannah RCAF,
Sgt Jack Loughran RCAF,
F/Sgt John Baird RCAF, Sgt Stan
Way RCAF, Sgt Geoff Maynard
RAF. Taken sometime during
October 1944 prior to taking off
on an operational sortie. *Courtesy of
David Langner*

7 F/O Lloyd Hannah, pilot of
Lancaster LL956. *Courtesy of David
Langner*

8 Pilot Officer Jack Ryan in front
of Halifax MZ672. *Courtesy of the
Bomber Command Museum of Canada*

1 MZ674: P/O Charles Maurice Crabtree. *National Archives of Canada*

2 MZ674: F/O Dell Alfred Butler. *National Archives of Canada*

3 MZ674: P/O Francis Harvey Eade. *National Archives of Canada*

4 MZ674: P/O Leonard Hunter Hogg. *National Archives of Canada*

5 Crew of MZ453, taken 1944 – left to right. F/O George Saunders, navigator, F/Sgt Al Ladner, wireless op and gunner, F/O Harry Rutter, bomb aimer, F/Sgt Jack Linstead, mid-upper gunner., F/O Frank Augusta, pilot. British officer, unknown flight engineer. Kneeling at the front – Sgt 'Mac' McLeod, rear gunner. *Courtesy of F/O Frank Augusta*

6 Believed to be the crew of PB357, far left to right, rear row P/O Eric Rivers, F/O Christopher Nigel Charles Crawford, Sgt Arthur Henry Frost, F/Sgt Thomas Edward Feaver, then three more unknown crew. *Photograph courtesy of Francis Rogers.*

7 PB357: P/O Eric Rivers. *National Archivesof Canada*

8 PB357: F/Sgt Thomas Edward Feaver. *Courtesy of Francis Rogers.*

9 PB357: Sgt Arthur Henry Frost. *National Archives of Susan Frost*

10 MM184: F/O Frank Dell. *Courtesy of Frank Dell*

1 F/O Ronald Naiff, navigator on MM184, rear row, second in from the left. *Courtesy of F/O Frank Dell and Chris Goss*

2 ME595: Rear row, left to right – Bill Ball, 'Moosh' Embury, Bill Pullin, Norman England, Wilson and Cyril Webb. Front row, left to right – George Boyd and Norman Hoad. Sgt Webb was given the nickname 'Lucky', Sgt Boyd was known as 'Hoppy' and Sgt Embury known as 'Moosh'. *Courtesy of Norman Hoad.*

3 ME595: Sgt George Patrick Boyd.
Courtesy of Paddy Boyd

4 Convicted war criminal Major Wilhelm Dinge.
Courtesy of the National Archives, Kew

5 Convicted war criminal Stabsfeldwebel Georg
Gawliczek. *Courtesy of the National Archives, Kew*

6 Convicted war criminal Stabsfeldwebel Josef
Bussem. *Courtesy of the National Archives, Kew*

1 MZ920: P/O Donald McLeod
Ward. *Courtesy of David George.*

2 MZ920: F/L Donald Zachary
Taylor Wood. *Courtesy of David George.*

3 MZ920: F/Sgt Geoffrey Davies
Grant. *Courtesy of David George.*

4 MZ920: F/O William Robert
Ewing. *Courtesy of David George.*

5 LL774: P/O Colin Charles Hunt.
Courtesy of Colin's family and Chris Hunt

air gunner's badge on 12 November 1943. He worked his way up from aircraftman to leading aircraftman and then to flight sergeant. Following training he was posted overseas to England, arriving at his OTU on 13 November 1943; he joined No. 419 Squadron on 21 June 1944.

The bomb aimer of this crew was Flying Officer Jules Napoleon Robert Therreault. Born on 24 February 1918 in Montreal, he was the son of Napoleon Alexandre and Marguerite Chatelain Therreault, who resided in Rosemount, in the province of Montreal, Quebec. He was their only child. His mother had been born in Switzerland, but his father was born in Quebec, a Canadian citizen. Robert was bilingual, speaking fluent English and French. He had spent two years in high school and was deemed as intelligent following his initial interview. On 19 February 1942 Robert enlisted into the RCAF, having no previous military experience. He had left school at the age of 15 and had had only one permanent occupation, as a clerk with a local wholesale jeweller, where he was engaged with watch repairs and accessories. He had worked there for eight years, his employer being a Mr C. E. Munger. Most employers guaranteed job security for people returning from active service, but in this case no guarantee was made. However, Robert stated he had no intention of returning to his previous employer after service. Robert initially enlisted for ground duties, but passed his medical with no problems and after interviews was quickly recommended for aircrew duties, and so changed his application accordingly. He had excellent hearing and vision, and the assessing doctor described him as physically fit, though perhaps slightly underweight at 134lb, and of average appearance. He also considered him to be very ambitious and willing to serve. At the end of these tests and interviews Robert was recommended for the position of pilot, but as not suitable for commission. Following the medical examination, he was interviewed by a board, who also recommended him for the position of pilot, describing him as very keen to fly and eager to study and learn more. It appears he was a motivated man from the reports studied. It is not known why he was not trained as a pilot. It is most likely there was a shortage of a particular trade elsewhere at the time. He was a medium-built chap, with his height standing at 5 feet 5 inches tall, with blue eyes and brown hair, and an interest in model building, roller skating and skiing. He was just what the RCAF was looking for to fulfil aircrew positions. Robert qualified as a bomb aimer on 3 September 1943, being awarded the bomb aimer's brevet. Shortly after, on 8 October 1943, he embarked from New York, arriving in the

UK eight days later on 16 October. He was initially posted to the RAF Bournemouth reception centre and then on to an OTU for further training with a crew, until being sent to No. 61 Base, arriving on 6 May 1944, prior to being placed with his squadron where he arrived on 21 June 1944. He remained there until he was killed on Saturday, 14 October 1944.

Pilot Officer Harold Sigal (R165010) was the bomber's navigator. His surname is unusual for a Canadian, and was originally a Jewish name, meaning 'treasure' in the Hebrew language. He and his parents resided at Claude Avenue in Toronto, Ontario. His mother, Racheal Sigal, was born in Russia and his father, Max Sigal, was originally from Austria. Harold was born on 20 June 1917, one of two children. He was among the eldest in the crew, at 27 years old. After matriculation, he worked full time as a shipping clerk with W. Pattenwick Stores and then became an assistant manager with his parents' shirt company. When he enlisted he stated that he wished to return to his parents' company to work, having spent the last seven years working for them, and had signed up only for the duration of the war. On enlistment he requested flying duties, listing pilot as his first preference with observer as his second. He was formally sworn into the RCAF on 22 April 1942, having signed up at a recruiting centre in Toronto. Standing at 5 feet 7 inches tall, with a weight at enlistment of 152lb, a good complexion, brown eyes and hair, and excellent vision, he suffered no medical problems and passed his examination on 23 August 1943. He was recommended for flying duties within the RCAF. Having trained at various OTUs, he qualified as an air navigator, gaining his navigator's badge on 3 September 1943. Harold was assessed again on 31 December 1943, and found to be competent and 'very good'. He left Canada to embark on a ship at New York on 8 October 1943, arriving in the UK on 16 October 1943. He was initially sent to the RAF Bournemouth reception centre and then moved to No. 24 OTU on 8 February 1944, where he spent a short time, before being posted to No. 61 Base and finally to his squadron on 21 June 1944.

One of KB800's air gunners was Pilot Officer Robert Henry Bowen (J92364), who was the son of Arthur and Lydia Bowen. He had a younger sister and brother who himself was already serving in the RCAF. Both of Robert's parents were English, his father being born in Ripon and his mother in London. At the time of Robert's enlistment they still held UK citizenship. When he was killed on air operations, he left behind a wife named Euphemia Margaret Bowen, whom he had married on 16 November 1943 while serving in the RCAF. They had no children. Robert left school at the age of 15, but then attended high school, where he completed an additional two years of study before seeking employment. Before signing up for service within the RCAF, he was employed locally in Alberta as a farmer, handling and looking after farm equipment and machinery. He spent a total of four and a half years here with his employer, but when interviewed he stated he was not interested in returning to his employer or to this kind of employment. Instead, he clearly expressed a wish to continue service within the RCAF and take up aviation as a career. Robert joined the RCAF at a local recruiting office in Edmonton, Alberta, on 16 April 1940, stating a preference for flying duties as an air gunner. He had no previous military involvement and only half an hour's flying experience as a passenger in aircraft. It appeared he was generally active in many sports, enjoying an interest in boxing and swimming and taking great interest in the mechanics and workings of combustion engines. On the initial selection board, Robert was not recommended for either selection or commission, having failed basic entry tests for aircrew a number of times. His CT score was unsatisfactory and his general education only just satisfactory. Having already completed a Lewis course and having passed this with excellent results, and having enormous hunting experience in Edson in civilian life and at stations, he was recommended by the interviewing officer for air gunner. It appears, though, that he only scraped through after numerous attempts. He stood at 5 feet 8 inches tall, was well developed, weighing 150lb, and had a fair complexion, brown eyes and brown hair. Robert finally achieved the position of air gunner, qualifying on 4 December 1942 and being awarded the air gunner's badge. He held the rank of sergeant, which was the minimum rank for active aircrew with a trade, having worked his way through the ranks and passing the air gunners' course. He then continued to proceed up the ranks, with comments of 'very good' for his character references. He embarked from Halifax to travel to the UK on 14 December 1943, arriving just seven days later on 21 December, and was sent to the No. 3 RCAF Personnel Reception Centre for a number of months, before being relocated to No. 24 OTU and then on to No. 61 base on 8 May 1944. He arrived at No. 419 Squadron on 21 June 1944, and it was here he served until his death a few months later on KB800.

The wireless operator on board that day was a replacement, Pilot Officer Lucien Charles Le Vasseur. He was born in Winnipeg, Manitoba, on 29 August 1920, the son of Albert and Carmen Le Vasseur, of Lac Du

Bonnet, Manitoba, both of whom were actually American citizens. Lucien was raised in his town and attended school from 1927, finishing his education at Lac Du Bonnet High School in 1936, where he reached Grade 10. On leaving school he carried out many odd jobs up until 1940. He then followed in the footsteps of his father and became a butcher, but only for a couple of months, covering for someone. In October 1940 he became a clerk in a hardware store with Lloyd Sinclair, but in 1941, at the age of 20, he took the decision to join the RCAF. Lucien specifically requested to enlist for flying duties as a wireless operator or air gunner and presumably showed a keen interest in this field of work. He took his oath to His Majesty on 26 July 1941, but had to wait until the following month to undergo his interviews. He succeeded in impressing the interviewing officers, showing an alert, sincere manner, with an easy approach. The officer summed him up as an 'alert, intelligent country lad that should do well as aircrew'. Lucien began his air gunners' course at the end of 1941, and on completion of this he was sent to the Wireless Operators' School in Calgary on 28 February 1942. His training was not completed until the summer of 1943, and he was sent to the UK on 14 December 1943. During the early months of 1944 Lucien spent time with the No. 7 Air Observers' School, No. 22 OTU, and an Advanced Training Unit, polishing up his skills and converting to heavy bombers with a crew. Finally Lucien was posted to No. 419 'Moose' Squadron on 24 June 1944, where he racked up a number of sorties before losing his life on 14 October 1944 over Duisburg.

No. 626 Squadron

Lancaster NE163, UM-T2

Pilot	Flight Lieutenant Reginald Major Aldus	KIA
Flight engineer	Sergeant Vernon Sheppard	KIA
Bomb aimer	Flying Officer John Mervyn MacMillan	KIA (RCAF)
Navigator	Flying Officer Thurston Culshaw	KIA (RCAF)
Mid-upper gunner	Sergeant Harry Jeffries	KIA
Rear gunner	Sergeant Joseph Marks	KIA
Wireless operator	Flying Officer Ronald Ernest Blake	KIA

NE163 was initially delivered to No. 460 Squadron in May 1944, where it took part in various actions. On 15 August 1944 it was transferred to No. 626 Squadron, based at RAF Wickenby, Lincolnshire. It was airborne at 0643 hrs on the morning of Saturday, 14 October.

NE163 came down at 0849 hrs in the main street of a suburb named Barmingholten, which is on the outskirts of Sterkrade Holten. The bulk of the wreckage came to rest in Holtener Straße, which runs in a north–south direction, approximately 3 kilometres south-east of Dinslaken. The debris was found just to the north of the junction of Leit Straße and Holtener Straße, close to one of the local flak positions. To one side of the road nowadays is a large quarry and hill, with deposits from the coalmines. In 1944 these were open fields, and it was there that parts of the aircraft were seen. An eyewitness by the name of Erwin Casper, who is now deceased but lived at the location where the aircraft came down, recalled two Merlin engines lying smashed up in a field, together with other parts of the wreckage.

The incident involving Lancaster NE163 was witnessed by Trevor Jenkins, another member of No. 626 Squadron:

This aircraft was my flight commander's aircraft, that being Flight Lieutenant Reginold Major Aldus. They were flying alongside us while on the bomb run up to the target, and it was close enough for me to read the lettering on the fuselage. I then saw the aircraft receive a direct hit from a flak burst and it just exploded into a large fireball and fell from the sky after flying straight for a short amount of time. All of this happened very quickly and there would be no chance of anyone having the opportunity to bail out. The aircraft then simply fell to earth in flames, leaving a long trail of thick black smoke.

Five members of the crew were placed in the Walsum/Aldenrade cemetery on Schul Straße, on the outskirts of Dinslaken to the south-west, in a communal trench, and were interred with members of another crew. The remaining two airmen were placed at the Park Friedhof (also known as Waldfriedhof) cemetery in Dinslaken, buried with two other crews.

This crew proved problematic for post-war investigators at first, as they were not all together in one location. It is likely that, as they were not interred together, not all were found at the scene of the crash at the same time. A number of eyewitnesses who have been spoken to around the Dinslaken and Holten area mention bodies being found on their streets, away from wreckage. Perhaps these airmen jumped or were thrown out if parts of the aircraft broke up as it came down to earth in flames. The communal grave at Walsum, which was exhumed on 24 May 1946, contained nine bodies in all. It supposedly contained all the seven missing crew members of Lancaster NE163, together with two other airmen, who were initially thought to belong to different crews. Two of the NE163 airmen, however, Flying Officer R. E. Blake and Flying Officer J. MacMillan, were later identified in the Dinslaken Waldfriedhof on Willy Brandt Straße, and were not the airmen originally thought in Walsum. This left only five airmen belonging to the crew of NE163 and not seven as originally thought.

The confusion was that seventeen airmen were reported to have been buried by German authorities in the Waldfriedhof cemetery, Dinslaken. However, when exhumations took place, mixed remains of two airmen (Flying Officer R. E. Blake (NE163) and Flying Officer H. J. Watts (NF928)) were found in the sixth grave, which was not in accordance with the German records. This meant that the total was in fact eighteen airmen and not seventeen.

The communal grave at Dinslaken's Waldfriedhof, to clarify, contained the seven crewmen of Lancaster NF928, seven from the crew of Lancaster JB297, two miscellaneous airmen, one from 10 April 1944 and one from 19 March 1945, and one positive identity, Flying Officer J. MacMillan from the crew of NE163; this made a total of seventeen. However, once the mixed remains in grave six had been discovered, and a second airman from NE163, Flying Officer R. E. Blake, had been identified, this brought the total to eighteen.

So there were two members of the crew of NE163 in the cemetery at Dinslaken's Waldfriedhof (Willy Brandt Straße) and the remaining five of NE163 located elsewhere at Walsum. In place of Flying Officer R. E. Blake at the Walsum cemetery was Flying Officer J. Lindsey of Lancaster NG190, who was positively identified. The cemetery at Walsum contained the five remaining airmen of NE163 and four of NG190, making a total of nine airmen. The remaining two deceased members of NG190 were buried elsewhere, while one was one never located at all.

When exhumations were conducted by the MRES teams, the first grave to be opened was the navigator's, Flying Officer Thurston Culshaw, and he was identified by a number of means: he had his Canada badge on his shoulders and his name displayed on his shirt collar and his name tag on the right breast of his uniform jacket.

Second was Sergeant Harry Jeffries, who was the mid-upper gunner. The only means of identification on his body was a faded name tag with the letters 'J' and 'FF', the rest having been covered up by blood. But this was enough for a positive identification, as he was the only crew member with this surname.

Sergeant Vernon Sheppard was next to be exhumed in the third grave. He was identified by a brevet along with his name and the three digits 335, which were last three digits of his service number (2211335).

The fourth grave to be looked at was that of Sergeant Joseph Marks. The only means of identification were the digits 1483 on his collar, which were the last four digits of his service number (1581483).

The next grave to be examined was assumed to be that of the wireless operator, Flying Officer Ronald Ernest Blake, but here there was only part of the deceased, showing a Canadian WAG brevet, the Canadian badge on his shoulder together with flying officer braid. However, this airman was found in the trench that made up the graves of the crews of NF928 and JB297 in the Dinslaken Waldfriedhof cemetery, and he was eventually identified by a process of elimination.

It was assumed, also by the process of elimination, that the next grave contained the body of Flying Officer John Mervyn MacMillan. At a later date this decision was amended, as MacMillan was positively identified by his disc elsewhere: in the Waldfriedhof cemetery at Dinslaken. The identity of the airman in the grave is not mentioned in the documents, but it later transpired this was an airman from Lancaster NG190.

The pilot, Flight Lieutenant Reginald Major Aldus, was located in the next grave. He did not have any blouse on, although a torn and ripped one was discovered in the grave with the deceased, and it bore the rank of flight lieutenant together with pilot's wings. He was wearing a pullover, which appeared to have a tape lying next to it and which seemed to have been previously attached, with the figures 1802985 and 58651. These numbers, however, are not his service numbers. An officer's shirt was also found on him, and this together with the pilot's wings confirmed that this was the body of the pilot.

The airman lying next to him was not affiliated to the crew of Lancaster NE163, but from the crew of Lancaster NG190. This airman was Flying Officer A. Picard. He had no blouse on, but between his body and that of the pilot was a flying suit, with a faded tape on it with the name 'A. Picard'.

The last airman to be exhumed from the trench was again a member of another crew, apparently an air gunner. He was still wearing his electrically heated flying suit. The airman's shirt was marked on the collar with a name and service number: Sergeant Hall, 1447469. This, however, eventually turned out to be Sergeant T. Alanson, the rear gunner of NG190. It transpired that he must have been wearing someone else's shirt.

Although two airmen from a different bomber had been located here, no one was able to give an account as to why, as most of the records had been destroyed under Nazi instructions. After the identification and exhumation process had taken place, the bodies were reinterred in separate graves with markers on them in the same cemetery. Flowers were arranged by the enquiry team and placed on the graves. The officer in charge of this exhumation and casualty enquiry was Flight Lieutenant K. Ramsden. All of the crew now rest together in Reichswald Forest War Cemetery at Kleve, after they were re-exhumed from their burial location sometime later.

The bomb aimer, Flying Officer John Mervyn MacMillan (J36883), was born on 21 July 1924 in Finch, Ontario, the son of Archibald Kenneth MacMillan and Muriel MacMillan. One of seven siblings, he had four brothers and two sisters. Like so many of the crewmen from the prairies, John was born and raised on a farm and had approximately two years' actual working experience on a dairy farm. He had completed five years at high school in Cornwall College Institute, Ontario, when he enlisted at No. 412 recruiting centre in Ottawa on 21 October 1942, aged just 17, with the ambition of becoming aircrew. However, he stated that after the war he wished to go back to college to take up employment within the field of science. He gained the rank of flying officer and qualified as a bomb aimer on 15 October 1943.

The navigator of NE163 was Flying Officer Thurston Culshaw (J/36932), who was born on 12 February 1922, the son of English-born Ralph Culshaw and Scottish-born Jessie Culshaw. He was brought up on the family farm in Alberta, in the suburb of Lougheed, with his five siblings, one brother and four sisters. He had a good general education, reaching Grade 12 matriculation in high school, and had worked as a farmhand for his father, with three years' experience. The family farmed mainly wheat. He told the recruitment officer for the RCAF that he wished to sign up for aircrew, showing a preference for pilot or observer, and crossing out both air gunner and wireless operator on the form. His initial assessment showed that he was heavy handed and a little awkward, but it was the view of the board that these things could be polished up and worked on, so he was put forward for selection, with a formal interview to follow. He enlisted with the RCAF at the Edmonton recruiting office on 24 July 1942 and qualified as a navigator just over a year later, on 15 October 1943.

Sergeant Henry Jefferies, one of the gunners on the bomber, was born on 9 December 1913 in Thornbury, Tabfield, Gloucestershire, and was the son of Frederick Francis and Kate Jefferies, of Malmesbury, Wiltshire. He grew up in the local area and was brought up on his parents' farm, Coldharbour Farm, located in Brokenborough, Malmesbury, Wiltshire, working within the farming industry after leaving school. He used to have a milk round in the village of Bisley, near Stroud, Gloucestershire. Henry enlisted as a volunteer on 2 June 1941 at the No. 1 Recruiting Centre in Marsham, expressing an interest in being an air gunner, for which he started training in December 1943. He completed his four-month course at the Air Gunnery School on 12 February 1944. Throughout his time in the RAF his character was shown to be 'Very Good'.

The pilot of NE163 was Flight Lieutenant Reginald Major Aldus, born on 12 April 1915 in Framlingham, Suffolk, and educated at a school in Grantham. He was very much a career man in the RAF and served with distinction for many years before his death in 1944. From school in 1931 he signed up for the RAF at the age of 16, but not to fly initially. He joined as an aircraft mechanic and metal rigger, and then began active service at the age of 18 in April 1933. In 1937 he commenced flying training and then gained his wings and served abroad, mainly in Palestine and Sudan, before returning to the UK to fly in wartime Europe. After completing two tours of duty by 1941, Aldus then instructed for some time before he volunteered for a third tour of operational flying.

No. 626 Squadron

Lancaster LM596 UM-V2

Pilot	Flying Officer James Commodore Campbell	KIA (RCAF)
Second pilot (Second dickey)	Flying Officer Robert Albert Charland	KIA (RCAF)
Flight engineer	Sergeant Sidney John Akhurst	KIA
Bomb aimer	Pilot Officer William Frederick Palmer	KIA (RCAF)
Navigator	Flying Officer Ross Cuthbert Clouston	KIA (RCAF)
Mid-upper gunner	Sergeant Thomas George Reynolds	KIA
Rear gunner	Flying Officer John Allan Orr	KIA
Wireless operator	Pilot Officer Roland Marcel Joseph Champagne	KIA (RCAF)

Lancaster LM596 was stationed with No. 626 Squadron at RAF Wickenby, Lincolnshire, which shared its base with No. 12 Squadron. The aircraft was delivered to the squadron from No. 101 Squadron on 6 June 1944.

The loss of this Lancaster was due to the heavy anti-aircraft fire in the area of the target. It is not known what happened on board, but it is most likely that the aircraft caught fire, with the crew struggling to clip on their parachutes and make their way to the exits amid the flames and smoke as it fell to earth. German documents mentioned that an aircraft was seen to explode and crashed at 0140 hrs, but it is unclear whether it blew-up right away or a short time later.

A number of days after No. 626 Squadron had reported that one of its Lancasters was missing, the IRCC forwarded a telegram to the Air Force headquarters reporting German information. It stated that Pilot Officer Champagne was killed on 14 October 1944, but his burial particulars were not given. The Air Force disregarded this telegram in view of the date and time of the aircraft's take-off. However, soon after a second telegram was received stating that Flying Officer Campbell and Flying Officer Charland were killed on 15 October 1944. In view of the evidence and the lapse of time, it was assumed that Flying Officer Charland, Pilot Officer Champagne and Flying Officer Campbell were killed and their deaths were presumed for official purposes. However, as there was no mention of the rest of the crew, they were assumed as still 'missing' until evidence showed otherwise. The crash investigation team looking into missing aircrew in the Ruhr area made enquiries at the beginning of May 1946 to ascertain the fate of this aircrew and found a handful of locals living in the area who were able to provide good information.

On the morning of 9 May 1946, the investigating officer, Flight Lieutenant C. A. Mitchell, went to the house at No. 11 Dickelbach Straße, Duisburg, and spoke with the occupant, Mr Stroucken, and his family regarding an aircraft that had crashed into his allotment site on the evening of 15 October 1944. The resident supplied the basic information that he knew and then arranged for his daughter, Maria, to take the investigating officer to the allotment site, which was situated approximately 15 minutes' walk away at 308 Heer Straße, near the junction of the main highway that led into Duisburg, formally known as Duisburg Straße.

Mr Stroucken advised the officer that a four-engined aircraft had crashed around the time of 2300 hrs (local time) that evening, and that eight bodies had been counted from the wreckage, six of them being removed by the Wehrmacht and the remaining two being buried at the scene, because they were already interred among the aircraft wreckage. The six airmen had been thrown from the wreckage upon impact and scattered over a short distance, so these were recovered, but it appears little or no effort was made to recover the other two, and the hole was simply filled in. Another point of interest to note is that the Germans recorded four of the bodies as unrecognizable, which probably explains why their names were not on the telegrams. The Germans recorded only the names of Flying Officer Charland, Flying Officer Campbell, Pilot Officer Champagne, and Flying Officer Orr, together with Flying Officer Batty, who was from another crew, so clearly their reports had got mixed up somewhere along the line. Statements from locals mentioned to the officer that the bodies that had been removed were left to lie in the street for up to four or five days before being taken for burial.

Upon visiting the area and the allotment site, which was in the rear garden of 308 Heer Straße, that also consisted of a large block of flats, the officer saw that the rear area was still being used for growing vegetables. However, in the middle of the area there was a small metal cross with the words of 'Two Unknown British Flyers' inscribed on it. Enquiries with the occupier, Mr Johann Hoegener, and his son and daughter revealed that on the morning following the crash an armed guard of Wehrmacht soldiers were placed around the crash site, after which two German soldiers and two Russian prisoners of war were used to strip the dead airmen of their possessions and remove six of the bodies from the wreckage. They also reburied the remaining two at the site. This was witnessed by the resident's children. The witnesses mentioned that the airmen were definitely Canadian, as they saw their flashes on their uniform.

A number of days later, on 15 May, following the visit when he had spoken to the eyewitnesses, the investigating officer returned to the site, together with a pathologist, and the two remaining bodies at the site were exhumed for examination. No real further identification was gained from this, as the airmen had been buried in the ground without a coffin or covering, and it was found that only an air gunner and pilot were present. Flying wings and braid on one of the shoulders showing the rank of flying officer were found on one body; the other showed an air gunner's badge. Both airmen were then buried in the New Waldfriedhof, Duisburg, one of the main cemeteries, the pilot being buried in Field 1A, grave number 330, and the air gunner in Field 1A, grave 331. This cemetery is located on Kreuz Straße, Hamborn.

The following year further investigations were still being made as to the whereabouts of this crew, and on 13 June 1947 the other six airmen from this crew were exhumed and the graves opened up in the New Waldfriedhof, none of which had any form of cross or grave marking. This was a common problem, which caused some airmen never to be found, especially if witnesses would not cooperate or simply had forgotten and records had been destroyed or lost. The witnessing officer to this was Flight Lieutenant L'Estrange.

One of the graves contained in plot 302 to 305, Field 1A, bore the shattered remains of four airmen, none of whom were individually identifiable, and only small broken masses of bones remained. However, some clothing did reveal a navigator holding the rank of flying officer. Among the torn clothing, parts of parachute harnesses and Mae West survival vests were found, together with a silk scarf.

One of the other graves contained an airman with the aircrew category of pilot and the rank of flying officer, identified by the pilot's wings brevet on the tunic. Many items of clothing were found, together with a parachute harness. However, positive identification of exactly which pilot this was was just not possible at this time, the situation being made worse by the fact that no coffins had been used for the burial.

The final grave exhumed in the cemetery contained the bomb aimer. Identification was by means of the clothing, which showed the rank of sergeant and bomb-aimer's badge. Items of clothing, including a white flying sweater and officer's shirt, together with a white silk flying scarf, were found. A parachute harness was also recovered along with his Mae West.

It is possible that these bodies were buried in a trench or mass grave to begin with, placed next to each other. Because some of the airmen's remains could not be separated, six of the crew were buried together in a single plot when reinterred in the Reichswald Forest Cemetery in 1949, with just Sergeant Reynolds and Flying Officer Campbell being placed in individually marked graves next to their crew mates. Flying Officer Campbell was eventually named positively by his identity discs, and Sergeant Reynolds circumstantially identified; hence their individual marking.

One of the pilots on this Lancaster, on board as a 'second dickey' on his first operation with an experienced crew before taking his own crew on operations, was Flying Officer Robert Albert Charland. He was new to the squadron and had been posted there only on 28 September. He was the son of Albert Louis Charland and Florence Mary Charland, both Canadian nationals, with his father being from Drumminville, Quebec, and his mother coming from Eau Claire. Robert was born on 22 June 1918 in Port Colborne. He was an only child, and lived with his parents in Ferris, Ontario, in their family home. He was brought up and educated locally, attending Harvey public primary school from 1927, from where he went to Worthington public school for his matriculation, which he completed in 1938, before taking up employment as an auto salesman with North Bay Garage in North Bay, Ontario. However, in late 1941 he went to work for Gamble Robinson Fruit and Vegetable company, also as a salesman. This job too was short-lived. War was being raged, and he decided to leave his employment in 1942 to enlist with the RCAF. Upon enrolment at a recruiting office in North Bay on 28 February 1942, he expressed a desire to fly and specifically to become a pilot, and therefore enlisted for flying duties. At his interview with the board on 24 December 1941, Robert impressed the interviewing officers with his persistence and desire to fly, despite having only a basic education and upbringing. Officers recognized his low to fair ability to learn and fair education, but his general background stood out to them. He was recommended by the board for pilot or observer, with comments 'an excellent lad who should do well' and 'believe he will try hard to qualify as Pilot Officer and very keen to fly'. He was accepted for pilot or observer, but he was to undertake pilot training when enlisted. He did, for an unknown reason, request to serve away from England, preferring to serve in Africa or Australia. However, he was eventually sent where aircrew were most required and that, of course, was Europe.

The pilot flying the bomber on the fateful evening was Flying Officer James Commodore Campbell. He was born in Canton, New York, on 9 October 1916, and, although he held Canadian citizenship, as his parents had then moved address to Sullivan Avenue, Thorold, Ontario, both of his parents had emigrated to the area from Scotland. His father was William Glen Campbell and his mother Mrs Margaret Campbell; James was one of six, having two sisters and three brothers. James spent his primary education at the Prince of Wales School from 1922 before moving to Thorold High School in 1930 to do his senior matriculation, where he spent three years, before finally completing a two-year course in 1935 at Welland Technical School, studying mechanics and aerodynamics. He appeared to have a love for machines and mechanics and sought to continue this route as a means of employment, but moved from job to job within a short period of time from 1935 to 1941. Straight from school he took up employment with Minty's Garage as an auto mechanic, where he stayed for approximately two years, before taking up a machinist's apprenticeship with Clark Machine Company. After this he worked again as a mechanic and then as a store clerk and machinist. James then chose to enlist in the RCAF, which he did on 4 February 1942 at the No. 10 Hamilton recruiting centre, enrolling for flying duties with the hope of becoming an observer or pilot. His preliminary interview was held on 24 December 1941, James, impressing the board with his excellent record in mathematics and aerodynamic courses and showing that he was capable of pilot training, which indeed he was recommended for by all interviewing officers. Despite his impressive schooling, he was rather reserved and quiet, but very keen.

LM596's navigator on that evening was Flying Officer Ross Cuthbert

Clouston, the son of a Canadian father named Charles Clouston and an English mother, Esther Clouston, who was originally from Middlesborough. Ross was born on 27 December 1921, in Bridgeburg, Ontario, which was part of Welland County, and he was one of two sons. Ross was educated at the Fort Erie High School, having completed his primary education, and finished his schooling gaining a junior matriculation in 1939. He did not continue on to any higher education or undertake any formal courses. Instead, he left school and gained an apprenticeship with a steel company named Horton Steel Works, but this was short-lived, as he was made redundant in 1940. But he soon took up employment again as an aircraft fitter with Fleet Aircraft Ltd in Fort Erie, and it was from here he moved into the RCAF in 1942. Perhaps it was the desire to fly that encouraged him while being employed within an aircraft company. He was enlisted on 15 May 1942 at the No. 9 recruiting centre, London, Ontario, seeking employment as a pilot or observer, but he was later to become a navigator.

The bomb aimer, Pilot Officer William Frederick Palmer, was born on 1 September 1923 in Magrath, Alberta. His father was John Frederick Palmer and his mother Flora Palmer, both of English heritage, having emigrated to Canada. William was one of many brothers and sisters. He was very well educated, being able to speak French as a second language, despite leaving school at the age of 17. He gained a senior matriculation at the Magrath High School, but also completed schooling in chemistry and had knowledge of bank keeping, having for a time been employed as an office clerk, although he was in this post less than a year, having joined in 1941. William was eager to take up employment within the RCAF, as he had made a previous application in Calgary on 2 July 1941, but this was rejected on the grounds that he was too young. As soon as he was old enough, he reapplied and was successful. On 15 October 1942, aged 19, he enlisted at the No. 2 Calgary recruitment centre, Alberta, exactly two years to the day before he would lose his life.

Pilot Officer Roland Marcel Joseph Champagne was the aircraft's wireless operator on board. He was born on 18 February 1920 in St Norbert, Manitoba, and was part of a large family, as there were seven sisters and four brothers. His father and mother were both Canadian. The family resided together in Manitoba and ran the family farm. Following his education, which finished in 1936 with Roland reaching Grade 10 at St Norbert Bay High School, he went into farming and spent many years there until his contract ended. He then drifted from job to job with none lasting more than a few months, and finished up as a sheet metal worker with the Western Steel Company in Manitoba. Then, in 1941, he enlisted in the RCAF. When Roland first enrolled, with no previous flying experience other than twenty hours as a passenger, he was one of the few airmen described in this book who chose ground duties instead of flying duties. He intended to train as an aero engine mechanic. However, he also stated that, if he was unable to achieve this role, he would like to become a pilot, if flight duties prevailed. Roland enlisted at a recruitment centre in Winnipeg, Manitoba, on 25 August 1941, and initially was trained as an aero engine mechanic, achieving a standard score in his testing. But he must have had second thoughts, as he then attended interviews, having asked for a transfer to flying duties. Upon his request, he was remustered for aircrew duties, and so began training, but undertook a wireless operator's course, together with an air gunner's course, which he took concurrently. He gained his wireless operator's badge on 1 October 1943 and then the air gunner's badge on 22 November 1943.

Flying Officer John Allan Orr was the son of Tasmanian Rhodes scholar, Professor John Orr, of 27 Queen's Crescent, Edinburgh. He was born at Stockport, Cheshire, on 28 February 1924. Entering George Watson's Boys' College in 1940, he achieved some distinction as a quarter-miler. John joined the RAF in August 1942. After training as a rear gunner, he was commissioned in July 1943. Flying in Lancasters, he completed his first tour of operations with No. 100 Squadron, and was awarded the Distinguished Flying Cross in April 1944.

No. 428 Squadron

Lancaster KB780 NA-T

Pilot	Flight Lieutenant William Harold Janney	KIA (RCAF)
Flight engineer	Sergeant Leonard Brotherhood	KIA
Bomb aimer	Flying Officer Archie Verdun Batty	KIA (RCAF)
Navigator	Pilot Officer Walter Henry Killner	KIA (RNZAF)
Mid-upper gunner	Pilot Officer Paul Reviere Jones	KIA (RCAF)
Rear gunner	Pilot Officer Francis Arthur Harrison	KIA (RCAF)
Wireless operator	Pilot Officer Albert Sydney McFeetors	KIA (RCAF)

KB780, another Canadian-manufactured Lancaster, was delivered to No. 428 Squadron, based at RAF Middleton St George, on 23 July 1944. On 14 October 1944 this aircraft became airborne at 0558 hrs and took off to attack the industrial target of Duisburg, but failed to return with the loss of all of its crew, all of whom are now buried together in the Rheinberg War Cemetery. KB 780 was hit by very heavy anti-aircraft fire on the morning raid, while over the target area itself. The Lancaster was seen to explode in mid-air in the area of Emmericher Straße, the waterways office and the Rhine Herne Canal, with many small pieces of wreckage falling to earth and becoming scattered over a wide area. The German reports list the crash site as 2 kilometres south of Duisburg-Meiderich, Rhine Herne Canal, with a crash time of 0853 hrs, and they state that the aircraft was approximately 95 per cent destroyed. Some of this wreckage was located by post-war investigators at the scene of the crash, but the majority was cleared away, with only fragments remaining. The claim for this bomber was made by No. 4 Flak Division. The aircraft was seen to explode over the target, as supported by an eyewitness account from one of the squadron, Ron Cassels:

I saw some aircraft being hit and two parachutes leave one of them. Then Stu pointed out NA-T from 428. It was being flown by Flight Lieutenant W. H. Janney. I was friendly with the navigator, Pilot Officer W. H. Killner, the only New Zealander on the squadron. They were about a 100 yards to our right and just above us. As they opened the bomb doors, the aircraft exploded and disappeared. They must have received a direct hit, which exploded the cookie. They certainly never knew what happened. They were close enough that the explosion gave us a severe jolt.

A telegram was sent to the UK via the Independent Red Cross Committee some weeks following the crash, stating that the crew were killed on 15 October 1944 at 0140 hrs. The names of certain crewmen were shown on the telegram, which meant the Germans must have identified the airmen following the crash, by either identification discs or personal belongings. However, the telegram mentioned no news of Sergeant Brotherhood, but included the name of a Sergeant Wills (known to be from ME748), with the names of the six other members of the crew. It did not refer to any burial particulars. Later on the death list became available, and it stated that some of the crew had been buried at the Parish Cemetery in Obermeiderich, with others at the Duisburg New Cemetery. The information, however, was disregarded by the Air Ministry, as the date was incorrect, as KB780 was missing from the morning raid on 14 October and not from the night raid. Eventually, on 16 April 1945 the Air Ministry finally accepted that the crew were dead for official purposes, and that their deaths had occurred on 14 October 1944, as no further news had been received. It appears the Germans somehow must have got their information confused, and mixed up the details of Lancasters ME748 and KB780. It also seems that the Germans mixed up Flying Officer Batty with the crew of LM596, reporting him as one of the crew they recovered from LM596's crash site. The investigating officers in charge of locating this crew and crash site after the war found the crash site only by process of elimination. Once all of the other aircraft had been located from the daylight raid, ND805 and KB780 were the only ones out-standing. ND805 was dealt with, which left the time and location of the remaining bomber from the German reports as KB780.

Sometime after the raid, during the day, a local police unit came across the bodies of the airmen, and a guard was placed around them overnight, with no one being allowed near. The wreckage was found very close to the waterway's office, completely destroyed. The guard remained in place until the military recovery team arrived on the following day.

The unit was thought to have come from Düsseldorf.

The seven airmen were recovered from the area of the crashed air-craft by a military team, but post-war investigators found it difficult to track down the whereabouts of the bodies. Initially all investigations carried out by Flight Lieutenant Tennison proved fruitless, with no graves located. Eventually in 1950 the case was closed, and all seven members of the crew are now commemorated on the Runnymede Memorial. The search for the graves was complicated by the fact that three heavy raids occurred on Duisburg, disrupting the police and civil defence records, with not all graves being marked adequately after mass funerals had taken place. Most of the local population, when interviewed, had no idea that an aircraft had even crashed, as they had been busy with their own troubles and in the shelters. However, German records listed the crew buried in various cemeteries including the Obermeiderich churchyard, the north cemetery of Duisburg/Hamborn and Meiderich. The post-war investigators found no trace of the crew in any of these cemeteries; all known Allied graves had been exhumed, and nothing had been found. What made the case confusing too is that some of these crew-men's names were mixed with the names of the crew from LM596, which were eventually located in Duisburg New Cemetery after the war. The reports had been mixed up.

German reports stated the following burial locations for each crewman:

Name	Cemetery as recorded by the Germans
Flight Lieutenant Janney	Obermeiderich
Flying Officer Batty	North Cemetery, Duisburg/Hamborn; New Cemetery, Duisburg
Pilot Officer McFeetors	North Cemetery Duisburg/Hamborn
Pilot Officer Jones	Obermeiderich
Pilot Officer Harrison	Obermeiderich
Pilot Officer Killner	Obermeiderich
Sergeant Brotherhood	Obermeiderich; North Cemetery Duisburg, Hamborn

The confusion can be appreciated, but, despite searches and exhumations of all Allied graves in these areas, no trace of the airmen was found. The investigating officers even enlisted the help of the police in the No. 2 Group Police District HQ, and they made enquiries on behalf of the investigation officers. They could find no trace of either aircraft, LM596 or KB780, nor could they locate any graves of the respective crews in the cemeteries listed in the enquiry above. The reason KB780 and LM596 are mentioned together is that the German report referred to a number of names from each crew, but how they came to mix these up is not known. All cemeteries within a twenty-mile radius were also visited, with negative results. The only information that could be established from the police enquiry was that nineteen unidentified bodies of airmen were buried at Duisburg New/Wald Cemetery (Stadt West Friedhof) on 20 December 1944, and a further five unidentified airmen were buried there on 21 February 1945. This enquiry opened up further discussion with regards to other crews from the night raids with missing aircrew members.

The reason for this is that, from the number of bodies buried, the enquiry concluded that at least two, possibly three, aircraft came down in the area at about the same time, which we know was the case with the Duisburg raids on the night raid on 15 October 1944. These nineteen bodies, all unidentifiable, possibly relate to the crews of LM165, ME748, and LM596, all of which crashed on the night raids to Duisburg. The German report also mentioned a Sergeant Wills, who was documented to have been buried in the Duisburg North/Hamborn Cemetery, while another report shows bodies being buried at Obermeiderich, one of which we know to have been a crew member from Lancaster ME748. It is possible the nineteen were originally buried locally and then moved to the Duisburg New Cemetery at a later date, possibly in December 1944, which is the date mentioned here. It is one of the largest cemeteries and is very close to the crash sites of LM165 and ME748, and other crews, such as those from PB357 and LM596, were found here. It is almost certain that five others from Sergeant R. Wills's crew, were buried here too. The seventh airmen of this crew, Flying Officer Shaw, was later found at an isolated spot in a cemetery in Essen; he had not been taken to a local cemetery, probably because his body had been found a month or so after the crash.

If some of these airmen were from Lancaster ME748, it would account for six of the unknown nineteen airmen in this cemetery. Furthermore, ME748 collided with LM165 and crashed very close to it, so it would make sense for the Germans to have recovered this crew and buried the bodies in the same cemetery as the crew of ME748. There would be no logical reason to separate them. What is known too is that all of the airmen located after the crash were removed on the same lorry. This now makes thirteen (six from ME748 and seven from LM165) unidentifiable and missing airmen, as Flying Officer Shaw from ME748 had not been found at the original time of removal. Lancaster LM596 had eight missing, although two were left at the scene, which makes nineteen airmen in total. Of course, this is only an assumption, but it is a theory into the identities of the nineteen missing airmen who were taken into the cemetery during December 1944. However, when the RAF teams arrived, they may have found more than nineteen airmen in this cemetery, but exactly how many is not known. It is also possible that not all of these airmen were identified by post-war investigators. The problem also to take into account is that sometimes the number of missing airmen listed is incorrect and a group of bones or body parts may constitute more than one airman, as was the case with LM596, when one grave was opened up to reveal the remains of four airmen. The crews of LM165 and ME748 are more than likely to make up some of the ninety-six unknown airmen currently resting in Reichswald Forest at Kleve, although some body parts from the crash of ME748 and LM165 are buried in Rheinberg, after being discovered by farmers after the war.

The investigation into the whereabouts of the crew of KB780 was closed in 1950, and a Final Graves Registration Report was drawn up, stating this particular crew had no known graves, and that their names were to be inscribed on the memorial to the missing. This report is dated 29 August 1950.

But, in fact, this crew's communal grave was in the Municipal Cemetery, Meiderich. This must have been completely overlooked, as MRES investigation officers attended this cemetery during their enquiries but found nothing. No doubt the grave was not adequately marked. It was not until the spring of 1957 that the commission discovered the remains of this aircrew. The cemetery authorities in Germany had been preparing an unused site in Duisburg at the Meiderich Municipal Cemetery, located on Varinzer Straße, and in doing so had stumbled upon the graves of seven Allied airmen. The airmen turned out to be the missing crew of Lancaster KB780, which were in an unmarked grave at the time of the original burial. Further investigations confirmed their identity. In two cases, personal effects were found in the form of a wrist bracelet engraved W. H. Janney and a gold ring inscribed A. S. McFeetors. Pilot Officer McFeetors's ring was returned to his family, and it is now in the possession of his son, Ray. The next of kin of each family was notified of this discovery. All of the seven crew members were exhumed from this cemetery soon after they were located, and then removed to their final resting place in the Rheinberg War Cemetery, Germany. They were interred into a communal grave as individual identification was not possible.

The wireless operator on this aircraft was Pilot Officer Albert Sydney McFeetors. He was born in Copper Cliff, Ontario, the son of Frederick and Annie Smith, both of whom were UK nationals living in Canada. He was also known as Bert. Fred and Annie had four boys and two daughters. Bert's mother died less than six months after he was born. Because of his mother's premature death and the difficult times for a large family, Bert was raised by neighbours, the McFeetors family. In 1939 he took McFeetors as his last name, partly to recognize his up-bringing but also to carry on that name, as the McFeetors's only son, Henry Earl, had died in 1922 as a result of injuries received in the First World War. In his adoptive family there were four surviving girls, Helen, Jessie, Pearl and Eva. Bert worked as a foreman, having been promoted from a machinist with INC Ltd, in Sudbury, Ontario. He was with the company for nine years prior to enlisting with the RCAF, which he did on 31 August 1942. Just over two years later he would be killed in action on active service in the skies over Germany. He had no previous experience in terms of flying, other than some ten hours' flying time as a passenger. Although Albert reached Grade 13 at school, he did not score well in his entry exam. He was seen as alert during the interview and specifically re-quested a position as wireless operator. He was deemed as physically fit with an even temperament, and was expected to develop well under training. In his spare time he enjoyed building model aircraft, and expressed a moderate interest in photography, fishing, baseball and skiing. Bert was accepted and trained with No. 3 Wireless School, Winnipeg, Manitoba, with the RCAF. He successfully completed this course on 9 July 1943 and was then sent on an air gunner's course, which commenced on 12 July 1943.

The mid-upper gunner on the aircraft was Pilot Officer Paul Reviere Jones (J92064). He was the son of farmer Robert Mckee Jones and Audrey Aline Jones, born on 19 December 1922 at the family farm in St Walburg, Saskatchewan, and was one of six siblings, having three brothers and two sisters. He worked on his father's farm straight from school. Paul enlisted with the RCAF on 13 November 1942 at a recruiting office in Saskatoon for flying duties, with no specific preference for a set position of aircrew. Following assessment, he was recommended for standard aircrew, and later went on to train as an air gunner. Being willing, alert and aggressive, he was assessed as good aircrew material and came across to the interviewing officer as being extremely keen, having lots of confidence and of a cheerful disposition. He also had a fair knowledge of mechanics and mechanical ability. For leisure and sporting activities Paul enjoyed softball and basketball, though he had limited experience, because of his background.

Flying Officer Archie Verdun Batty (J21182), the Lancaster's bomb aimer, came from a slightly different background than most on this raid. He was a schoolteacher and a store manager before enlisting in the RCAF. Archie was the son of Samuel Batty and Agnes Jane Maxwell, who resided in Limerick, Saskatchewan. They both worked on the family-owned farm, specializing in grain farming. Archie was born here on the farm on 13 March 1916, being one of seven children, having three sisters and three brothers, although sadly one of his brothers died just a few years after Archie was born. Despite his early farming background, he completed a full education, moving from primary school, in 1921–9, to Limerick Secondary School, in 1929–34, where he achieved Grade 12, before undertaking a university course at Moose Jaw Normal University, where he studied to become a teacher. He taught for a total of three years at the Lynthorpe and Stonehenge schools until 1939, where he changed roles and left teaching to become a manager with a company called Limerick Co Op Association Ltd, in return for a higher salary. It was from here in 1942 he left and joined the RCAF.

The pilot of KB780 was Flight Lieutenant William Harold Janney. William was born on 12 February 1915, to Flossie Belle and William Ernest Janney. He was one of three children, two brothers and a sister. He lived with his parents in Toronto, Ontario, and attended school there, continuing all the way through to university. He then worked as a clerk with HEPC, which specialized in the sale of hydro-electric energy, leaving to join the RCAF on 2 March 1942 in Toronto. His pastimes included building model aircraft and ships, but William also enjoyed skating and golf.

KB780's rear gunner was Francis Arthur Harrison, DFC, who was born in Cranbrook, British Columbia, on 3 May 1917, the son of Robert Henry and Maude Harrison. His father worked locally as a train conductor. He had two brothers and one sister of similar age. Francis was raised in Cranbrook and he began his education in 1924, completing it in 1937, when he went to work as a first-aid man for a local company and the government. In 1940 he changed positions and left for Banff Hospital as a repair man, although he was there for only a year before he moved jobs again, this time as a labourer. The same year, 1941, he trained as an assistant electrician with the West Kootenay Power and Light Company.

Pilot Officer Walter Henry Killner was the only member of the crew from New Zealand. He was an experienced navigator, with twenty-seven sorties behind him. Born in Christchurch on 2 November 1908, Walter received his secondary education at Christchurch Boys' High School. A keen sportsman, he undertook tennis, golf and yachting in his spare time, while he spent his working life after school employed by Lever Brothers Ltd as a company representative. In March 1941, with war already raging, Walter applied for war service with the RNZAF. On 18 April 1942 he was finally enlisted for aircrew training at the Initial Training Wing, Rotorua, and on 22 June he embarked for Canada under the Empire Air Training Scheme. In total he had served 561 hours as a navigator.

No. 153 Squadron

Lancaster NG190 P4-T

Pilot	Flying Officer Joseph Ross Eugene Brouillette	KIA (RCAF)
Flight engineer	Sergeant Arthur Scammell	KIA
Bomb aimer	Flying Officer Glenn Crawford Bellamy	KIA (RCAF)
Navigator	Flying Officer Alfred Alexander Picard	KIA (RCAF)
Mid-upper gunner	Flight Sergeant William Greene	KIA (RCAF)
Rear gunner	Sergeant Thomas Allanson	KIA
Wireless operator	Flying Officer James Lindsay	KIA (RCAF)

Stationed with No. 153 Squadron at RAF Kirmington, this Lancaster arrived on 7 October 1944, having been moved from No. 166 Squadron, where it was initially delivered on 3 October 1944, when No. 153 Squadron was formed from previous members of No. 166 Squadron. NG190 became airborne at 0655 hrs and was one of the later Lancasters to become airborne in fair weather, flying most of the route above cloud in clear skies, and was shot down less than two hours later with the loss of all the crew, one of whom has no known grave.

NG190 was lost to the heavy flak that was engaged over the target. Captured German documents reveal that this bomber exploded in mid-air and broke up, with the bulk of the wreckage falling down into Schloss Straße, Aldenrade, approximately 1 kilometre south of Dinslaken at 0848, with the wreckage being cleared by German police and German troops. Parts of debris also turned up at Mattler Busch, which is located 4 kilometres south-east of Walsum, and is very close to the river Rhine. This area is made up of a maze of tributaries between the Emscher Canal and the River Elper, which are approximately 1 kilometre apart. A claim by No. 4 Flak Division was made for this bomber.

Despite visiting the crash site and speaking to a number of elderly residents who reside in the street, I found no one who could confirm exactly where in the road the bulk of the wreckage had fallen; they did confirm that an aircraft had crashed in October 1944 following a heavy raid to Duisburg.

The aircraft that came down here is almost certain to be that of Lancaster NG190. Although investigators were unable to locate the official register of crashes, other documents point towards this crash site being that of NG190. This was the view of the investigation teams, once they had taken into account the other crashes of this date, together with other circumstantial evidence. However, initially only some of the crewmen had been found, and a search for the others proved fruitless.

Four of the crew had been recovered from the main crash site and taken for burial at the Walsum/Aldenrade cemetery, which was the nearest available cemetery to the crash site itself. Although no burial documents could be traced for them, exhumation at the cemetery showed that the Germans had buried the airmen they had recovered with five members of another crew, with the collective grave containing nine airmen in total. The other airmen were five crew members from Lancaster NE163, the remaining two of this crew being found at the Dinslaken Waldfried-hof cemetery. The Walsum cemetery is located on Schul Straße in Aldenrade, and the field within the cemetery where the communal grave was found is named Ehren Friedhof.

At the exhumation, the first five bodies recovered belonged to the crew of Lancaster NE163. But the sixth grave contained the body of a Canadian wireless operator, and the only airman missing from Lancaster NG190 who was Canadian was Flying Officer James Lindsay. He was then identified.

The airman in the next grave was Flying Officer Glenn Crawford Bellamy. The body had a bomb-aimer's brevet on his tunic and flying officer rank displayed with Canadian flashes. His collar bore no name but showed a laundry mark, either B26X or 826X. It is possible he had red hair, but the officer was not certain of this. But there was only one flying officer Canadian bomb aimer lost in this area on 14 October 1944, so there was no doubt that this was Flying Officer Bellamy.

Flying Officer Picard was found in grave number eight, and he was positively identified by his service number, J37732, which was written into the waistband of his flying trousers. This had first been misread as J87732.

The next grave to be exhumed was the air gunner's, Sergeant Thomas

Allanson, who was discovered in grave number nine. There was initially some problem with this identification as, although the grave contained an airman bearing the rank of a sergeant and air gunner's brevet, the collar on the neck revealed the name 'Hall 1447469'. It transpired that this airman was believed to be wearing someone else's shirt, and no one by this name was reported missing in this area near this date. It was the opinion of the investigating officer Flight Lieutenant L'Estrange that this was definitely the body of Sergeant Thomas Allanson.

Further enquiries made by the investigation units found that the pilot and mid-upper gunner had been laid to rest in a completely different location at a cemetery on Casper Baur Straße, Wesel. This was because the bodies had been located many weeks later by the Germans, having been found near the Rhine.

The pilot of the aircraft, Flying Officer J. R. E. Brouillette, was washed ashore from the Rhine on 29 October 1944 at Mlenkopf Rhein Lippe and then laid to rest at Wesel, where a cross was erected for him, showing his name. The mid-upper gunner, Flight Sergeant W. Greene, who was also washed ashore from the Rhine at a later date, was buried here too. He was identified by the Germans from a handkerchief found in his pocket and his uniform, which showed an air gunner's badge with Canadian shoulder flashes.

When investigation teams located the caretaker of the cemetery, whose name was W. Sardeman, many enquiries were made as to when the airmen were received into this cemetery, as the dates varied. It was confirmed that Flying Officer Brouillette came from the German Air Force at Bonninghardt and was received by the cemetery on 3 November 1944; it was also confirmed that he was recovered from the river. All clothing, except for a black tie, had been removed from the body. He was later buried at the cemetery on 4 November 1944. Flight Sergeant Greene was also received into the cemetery from the German Air Force unit stationed at Bonninghardt, on 22 November, with his remains interred in a coffin and his cause of death stated as unknown. He was buried on 23 November 1944 at this cemetery.

The last remaining crewman was Sergeant A. Scammell, the flight engineer, but despite numerous enquiries and searches his body was sadly never located. It is thought he was either washed away when parts of the aircraft went into the river Rhine with the pilot and rear gunner, or possibly was still buried in part of the aircraft remains at the bottom of the Rhine. Alternatively, he could have been removed later from the scene of the crash and buried in an isolated cemetery. All investigations into his whereabouts proved fruitless, and hence he is commemorated on the Runnymede Memorial on panel 237, as he has no known grave.

During investigations of this aircrew at Wesel on 29 September 1945, the investigation teams were shown an airman who remains unidentified. He had been discovered in the corner of a cornfield and was in an isolated grave. No identification could be established, as it appeared the airman had been looted of all items. He was located in a field three miles south of Wesel, on the Wesel to Dinslaken road, and it was apparent to the local civilians that he had been there for about six months when he was found in March 1945. It is possible that this could have been Sergeant Scammell, but without any form of identification, this airman was never named.

Meanwhile, a report was also made about the mistreatment of airmen in the area of Wesel. It emerged that a local by the name of Kurt Reinicke had made an allegation of ill treatment of aircrew against official Geerg Gillman. It was said that on one occasion he had paraded an Allied airman through the streets with a label hanging around his neck with 'Murderer' written on it. Nothing specific was discovered to link this treatment to the crew of NG190, but the investigators were not entirely happy with the way the Dutch army lieutenant was handling the case and recommended that Gillman should be questioned further.

Mid-upper gunner Flight Sergeant William Greene, service number R224448, was the son of Mary and David Greene, who resided in Drolet Street in Montreal, Quebec, and was born in Montreal on 28 March 1924, one of four brothers and a sister. Despite the family all having Canadian citizenship, his father was born in Ireland. William remained at this address for his childhood, attending school and gaining one year at high school, from where he went to work as an office boy in 1941 with Bepco Company Ltd, later moving to Alcoa Steamship Company as an office clerk. In 1942 he joined the Army and enlisted in the Black Watch Reserve at the rank of private in June 1942, prior to leaving and enrolling with the RCAF on 9 April 1943. He had no previous experience with flying, but had a great interest in model aircraft. At the time of the application he was 19 years old, with a height of 6 feet and a weight of 149lb, and so was reasonably built and had excellent vision. He was assessed as being mentally capable for the tasks of aircrew and having a rather likeable and pleasant personality, with a keen drive to learn. His complexion was described as medium and he had long swept-back brown hair with blue eyes. Having enlisted in the RCAF, he completed his air gunner training and was awarded his air gunner's badge on 14 January 1944.

Flying Officer Glenn Crawford Bellamy, service number J37834, was the bomb aimer on Lancaster NG190 and as such was largely responsible for the success of the sortie once the aircraft arrived at the destination. Glenn was the son of farmer Alexander McPhail Bellamy and Anne Jane Crawford who were both born and raised in Canada. They ran the family farm in Mckague, Saskatchewan, and had a large family. Glenn was born on 15 December 1915 and had no less than four sisters and six brothers. Glenn left Beech Grove School having completed Grade 10 and went straight into farming with his parents. They employed him from 1932 until he enlisted into the RCAF on 2 June 1942 at the No. 4 recruitment centre in Saskatoon. Having previous experience with farm machinery he was mechanically inclined and applied for flying duties, specifying either pilot or observer at his initial interview, although he had no previous flying or military experience. He also mentioned in his interview that he would like to return to his previous occupation of farming after active service. It is not known why he decided to leave the farm and enlist for active service. Perhaps his brothers, who were already engaged in the armed forces, with one serving in the Canadian army and two in the American army, influenced him. Despite wishing to be a pilot, he unfortunately did not make the grade for this position, with his education letting him down, as he proved to be deficient in English, Mathematics and Physics. He was described as being of satisfactory material for standard aircrew, being quiet and rather reserved, but having a good-mannered personality, accompanied with a keen fighting spirit and a neat and tidy appearance. The medical officer found no unusual conditions and declared him physically fit for full flying duties. He stood at 5 foot 4 inches tall, and had developed well, and had dark brown hair and hazel eyes with a good complexion. The interviewing officers con-cluded that he would not be suitable for a commission and he should prove satisfactory only for pre-enlistment material. Having completed basic training, Glenn undertook extra exams in Physics and English and obtained passes on these courses on 18 August 1942, continuing his training by embarking on a bomb-aimer's course from 19 May 1943 and qualifying on 29 October 1943, being presented with his bomb aimer's badge.

The wireless operator on NG190 was Flying Officer James Lindsay, service number J19994, the son of British-born Margaret and William Lindsay. He was one of seven siblings, and had one brother and five sisters. James was born on 17 December 1919 and was raised in Manitoba, Winnipeg. He left school after finishing Grade 10 and completing only part of Grade 11. From graduation he went from job to job throughout the period 1937–41, being mainly employed as a general labourer or office clerk. He had a brother already serving in the RCAF, so it was perhaps this combined with dead-end jobs that led him to enlist with the RCAF himself. He did so on 12 June 1941 at the local recruiting centre in Winnipeg. His brother, Flying Officer Alexander Lindsay, held a position of a bomb aimer with No. 630 Squadron and was shot down and killed on 27 July 1944, just a few months before James met the same fate. On enlistment, James specified flying duties, with a particular interest in becoming a wireless operator. It appears he had no other interest to enlist in other occupations within the RCAF. At the age of 21, he was the typical age for aircrew, and after the interviews and selection process he was deemed best suited for aircrew duties, particularly as wireless operator, air gunner or observer. He had no previous flying experience, other than being a passenger in aircraft no less than five times.

No. 153 Squadron

Lancaster JB297 P4-B

Pilot	Pilot Officer Cornelius George Draper	KIA
Flight engineer	Sergeant Arnold John Porter Panther	KIA
Bomb aimer	Sergeant Cecil Wilkinson	KIA
Navigator	Sergeant Robert Charles Ernest Lammas	KIA
Mid-upper gunner	Sergeant Dennis Robert Gordon Watkinson	KIA
Rear gunner	Sergeant Neville Lawrence	KIA
Wireless operator	Flight Sergeant Albert Henry Kerfoot	KIA

JB297 was initially delivered to No. 405 Squadron, based at RAF Gransden Lodge with No. 8 Group, on 28 September 1943. On 7 October 1944 the Lancaster was transferred to No. 166 Squadron, which was made up from crews from 'C' flight of No. 153 Squadron, the squadron being reformed as a heavy bomber squadron but still stationed at RAF Kirmington, Lincolnshire.

JB297 was part of 'B' flight, commanded by Squadron Leader J. W. Gee, DFC. It will be noted that NG190, which was based with the same squadron, was also part of this flight, and together with JB297 was lost on its first operation with the newly formed squadron.

This Lancaster took off from RAF Kirmington at 0640 with twelve other bombers, into fair weather conditions. It climbed through the cloud into clear skies and then proceeded towards the first waypoint with the rest of the stream. It was never heard from again.

The aircraft is known to have crashed at Dinslaken, but very little else is known regarding the crash itself. However, during my investigations I have discovered a crash site that was initially overlooked. This crash site is not 100 per cent confirmed as that of JB297, but the information certainly points in that direction, taking into account the other known crash sites.

On 19 July 1946 Flying Officer Myhil, an investigating officer of the No. 4 MRES enquiry team, was looking into the crash of another Lancaster crew – NF959. Although he found little intelligence regarding the crew he was seeking, he did stumble upon information in the Dinslaken area, which, by a process of elimination, he has given as the most probable location for the crash site of JB297. The investigating officer spoke with a Mr Albert Stein, who resided at number 14 Blucher Straße, who informed the officer that on the morning of 14 October 1944 he was on Luftschutz duty at his factory, the August Thyssen Works, situated in Thyssen Straße, Dinslaken. Albert described how on the morning of 14 October a four-engined heavy bomber came hurtling down and smashed into the roof of his rolling mill at the factory, killing all of the crew; he also mentioned that the wreckage did not burn. He personally assisted in the removal of the seven dead airmen from the tangled wreckage of the Lancaster; they were then interred in the Dinslaken Waldfriedhof cemetery nearby. Albert recalled quite clearly that the pilot was very tall, believed to be over 6 foot and had dark black hair; further-more he also reported that another member of the crew was a very corpulent airman. He was also certain that one other aircraft crashed on this morning not far away but also in Dinslaken itself, with the crew being buried nearby.

An eyewitness I spoke to also recalls a four-engined bomber crashing down into the railway centre during October 1944. As this is next door to the factory and steel mill, it is quite possibly the same bomber that Albert mentioned to the investigating officer. On a sunny afternoon in March 2010, I arrived at Thyssen Straße, Dinslaken, in search of the old steel mill. The area is now an industrial estate, home to many ware-houses and various businesses, and very built up. The steel mill that was there in 1944 has since closed down, but many derelict chimneys and factories remain. The group of factories and mill had been located directly next to a marshalling yard and railway line, presumably for transport of raw materials.

The investigating officer was shown the plot in the far corner of the Dinslaken Waldfriedhof cemetery (now known as Park Friedhof) that held the mass grave of airmen, located just outside the cemetery proper, in a small wooded area. Albert Stein took the officer there and described the area where they had been buried. He was also aware that another crew who had been killed on the same day in a crash in Dinslaken were also buried there. Albert had been present at the exhumations, in an attempt to assist with identification.

From the records and research conducted, we know that two Lancaster bombers crashed at Dinslaken that morning – JB297 and NF928 – and that both of these crews were located by post-war investigators in the same mass grave at the Dinslaken Waldfriedhof, together with some members of the crew of NE163.

With the crash sites already confirmed for NE163 at Barmingholten and NF928 at Hiesfeld, it means that JB297 must be the aircraft that crashed into the factory on Thyssen Straße, Dinslaken. We also know that the pilot of NF928, the only other Lancaster to crash at Dinslaken, had blond hair and not black hair.

Lancaster JB297 was brought down by heavy anti-aircraft fire. The crew of JB297 were buried together in Reichswald Forest War Cemetery, located at Kleve, having previously been located by post-war investigators at the Waldfriedhof cemetery at Willy Brandt Straße, Dinslaken. They were found in the same trench as the crew of NF928, together with two members of NE163. When post-war investigators initially opened the trench with the airmen in it at Dinslaken, they could confirm the identity of only five members of the eighteen total dead. Only one of the crew of Lancaster JB297 could be named initially, and that was flight engineer Sergeant A. J. Panther. He was identified by his collar number, which showed 1880849. It is not known how the other members of the crew were identified. At the time, they were still listed as missing, while awaiting identification, as they did not appear on the German death list. Further exhumations took place and eventually all the identities were discovered.

The graves of the crew of JB297 were on the right-hand side of the trench, being counted from right to left by someone standing in front of the trench on the approach path on the outside of the cemetery in the wooded area at the rear. The exhumation that took place on 17 July 1946 revealed the following details.

Grave number one (number three in the row) was believed to be the pilot, as the body had pilot's wings on his clothing. The body was fully dressed and the airman was reasonably intact, although the limbs were broken. No other identification was possible at this time.

The second grave revealed an identifiable sergeant, as he had three stripes clearly present on his arm. He was wearing full battle dress. No other forms of recognition were available.

The third grave contained an airman with a 'B' brevet on his chest tunic, so was obviously the bomb aimer. Three stripes were also found on his arms, reflecting the rank of sergeant. There was no other identification possible on the remains.

The fourth grave contained remains, but identification was impossible. However, sergeant stripes were shown on his arms, but no brevet was seen on the tunic. He was dressed in an electrically heated flying suit, so was quite possibly the mid-upper or rear gunner.

The fifth grave contained the body of the flight engineer, bearing the rank of sergeant. He was named as Sergeant Panther by means of his collar, showing his name and service number 1880849.

The sixth grave to be examined contained one of the air gunners, as an air gunner brevet was found on the tunic. There was no other identification except for a shirt collar size of 15 inches and someone holding the rank of a non-commissioned officer.

The last grave to be opened up revealed the remains of an airman. No identification was possible, except that he was a sergeant according to his uniform stripes on his arms.

All airmen now rest in Reichswald Forest Cemetery, Kleve, and they have named graves. Confirmation of names must have taken place upon further exhumations.

No. 166 Squadron

Lancaster PD224 AS-K2

Pilot	Flying Officer Andrew McNeill	KIA (RCAF)
Flight engineer	Sergeant William George Angles	KIA
Bomb aimer	Flying Officer Edward Roger Lambert	KIA (RCAF)
Navigator	Flying Officer Bryn Evans Roberts	KIA (RCAF)
Mid-upper gunner	Sergeant Sidney Sutherland Harper	KIA
Rear gunner	Flight Sergeant Leonard Schaff	KIA (RCAF)
Wireless operator	Flight Sergeant Joseph William Powell	KIA (RAAF)

Stationed with No. 166 Squadron based at RAF Kirmington, Lincolnshire, this aircraft was received by the squadron on 4 August 1944 direct from the factory.

PD224 became airborne from RAF Kirmington on 14 October 1944 at 0630 hrs and flew without incident to the target area of Duisburg, but it failed to return, with all seven crew members killed. The bomber encountered heavy flak north of the target area, and it was fatally hit, causing it to crash at 0849 hrs, although the flak was not the direct cause of the crash.

It is thought at first that the loss of this bomber was due to flak, but some sources stated it was hit by falling bombs from another aircraft. A claim was also made for the bomber by Company 8/1 of the No. 4 Flak Division. The incident was witnessed by a No. 576 Squadron member flying in Lancaster LM594, Flying Officer C. F. Phripp of the RCAF. He was a close friend of Flying Officer McNeill, the pilot of PD224.

However, another twist of fate was that on the original crew of Flying Officer McNeill was a flight engineer by the name of Sergeant Albert Amos. He was the crew's normal flight engineer. On the day of the raid to Duisburg, Albert could not take part, for some reason, most likely owing to sickness, and hence he was replaced for the raid by Sergeant William George Angles.

When this aircraft came down, it is believed it still had its bomb load on board, which exploded with the impact of the bomber hitting the ground. Wreckage would have been spread over a wide area as a result of the impact and following explosion. Thousands of pounds of bombs and ammunition combined with thousands of gallons of fuel would have destroyed much of the aircraft, and, to support this, the Germans record the wreckage being 98 per cent destroyed. It can only be presumed that the aircraft caught fire when hit by bombs perhaps, or possibly that the hit caused large parts of the aircraft to be damaged,such that it lost control quickly, which did not give the crew time to escape. The bomber came down at 0849 hrs, 1.5 kilometres south-east of Eversael at Michplatz, Orsoy, which is approximately 5 kilometres west of Dinslaken. The crash site itself was visited by investigators when teams were searching for the crew. Little was recovered or found, as most of it had been removed by German soldiers, but part of a blade from the airscrew was located, and so were other small parts that had serial numbers on them – namely, D H 148 and N.E 81740. This site was then confirmed as the crash site of PD224.

Following the crash, all seven of the airmen were recovered, although not all from the same site. Some were discovered further away from the crash site itself. The bodies were interred in the village of Orsoy, the main town just a few minutes' drive from the crash site. Some were placed in the Protestant cemetery and others located in the Catholic cemetery in the town. It is not known why the remains of the crew were separated, but it may have been because they were not all found together. The original grave from 14 October was not opened up or disturbed when the other bodies were found.

Five members of the crew were located by post-war investigators in a small churchyard in Orsoy. This was the Catholic cemetery and the airmen had been buried in a communal grave. The other two airmen from PD224 were buried in a Protestant cemetery, in the same grave.

Investigators visited the Catholic cemetery in Orsoy with the help of the 'parson' (as recorded in the report) and discovered five graves in the far corner of the cemetery on the northern side. The 'parson', cemetery burgomaster and chief grave-digger all verified that the five airmen from this Lancaster had been brought to the cemetery directly from the crash site on 14 October 1944 and had been buried the day they were killed. Their identification had been simple. Many had their ID tags or other documents and belongings on them, but these had been removed and sent to the Luftwaffe headquarters. It was assumed that, because the aircraft had exploded with its bomb load upon hitting the ground, Powell and Roberts had been obliterated, as only five members were located from the wreckage. However, it later became apparent that this was not the case.

Investigators spoke to the mayor's courier, Mr Wilsing Gerhard, and he stated that two bodies of Allied airmen had been found and brought in for burial a short time afterwards, on 17 October. They had been discovered together in a meadow approximately 3 kilometres south-west of Orsoy, 6 kilometres south-south-west of Milchplatz. He mentioned to the investigators that the airmen were almost complete, with some clothes on, but were assumed to have fallen from a great height with no parachute and had partially buried themselves in the ground on impact. But, when the graves of these two airmen were examined, many of the clothes were missing, presumably because they had come off in the fall to earth.

All the airmen at the Catholic cemetery were exhumed, and it was found that the five airmen buried there were in a mass grave with no coffins; however, all had crosses above them, showing who they were. These would have been erected by the Germans at the time of burial. Despite this, each had to be identified.

The first to be examined was Sergeant William George Angles. There was no positive explanation to confirm his identity other than the officer's-type shirt that he was wearing, and the same followed for the next grave for Flying Officer Andrew McNeill.

The third body was the remains of Flying Officer Edward Lambert. He was identified by his officer's shirt and his bomb-aimer's brevet on his battledress. The fourth was Flight Sergeant Leonard Schaff. Again, identification was by way of his type of shirt but also by his personal number, the last four digits of which were written on his shirt. The last grave to be opened was that of Sergeant Sidney Harper, and he was singled out by his personal number, written on his officer's shirt.

As for the bodies of Flying Officer Roberts and Flight Sergeant Powell in the Protestant cemetery, the MRES teams trying to name them had problems, as there was no positive identity visible, in terms of markings or clothing, and both bodies were buried in the same grave, No. 10, Field 2. However, the airmen's teeth charts from their medical records were used to identify one of the airmen, and thus, when they were reinterred in the Rheinberg war cemetery, they were put into separate graves under their own names. Many of the clothes were missing and in rags, although three Australian uniform buttons were found with Flight Sergeant Powell. It is likely they ended up here after being located at a later date than the other five crew members.

Flight Sergeant Powell's dental chart, which was used by investigators, did not entirely match that of the deceased. Yet there was a strong resemblance, and in view of the fact that small parts of RAAF blue sweater were found on the body and the German cemetery records stated that one body was that of an Australian, and the other was a Canadian, one body in the grave was accepted as that of Flight Sergeant Powell.

In the case of Flying Officer Roberts, however, parts of wire and his electrically heated flying suit were found with him, but his flying boots were missing. This airman was accepted as Flying Officer Roberts following the identification of Flight Sergeant Powell, as the other crew members had already been named. Before they were moved, it was noted that all of the graves of these airmen from PD224 were neatly looked after and had flowers placed on them. These two are now buried in the Rheinberg war cemetery, with the other five being buried in Reichswald Forest War Cemetery.

The investigating officer did suggest to the Air Ministry that these two airmen should be transferred to the Reichswald Forest Cemetery, so that the crew could be placed together, side by side, but this was refused for unknown reasons. Despite individual identities of Flight Sergeant Powell and Flying Officer Roberts, they share a collective grave, as it is likely the remains could not be positively separated.

The rear gunner of this bomber was Flight Sergeant Leonard Schaff (R213524), who had originally come from a background of farming, like so many other Canadian crewmen. He was one of eight children, three of whom were stepchildren from a previous relationship. He was the son of Rita Wagner (her remarried name) and John Schaff of Saskatchewan; his father and mother were of Russian citizenship. He lived at the family home with his mother and stepfather, Kasper Wagner, in Burstall, Saskatchewan. Leonard was born in Saskatchewan on 9 January 1923 on the family farm and spent his school years from 1930 to 1940 at the

Prelate School in Saskatchewan, reaching Grade 10. From there he went on to work as a farm labourer for two separate employers, Joseph Mitzel in Nemiskam from 1940 to 1941, and then Mike Ondrick at Etzikom. He left to join the RCAF, enlisting at the age of 19 on 11 January 1943 at a recruitment centre in Regina. He applied for aircrew duties but stated no particular trade. On initial application he was assessed as being rather neat in his appearance, well motivated and of good material, and so was recommended for aircrew duties. His interests included hockey, swimming and baseball.

The bomb aimer was Flying Officer Edward Roger Lambert, J35772, the son of Edward Lambert and Delina Maillargeon, born on 18 February 1918 in New Market, in the state of New Hampshire, USA. His mother was from that area, but his father was of Canadian citizenship and came from the area of St Valere, Quebec. Lambert lived with his parents at Rue Academie, Victoriaville. He achieved two years of higher education after normal schooling and attended the Montreal University before taking up employment as a polisher with the Eastern Furniture Company, between 1933 and 1941. From there he took employment with the Sterling Furniture Company until his enlistment with the RCAF. His main language was French. He enrolled with the RCAF on 6 May 1942 at a recruiting office in Montreal aged 23 and applied to be either an observer or pilot, but he later ended up as a bomb-aimer, despite being recommended by the interview board for pilot. The interview board deemed him as having a very alert and confident manner, with a neat appearance and confident approach to tasks, but overall was regarded to be of average material.

PD224's navigator was Flying Officer Bryn Evans Roberts (J36862), one of the youngest of the crew, having been born on 14 July 1924 to John and Eleanor Roberts, who were both of English citizenship. His father was from north Wales. He was their second son to them, and they also had two daughters, although one of them died. Bryn was well educated, having achieved a senior matriculation and then attended university to study chemistry in 1941, but he decided to enlist in the RCAF when at school and at the time of enrolment was still a student and only 17 years old. He filled the application forms out just before his 18th birthday. His schooling began at the local primary school, where he gained a good basic education from 1931 to 1938, before attending the Holden Riley Secondary School, where he completed the twelfth grade and a senior matriculation. He then attended Riley University to study chemistry, completing this in 1942. He held a part-time job on a local farm when not at school and after school hours to bring in some small earnings, and also worked for a Mr J. E. Roberts, but left that following schooling to enlist with the RCAF on 18 April 1942.

The pilot was Flying Officer Andrew McNeill, the second son of Hugh and Margaret McNeill, who were both Scottish but had moved to Canada. They lived at Eglinton Avenue, Toronto, Ontario, and Andrew was born in Toronto on 1 January 1918, himself becoming a Canadian. It will be noted that the family lost both of their sons, the other being William Craig McNeill, who was killed on 9 May 1945. He was a lieutenant in the Queen's Own Cameron Highlanders of Canada. Andrew was well educated, having attended high school and university (the Institute of Science and Technology), where he studied aeronautical engineering, which put him in a great position on applying for a pilot's position within the RCAF. He completed his standard matriculation at high school in 1934, but moved to university a number of years later, completing this course in October 1941. His employment after leaving school in 1934 covered various positions, including a machine operator with the Canadian National Carbon Company and later a woodworker for the De Havilland Aircraft Company, and it was from the latter position that he went into the RCAF.

No. 166 Squadron

Lancaster ME748 AS-Q

Pilot	Flying Officer George Kenneth Shaw	KIA
Flight engineer	Sergeant Sydney Dennis Starbuck	KIA
Bomb aimer	Flight Sergeant Edward Frank Rogers	KIA
Navigator	Sergeant Godfrey Joseph Spillman	KIA
Mid-upper gunner	Sergeant Robert Thompson	KIA
Rear gunner	Sergeant K. K. Nagalingham	KIA
Wireless operator	Sergeant Robert Wills	KIA

ME748 was a Mk 1 Lancaster based with No. 166 Squadron; it had been delivered to them on 22 April 1944. The aircraft was based at RAF Kirmington, located in the Humberside area. This bomber was one of many detailed with the task of going back to Duisburg to finish the job on the night of 15 October. It became airborne at 2215 hrs, but failed to return, with the loss of all of her crew.

The main bulk of the wreckage from Lancaster ME748 was found on the border of the road and the flak battery on Neumuhler Straße, Meiderich, Duisburg. Other parts of the aircraft were discovered nearby at the Harbour station, indicating that it had quite clearly broken up in flight. This Lancaster was involved in a mid-air collision with Lancaster LM165. Full details are given in LM165's report.

All of the crew from ME748 are still listed as missing, with no known graves, with the exception of Flying Officer Shaw, who was found in an isolated grave in a cemetery in Essen after the war by post-war investigators. Nothing is known of the fate of the other crewmen, although it is most probable they were interred at the Duisburg Wald Cemetery, together with the crews of PB357 and LM596, two other aircraft lost from the night raids. It is highly likely that they were recovered from the nearby cemetery and placed in the Reichswald Forest Cemetery or Rheinberg Cemetery as 'unknown airmen', as we know from all other investigations. No successful identification was made on any bodies recovered from these crashes, other than Flying Officer Shaw, but we know from eyewitness reports that the aircrew from both this bomber and LM165 were badly burnt. Flying Officer Shaw is interred in the Reichswald Forest Cemetery at Kleve, and the missing are all commemorated on the Runnymede Memorial.

No. 625 Squadron

Lancaster LL956 CF-Q

Pilot	Flying Officer L. A. Hannah	KIA (RCAF)
Second pilot	Sergeant D. R. Paige	Unharmed (RCAF)
Flight engineer	Sergeant R. B. Bennett	Unharmed
Wireless operator	Flight Sergeant J. Bilan	Unharmed (RCAF)
Navigator	Flight Sergeant K. R. Strachan	Injured (RCAF)
Bomb aimer	Flight Sergeant L. D. Bennett	KIA (RCAF)
Mid-upper gunner	Sergeant J. K. McRone	Unharmed
Rear gunner	Flight Sergeant J. Loughran	Unharmed (RCAF)

Lancaster LL956 was delivered to No. 625 Squadron at RAF Kelstern in April 1944. The base had been open for only about a year, and had acquired a reputation for being very efficient. The crew flying on 14 October 1944 was not the original crew; only some of the original crew members were flying that morning with Lloyd Hannah.

In the days before the mission to Duisburg, the aircraft was reported to have suffered from higher than normal oil and engine temperatures on the starboard inner, and so had been taken out of service while the fault was rectified by the ground crews. The pilot had previously questioned them when about to leave on a raid and had consequently missed the flight. He was halfway through his tour of operations and had trained as both engine mechanic and pilot, so had plenty of experience behind him. As it was the aircraft was deemed fit to fly again just before the raid to Duisburg. With the crew boarding at just before 0530 hrs, they prepared to leave for the raid, but were delayed and thus had to wait around a short time before they could depart.

At 0628 hrs, with a full load of bombs weighing in at approximately

16,000lb, 1,400 gallons of fuel and a take-off weight at 65,000lb, LL956 thundered down the runway, with other aircraft due to follow in turn. As the aircraft gained speed at full throttle, the unthinkable occurred: the starboard inner engine burst into flames and lost power, causing the air-craft to underperform and struggle, with only three engines delivering power, and the aircraft at its maximum weight. With the aircraft heading towards take-off speed, a decision had to be made to take off or abort. A decision to abort could have left the aircraft leaving the runway and crashing, which would have been catastrophic, and the pilot chose to take off to give his crew the best chances of survival and to avoid an explosion at the end of the runway.

With a full load, the aircraft struggled to climb on three engines, as there was insufficient power – the starboard inner engine was still ablaze as it lumbered skyward. The fire was spreading and it was becoming apparent that the aircraft would not be airborne for long. The pilot attempted to bring the aircraft back round and turned right after take-off. Time was running out with fire eating away at the superstructure and the wing. With the aircraft gaining just 600–800 feet in altitude, as noted by the flight engineer, the pilot gave the order to bail out, just two minutes into the flight. There was no chance of the pilot escaping, as he was struggling at the controls to give the others enough time to jump. The aircraft flew over the village of Fotherby, near Little Grimsby, and it was here the rest of the crew bailed out. Shortly after the aircraft was wit-nessed to dive steeply from approximately 2,000 feet into the ground, exploding upon impact. The Lancaster crashed at 0634, just six minutes after take-off, at Bradley's Farm, with the captain still at the controls. The resulting explosion caused substantial damage to a nearby farm building, taking off its roof. Today there is a large pond at the crash site, filling the crater caused when the aircraft hit the ground.

The second pilot on board that morning, Sergeant D. R. Paige, on his first trip prior to taking his own crew, supplied the following statement after the incident.

As second pilot I helped the captain with the run-up, which was satisfactory. There was no trouble while taxying or until we were three-quarters of the way down the runway, with full power on, when there were two loud reports from the starboard inner engine. This engine was throttled back slightly and the detonations stopped. Just as we left the ground, the flight engineer, who was behind me, reported a fire in the starboard inner engine. The engine was feathered at this point, and, as the fire was still going, the extinguisher was used. It put out all of the flames except in the air intake, which continued to smoulder. After about two minutes the engine burst into flames again and the captain gave the order to bail out. All of the other engines operated OK.

Following the incident, on 17 October 1944 a court of inquiry was opened at RAF Kelstern by order of the Air Vice Marshal of No. 1 Group, in order to establish the facts and to allocate responsibility to any persons if possible. A total of twelve witnesses were called to the court, including a number of the aircrew. The court established that on the morning of the incident LL956 took off in reasonable weather with 6/10 stratocumulous cloud at a base of 1,600 feet, 10/10 stratocumulous cloud with a base between 2,000 and 3,000 feet, 5 miles visibility and gusty winds blowing from the south-west at 27mph. All of the aircraft and engine mainten-ance log books were satisfactory, and all necessary inspections had been carried out. This included the changes made to the starboard inner engine on 6 October 1944, when the aircraft could not fly because of a faulty magneto. The exhaust plugs and magneto were changed on this day, and everything was deemed acceptable, and in fact the aircraft had flown twice since this date, one of which was an operational flight.

Upon inspection of the badly smashed starboard inner engine at the scene, it was noted that it definitely showed signs of being subjected to intense heat, but unfortunately it was too badly damaged to ascertain the exact cause of the fire. It was presumed that the fire in the starboard inner engine was caused primarily by failure of an inlet valve, causing flame trap failure and consequent ignition of the gases in the starboard induction systems, during take-off, which in turn led to the fire in the carburettor. The lapse of time between the start of the fire and the employment of the graviner extinguisher – about three minutes – allowed the fire to gain to such an extent that the extinguisher was not sufficient to put it out completely.

The Group Commander agreed with the findings of the court, although stated that the manipulation of the throttles on take-off appeared to have been most irregular, and he was ensuring action was going to be taken to avoid any reoccurrence of this practice. The 'Forwarding Remarks of Commander-in-Chief' concurred with the findings of the court. They mentioned that, from the technical aspect of the incident, the findings must remain inconclusive, as the engine was too badly smashed to gain any concrete evidence of what had actually caused the failure. They indicated though, that the second pilot on this occasion was acting as flight engineer, and this was not good practice, and steps were going to be put in place preventing this being the case again. The Commanding Officer of the RAF Station, Group Captain, R. H. Donkin, stated the following:

I have to concur with the findings of the court. The only irregularity appears to be that the second pilot was acting as flight engineer and steps are being taken to prevent a repetition of this. The captain (Flying Officer Hannah) appears to have acted with commendable coolness in a very awkward situation. I do not consider that the maintenance staff can be held in any way to blame.

An eyewitness to the crash by the name of Mr Wilf Brader, who was in a farmhouse at the time, approximately 500 yards from the sight, remembers a huge flash, followed by an explosion, with clay and soil being thrown about and crashing through the roof of the house, which had been blown off. Mr Brader recalls arriving outside his house and seeing the surrounding fields littered with aircraft wreckage, with large sections of the wings and fuselage in the field, together with an engine that still had its propeller attached in a field just a short distance away. The aircraft itself left a huge crater, which later became a pond.

   The remainder of the crew managed to bail out of the aircraft, but the bomb aimer became a further casualty when his parachute did not open in time before he hit the ground. The navigator also had an end to his full flying career, as his parachute only partially opened, and he fell to the ground with his chute trailing behind him. He suffered extensive damage to one of his legs, which was badly broken. The pilot and bomb aimer are now buried in Harrogate in a local cemetery.

During the month of January 2010, following correspondence with the relatives of the pilot of LL956 and the landowners where the crash site is located, I made the journey to the site on a crisp cold morning and met the owner of Bradley's Farm. They had been extremely kind in giving me permission to access the site and also to explain further the story of the sacrifice.

   Flying Officer Lloyd Albert Hannah, the captain of LL956, was born in Saskatchewan on 18 June 1918; he was one of nine children, having three brothers and five sisters. He resided with his family at Alder Avenue, Moose Jaw, Saskatchewan. His mother, Mary, and father, Allen, both

Canadian citizens, had been born and brought up in Canada themselves. Lloyd was raised on the farm where his parents lived, educated locally and began his schooling years in 1926 at West Lake School, where he achieved Grade 10. He then continued his education at a central college, where he took part in an aero engine and aeronautics course His parents owned and operated the family wheat farm, although it would seem that Lloyd wanted to follow in his brother's footsteps. So he gave up working as a labourer on the family farm and joined the RCAF, enlisting for ground duties as an aero engine mechanic. At the time Lloyd enlisted on 5 September 1940 at a RCAF recruiting office in Regina, his three brothers were already serving in the RCAF. Having undertaken training within the RCAF to become a fully qualified aero engine mechanic, Lloyd continued to work in this trade at an RCAF station in Vancouver until the beginning of 1943, where he volunteered for flying duties. It was also during this period that Lloyd married his wife, Margaret.

The crew's bomb aimer for that day was Flight Sergeant Lloyd Douglas Bennett. One of four siblings, two brothers and two sisters, Lloyd was the son of Frank Ayearst and Sadie Bennett. He was born on 6 November 1916 in St Thomas, Elgin County, Ontario. Lloyd was raised in this town and he began school in 1925, finishing his senior matriculation in 1937, before continuing his education with the University of Toronto, where he studied pharmaceutical medicine. In between going to university and leaving high school he undertook an apprenticeship with L. M. Heard St Thomas from 1937 through to 1940, and he left here to attend university. He graduated in 1942 and then went on to work for L. K. Liggett and Company as a druggist, obtaining the position of assistant manager. He began work here in 1942. However, this was short-lived, and he applied to join the RCAF, with a specific request for flying duties as a pilot. Following the accident, it was discovered that he had delayed pulling his parachute ripcord too long, and the chute had not fully opened when he hit the ground.

No. 425 Squadron

Halifax MZ674 KW

Pilot	Flight Lieutenant J. Galipeau	POW (RCAF)
Flight engineer	Pilot Officer Francis Harvey Eade	KIA (RCAF)
Bomb aimer	Flight Sergeant Charles Frederick Williamson	POW (RCAF)
Navigator	Flying Officer Dell Alfred Butler	KIA (RCAF)
Mid-upper gunner	Sergeant Joseph Leo Marcel Pare	POW (RCAF)
Mid-under gunner	Flight Sergeant Joseph Omar Bazinet	POW (RCAF)
Rear gunner	Pilot Officer Charles Maurice Crabtree	KIA (RCAF)
Wireless operator	Pilot Officer Leonard Hunter Hogg	KIA (RCAF)

Halifax MZ674 (named 'Willie the Wolf from the West') was a Mk III variant, with a seasoned crew who had flown an average of nineteen operations. The bomber took off from RAF Tholthorpe at 0605 hrs on 14 October 1944 to bomb Duisburg but failed to return. The four crew members who perished on the raid, when they were unable to exit the aircraft as it was crashing towards earth out of control, are buried in the Reichswald Forest Cemetery at Kleve. The remainder bailed out on the command of the captain after various attempts had been made to save the bomber. It was as they were approaching the target area that the pilot, Flight Lieutenant J. Galipeau, saw about five large explosions in the air, ahead of his aircraft, which he presumed to be exploding aircraft, and then confirmed two Lancaster bombers spinning down, one of which was engulfed in flames. By this time the bomber had commenced its bombing run and the bomb doors were open, with the bomb aimer giving commands to the pilot. This was always one of the most vulnerable parts of the flight for the crew. The bomb aimer success-fully released the bombs but it was just after the release that the bomber and crew ran into trouble. A direct hit was received in the starboard wing of the Halifax from flak, with the shell passing through the wing without exploding. Further shells then exploded very close by. Shortly afterwards the two starboard Merlin engines were in trouble, with the boost gauges showing -6$\frac{1}{2}$, although the rpm remained fine. However, the mid-upper gunner then notified the pilot over the intercom that a fire had begun in the wing.

The pilot attempted to shut down the damaged and now failing engines and feather the propellers, but without success. At this point the flight engineer advised the pilot that one of the fuel tanks in the wing was draining fast. With a fire in the wing that could not be extinguished, the pilot had to consider his options. He informed the crew that they might have to bail out of the aircraft, but decided to take a chance and try the dangerous option of putting the aircraft into a dive, in a bid to put out the flames. When this was unsuccessful, there was no option but to bail out. By this time the wing and fuel tank were ablaze and the fuel tank almost empty, so the aircraft could explode at any time. They had to get out quickly. The pilot reduced the speed out of the dive to approximately 160mph to enable the crew to exit the aircraft safely and then informed the crew to bail out. The two starboard propellers were by this time just windmilling, and without the blades being feathered the aircraft was hard to control and creating lots of drag, which made it lose height very rapidly. The pilot watched the bomb aimer leave the aircraft and checked the intercom to see if any other crewmen remained. When he got no answer he began to leave his seat. Looking back down the fuselage, he saw lots of smoke and but no crew members, so the pilot bailed out through the forward escape hatch. With the pilot now on his parachute and drifting down, the aircraft was heading towards the ground in a spiral dive, and it was seen to enter a thin layer of cloud. Three parachutes were visible drifting downwards.

At this point the Germans began to open fire on the pilot with small-arms fire, so he spilled air from his chute to increase his descent rate and hit the ground, where he was immediately captured by the Germans. He was not injured from the small-arms fire.

Eyewitness Flying Officer Augusta, the pilot of Halifax MZ453, was flying next to Halifax MZ674, at a distance of approximately 100 yards when it was hit.

As we were heading towards a target that our bomb-aimer had spotted through the clouds, which appeared to be a factory of some kind on a bend in the river, there was a large explosion slightly in front and to the left side of us. We then became enveloped in a large white cloud of smoke, which rocked the aircraft. Upon flying through it and looking out of the cockpit to my right, I could see the Halifax next to us had been hit. I knew there was an explosion and I could now see lots of flames coming from the starboard wing, which had been set on fire, the engines burning, and it began to descend rapidly and break away from me, with pieces of wreckage beginning to fall from the aircraft.

Flying Officer Augusta caught only a glimpse of this, as he and his crew had their own problems on board, both because they were themselves hit by flak shortly after and because they were on the bombing run, with the bomb aimer keeping the pilot busy with his instructions. Flying Officer Augusta completed the bombing run at 0848 hrs, having been hit by flak. It would appear that Halifax MZ674 would have completed its attack at the same time, as they were converging on the same target through the gap in the clouds. The stricken Halifax that Flying Officer Augusta saw after it had been hit had banked away and begun to lose altitude rapidly. It is believed that NF928 (identification is unconfirmed as no number was seen) had gone down in flames and with the wing breaking off just minutes before. This, MZ674, and MZ453, the Halifax flown by Flying Officer Augusta, had been in a formation on the bombing run. With the loss of NF928, there were just two Halifax bombers together. It was just after the bombing run at approximately 0848 hrs that MZ674 ran into trouble, when it was hit in the wing. This corresponds with what Flying Officer Augusta saw from his cockpit.

MZ674 then dived away out of the area, in an attempt to put out the flames. When this had failed and with some of the crew having bailed out, the bomber hit the ground, having flown a short distance. This would perhaps explain why it is some way from the target area. It is possible this Halifax turned to starboard from the target and began to head west back towards Belgium.

The Halifax came crashing down at Breyell Bracht, which is approximately 20 kilometres north-west of München Gladbach, hitting the ground at around 0900 hrs. The members of the crew who did not manage to exit the stricken aircraft were found at the scene of the crash. It came down in the corner of a small field, with wreckage spread all over the location. The area has since been built on and the actual crash site has been replaced with houses.

However, two of the airmen were not removed from the aircraft crash site and were reburied in the wreckage that was left at the site by the Germans. Post-war investigators located numerous pieces of the aircraft at the site when it was fully excavated on 13 June 1949, and located two crew members, having found the other two at the nearby Dreyelle cemetery. This accounted for the number of missing airmen from this aircraft. The salvage of the aircraft took some four or five days to complete fully and was conducted by the BR and SD unit of No. 4 MRES unit, with them discovering some human remains together with minute portions of torn and decayed clothing.

Earlier enquiries in 1947 revealed that two airmen, namely Flying Officer Butler and Pilot Officer Hogg, had been taken from the crash site by the Germans, identified, and buried in the Honour Cemetery, at Breyell, not far from the site itself. The remaining two crewmen, Pilot Officer Eade and Pilot Officer Crabtree, were removed from the aircraft crash site after they were found within the wreckage when excavation took place by No. 4 MRES after the war.

Exhumation of all of the remains proved fruitful, with positive identification being completed. Flying Officer Butler had his service number written on his shirt, and Pilot Officer Hogg had a cross marked with his name and service number. These were both exhumed by the MRES team from the graves in the Breyell cemetery. Pilot Officer Hogg was found in the grave under his own individual marking, as the Germans had positively identified him following the crash from his identification disc. He was clothed in his flying suit, wearing his dark blue flying sweater and Canadian tunic, bearing Canadian and US shoulder flashes; his body was completely intact. A written mark was also found on his shirt collar just below the neckband, showing Grovers Mill Ltd, Montreal.

The remains of the two airmen recovered from the scene of the crash itself comprised many bones and minute decayed portions of clothing from an aircrew sweater and an RAF battledress. The problem was that there were no indications as to who these men were, although it was obvious they were the two remaining airmen, as two others had been found and identified and the rest were safe after bailing out. The airmen were in the wreckage but not at their respective stations, the rear gunner's and engineer's positions respectively, so if possible a means had to be found to separate the two to avoid them having to be buried in a joint grave. Among the remains was a smoking pipe, very ancient in appearance, having been repaired twice over, which would indicate one of the persons was a seasoned pipe smoker. This was the only thing of any use to be found.

The MRES teams recovered everything and sent the details to the Air Ministry in London, and together they made enquiries with the RCAF, who in turn contacted the next of kin of each airman. One of the relatives confirmed his relation had been a pipe smoker and had also written a letter back home requesting a new one be sent, because he had damaged his. This tied in with the fact that the pipe had been found to be broken but then repaired. The Air Ministry accepted this as good enough evidence to identify one of the men, and hence the other was named by process of elimination. Pilot Officer Crabtree and Pilot Officer Hogg are now buried in individually marked graves in the Reichswald Forest Cemetery at Kleve.

The three other crewmen who were lucky enough to get out in time were all captured by the Germans shortly after landing by parachute. Flight Sergeant Charles Williamson, the bomb aimer, was captured near Aachen and was sent to Stalag Luft VII prison camp at Bankau after interrogation at a transit camp, arriving there just eight days after he had been shot down. However, on 19 January 1945, Charles began a march to Stalag Luft IIIA, Luckenwalde, with many other prisoners, reaching there on 5 February 1945. He was kept there until the camp was liberated in April 1945. Before the war Charles had been a student living in Dorval, and signed up with the RCAF on 3 May 1941 at the age of 21.

The mid-upper gunner, Sergeant Joseph Leo Marcel Pare, exited the aircraft and was captured the same day after landing somewhere near Düsseldorf. He was uninjured and surrendered to his captives, but was then transported to the interrogation and transit camp in Frankfurt. He spent a total of five days there in solitary confinement while undergoing interviews. He was released a few days later, arriving in Stalag Luft VII at Bankau, the same camp where his comrade Flight Sergeant Williamson was sent. Joseph was kept there until 19 January and then he too marched to Stalag Luft IIIA. A carpenter living in Montreal before enlisting, Joseph volunteered to serve in the RCAF on 18 July 1942, aged 21.

The mid-under gunner lucky to escape by parachute was Flight Sergeant Joseph Omar Bazinet. He was captured close to a village named Mulhausen, suffering injuries, and so was confined to a civilian hospital the same day for the next ten days. On 24 October he was moved to Düsseldorf, where he was again confined to a POW hospital and was not released until 20 November. His next stop was the prison camp at Bankau, Stalag Luft VII, although he spent only a month there before being moved again to Stalag Luft IIIA in Luckenwalde. Joseph states that he was force-marched along with other prisoners, a distance of approximately 340 kilometres, in intense cold and poor weather, with practically no food and little medical equipment. The sleeping conditions en route were also described as poor. It was here Joseph remained until he was liberated. Joseph joined the RCAF on 10 October 1942 at the age of 22, and before this he had been a student residing in Ontario.

Pilot Officer Leonard Hunter Hogg of the RCAF was the wireless operator on board this Lancaster and came from San Francisco, living with his parents, Mr Leonard Sebastian Hogg and Mrs Jessie Thompson Hogg. His father was American, although his mother was English. Leonard was born on 22 January 1923 in northern Vancouver. He had only one brother, named Lawrence. Leonard began his primary education in 1930 at the Kelowna Public School, but then went onto the Edison Grammar School to study for his matriculation. When he finished this in 1935, he chose to further his education, studying at the Everett school and Polytechnic High School, learning Physics, Mathematics and History. He finally left in 1941, when he took up his first employment as a meat packer with Safeway Inc. in San Francisco. However, he was there for only a number of months before moving into an office environment, carrying out general office work with Zellerbach Paper Company. In the next year he had two jobs, the first as a truck driver with Westbrook–Fredrickson Company and then employment with the W. A. Bechtal Shipbuilding Company. From there he went on to enlist with the RCAF in November 1942.

Pilot Officer Charles Maurice Crabtree was the aircraft's rear gunner; he transferred from the Canadian Army Corps to the RCAF to become an air gunner, but was killed when he was unable to exit the aircraft when it was shot down. Charles was born on 28 January 1921 in Toronto, Ontario, the son of Maurice and Edith Evelyn Crabtree. At the time of his enlistment with the RCAF he was still in the Army. He was essentially a military man with a liking for service life. Following his education at the Forest Hill Public School, which he completed in 1935, he attended the University of Toronto to study an arts course, having achieved a senior matriculation, but from here in 1939 he enlisted in the Canadian Army Corps, and was accepted for service on 1 October 1939 following his medical and interviews. He had, in fact, already applied to the RCAF, but joined the Army while waiting to be called up for the Air Force.

The aircraft's navigator was Flying Officer Dell Alfred Butler, who was one of three sons to Martha and Alfred Butler. He had been born in Toronto on 15 December 1909, and, at the age of 34 years, was one of the older members of the aircrew. Dell attended school in Chamberlain, Ontario, until 1923, leaving at the age of 14, but appeared not to have a full-time job until April 1927, when he worked as a night storeman, but was promoted to baggage man in October 1929, where he stayed until his position was abolished in July 1931. From there he worked in various jobs, including as a checker and an accountant, until 1940, where he enlisted with the RCAF at the centre at North Bay on 4 June 1941, applying for the role of ground duties as an equipment assistant. He was later to move to aircrew duties as navigator, following a request by himself for transfer.

The flight engineer on board that day was Pilot Officer Francis Harvey Eade, one of four children of Mr Matthew Henry Eade and Mrs Eade, of Laurier Avenue, Timmins, Ontario, who had two sons and two daughters. Francis was born in this town on 13 November 1922. His parents were not of Canadian origin, but had both been born in Cornwall in England. Francis was brought up and attended school in Timmins until 1937, when he left at the age of 15 to attend a technical school, where he studied to become an electrician, completing the course in 1940 at the age of 18. His employment in civil life was short, just a number of months, but he undertook an apprenticeship with a local machine shop company. He left in the middle of 1941 to join the RCAF, enrolling for ground duties as an electrician. His schooling placed him in good stead, so he was accepted on 13 June 1941. He undertook courses and qualified as an airframe mechanic, but was later to apply for flying duties.

No. 429 Squadron

Halifax MZ453 AL-J

Pilot	Pilot Officer F. K. Augusta	RCAF
Flight engineer	Sergeant A. H. Henderson	
Navigator	Flying Officer W. H. Potts	RCAF
Bomb aimer	Sergeant F. G. Gear	RCAF
Wireless operator	Flight Sergeant A. Ladner	RCAF
Mid-upper gunner	Flight Sergeant J. B. Linstead	RCAF
Rear gunner	Flight Sergeant H. D. McLeod	RCAF

This heavy bomber was a Mk IIIB Halifax based with No. 429 Squadron, which flew out of RAF Leeming. It became airborne at 0627 hrs and had an uneventful flight all the way to the target area but then ran into trouble in the final stages of the run-up to the target.

The aircraft was struck by flak while approaching what was thought to be part of an industrial target located by the bomb aimer by the river Rhine after the Master Bomber had given freehand. The Halifax was on the bomb run at approximately 18,500 feet when it was hit by flak in the wing and the nose section. The pilot was initially unaware of the full extent of the damage, as he was concentrating on the instruments, keeping to the bomb-aimer's requirements. He acknowledged the aircraft had been hit, however. The aircraft's right wing was set ablaze, but this was not too visible from the cockpit. By the time the pilot saw the damage, the paint had been burnt off the wing, which was black, with the oil tanks burning and oil together with fuel flowing down the wing.

The navigator was hurt by fragments of flak and metal from the aircraft and suffered injuries that caused him to bleed profusely and he sat wounded at his station. The wireless operator was so shocked and shaken by this that he had to look away out of his window. The navigator was the only crew member to receive injury from the initial flak hit.

Despite the aircraft being hit and on fire, with thick black smoke trailing from the starboard main plane, the captain took the decision to go ahead with the bombing run and release the bomb load to minimize the chance of an explosion from the bomb load going up. The crew completed the bombing run at 0848 hrs and then followed the bomber stream out of the target area. The rear gunner was asked for a damage report and he told the pilot that the aircraft was trailing thick black smoke. Another Halifax that was flying close to Pilot Officer Augusta's crippled aircraft was piloted by a friend. Augusta asked over the radio what was wrong with his aircraft and whether the other pilot could see the damage.

The friend advised 'Get out'.

Not knowing exactly where they were other than with the stream heading westwards, the crew bailed out. The pilot stayed at the controls until everyone had passed by the cockpit area, leaving his seat only when he was satisfied everyone was out of the aircraft and the autopilot had been set to fly straight and level. They all exited the aircraft via the front escape hatch, Flying Officer Augusta being the last out, hanging his feet out of the hatch and his hands on the lip of the hatch. He then let go and began to tumble towards the ground. The crew were spread out over a wide area.

The aircraft was therefore successfully abandoned at approximately 0915 hrs over the town of Keerbergen in Belgium, some 26 kilometres north-east of Brussels. Four days later the crew were flown back to England in an American aircraft.

Pilot Officer Augusta recalled his experience in correspondence.

Our trip to the target was uneventful; no enemy aircraft were identified en route via the route in over Belgium and only sporadic flak was encountered until about fifteen minutes to run to the target, when it increased. I heard the Master Bomber over the radio repeat that the target was obscured and under heavy broken cloud cover and that aircraft were to choose any target we could see. A short time later our bomb-aimer reported a large factory building on the edge of the river in the target area and we then made way to head toward this target. At that time a Lancaster was converging on us from the left. I was able to see it and was watching it closely, as it was getting quite close. At the same time our mid upper gunner reported a Halifax aircraft converging from our right. It appeared the three of us had chosen the same target. It was then I saw a Lancaster and Halifax get shot down. [These were Halifax MZ674 and Lancaster NF928.]

The bomb-aimer then shouted his directions to the target, at which time I went onto instruments to follow his commands. It was shortly after that he said we were lined up for the bombing run and I opened the bomb doors and as we moved to the right a bit, it was then we were enveloped again in more dense smoke and were hit. When we were well clear again, we entered the target area and the bomb-aimer repeated the command 'bombs gone'. It was then I turned the aircraft to leave the target area, and the wireless operator came over the intercom and reported that the navigator had been wounded and was bleeding profusely from his chest area. The wireless operator did what he could to bandage the navigator, but there was a lot of confusion among the crew, as the rear gunner was reporting that there was lots of black smoke coming from the engines and trailing behind the bomber, and it appeared we had been badly damaged, but we continued to head home. Very soon both starboard engines were causing problems and they began to lose power, which was shaking the airframe, and it was then both of the fire warning lights came on. I then had immediately to stop both of the starboard engines and began a slow descent from 18,500 feet to maintain flying speed and also to get out of the height where oxygen masks were needed.

On the squadron I had a good friend called Johnny Barstow, and we had given him the nickname 'Doc' from the famous Bugs Bunny cartoon. Unaware of the exact condition we were in, I broke radio silence by saying the famous words: 'Hey Bugs Bunny, what's up Doc?' He replied: 'Not much, you?' I replied back: 'We are trailing black smoke.'

A moment or two later Johnny replied back to me over the wireless: 'I see you now. I'll come over and take a look, hold on.' A short time later he flew over to us and took a look at our stricken bomber, which was still slowly descending. A very short time later he came over the wireless again and said just two words: 'Get out!'

Looking back over the years that have passed, those two words probably saved the life of me and the crew. All of the crew landed safely by parachute behind Allied lines and the navigator was taken to hospital in Luvain, Belgium, and was released a few days later, before we were flown home.

This was the second serious incident the crew had been involved in within a week, demonstrating the hazards that Bomber Command crews faced. Flying Halifax LV965, they had been sent to bomb Bochum. The crew bombed from 18,000 feet at 2032 hrs, but the Halifax was hit by flak and the No. 4 fuel tank was badly damaged and leaked much of the fuel. With little fuel remaining, the aircraft landed at 2222 hrs at the USAAF Base at Old Buckingham. A locking pin had detached from part of the engine throttle controls as a result of flak damage, and it prevented the pilot from closing the throttle for the port outer engine. When the bomber touched down on the airfield, it ground-looped violently, causing the starboard undercarriage to collapse. Travelling at speed, the Halifax skidded across the airfield, substantial damage being caused to its under surfaces. When it finally came to a stop, a fire broke out in the port outer engine. The aircraft was a write-off.

The location of Flying Officer Augusta's Halifax bomber has not been fully established, although it is known to have come down in Belgium, near the town of Baal.

No. 7 Squadron

Lancaster PB357 MG-S

Pilot	Flying Officer Christopher Nigel Charles Crawford	KIA
Flight engineer	Sergeant Arthur Henry Frost	KIA
Bomb aimer	Pilot Officer Thomas Donald Lawson Mason	KIA
Navigator	Pilot Officer Eric Thurston Rivers	KIA (RCAF)
Mid-upper gunner	Flight Sergeant Norman Heslop	KIA
Rear gunner	Flight Sergeant Ralph Phillips	KIA
Wireless operator	Flight Sergeant Thomas Edward Feaver	KIA

PB357 **was a** Lancaster Mk III, initially delivered to No. 35 Squadron before joining No. 7 Squadron at RAF Oakington. It was the only heavy bomber to be destroyed by an enemy fighter during Operation Hurricane. The Lancaster was brought down by Lt Arnold Doring of 7.NJG 2 in the Venlo-Goch area from 16,500 feet at 0343 hrs. Venlo is some 40 kilometres to the west of Duisburg. Doring was flying a Messerschmitt BF110 twin-engined nightfighter. His only known confirmed victory was Lancaster PB357 on the night in question.

It appears that this bomber proved difficult to locate when the MRES teams arrived in the area. They attempted to follow many avenues, but each failed to turn up results. On 21 May 1946 the investigating officer in charge of this case, Flight Lieutenant K. M. Ramsden, visited the north cemetery at Duisburg/Hamborn (in Bluten Straße) and discovered that, according to the cemetery records, no Allied aircrew at all had been buried there. A search of the cemetery also revealed no results. The records office at Hamborn informed the investigating team that it had records of a majority of cemeteries north of the Ruhr and there was no record of any Allied airmen buried in these cemeteries and none in the Meiderich

area either. The team visited the Meiderich police station, but were
unable to confirm that a crash had taken place on the date given. However, some information regarding an airman did come to light: that an
Allied flyer had been buried behind the Flak Kaserne, but had already
been identified by another investigation team and confirmed as a flyer
they had been looking for. This airman was named as Sergeant R. Wills,
from Lancaster ME748 with No. 166 Squadron, flying on one of the
night raids to Duisburg. This body came from the crash near the
Harbour station, located at Meiderich. The local police at Meiderich
advised that, according to their records, no crash took place at Morian-
Muhle, as originally thought by the RAF. Bodies from crash sites in this
area were normally transported to Düsseldorf, but there was no mention
of airmen by the name of Rivers or Phillips. The final cemetery to be
visited by the team was the main one in Sterkrade Holten located in
Sieges Straße, but they found the area had been bombed out. The
burgomaster stated that no Allied airmen had been buried there at all,
but did say that eleven airmen had been collected from crash sites nearby
on 14 October 1944 and buried in the small Jewish cemetery in Holten.
Upon visiting the area, the team found that some were victims of the
raid on 6 October 1944, but the eleven airmen from 14 October had
been exhumed on 3 May by the Americans and taken away. It was not
known where they had been conveyed at the time of this particular
enquiry. The investigating team could find no information as to the
whereabouts of the crew of PB357, despite visiting numerous cemeteries.
This enquiry therefore remained open until a full sweep of the area had
been done. It was not until the spring of 1950 that the crew were located
and accepted as those from PB357; up till then they had been buried as
'unknown airmen'. Investigations by the search officers, the cemetery
records office and the exhumation reports eventually identified which
aircraft the missing men had come from.

PB357 became airborne on 14 October at 2330 hrs and crashed a few
hours later on 15 October after it was shot down by a nightfighter, crashing
at Duisburg Beeck, beside a junction with Karl Albert Straße, in the area
of Meiderich. The fuselage and wings were located here in the road and
the engines were discovered in the centre of the market area, with one
engine being found next to the nearby post office. Nothing was found of
the aircraft when post-war investigators attended the scene years after
the war, as it had all been removed by the German recovery teams. It is

almost certain this aircraft exploded or broke up as it neared the ground, as the wreckage and airmen were scattered over a small area.

The crew were carried from the scene. Some were in nearby gardens and in the road with the wreckage, and they were initially buried in various locations locally, before being moved into the Duisburg Stadt West Friedhof Cemetery, all being transferred at different times. It was discovered after the war that the five bodies originally buried in this cemetery in Plot 1A, graves 340 to 344, together with the remains previously buried in Plot 1A, grave 336, constituted the remains of the crew of Lancaster PB357. The bodies in Plot 1 A, grave 336, were of two airmen who had originally been interred by a local Dutchman without record, and these two were buried in Duisburg Stadt West Friedhof Cemetery sometime during May 1946, having been exhumed from isolated graves by the German authorities.

Five of the crewmen had originally been buried in a collective grave in a meadow in Alsumer Straße–Nattenbergshof Straße, which is near to the crash site. These were thought to be English or Canadian airmen, but were undoubtedly from PB357, and were located by the German authorities on 3 July 1946 at this site. All of these bodies were exhumed by order of the governor of Hamborn, in an examination by a German doctor on 7 July 1946. All five airmen from this collective grave were then removed to the Duisburg North/Hamborn Cemetery for examination and then reburied again later in the Duisburg Wald Stadt West Friedhof Cemetery on 16 July 1946. The reason for the movement between numerous cemeteries is not known. The two airmen buried by the Dutch-man, plus the five from the meadow, made up the total crew of PB357. When all of the crew members were moved from their original burial locations to the Duisburg North/Hamborn Cemetery and then taken to Duisburg Wald Cemetery (Stadt West Friedhof), the RAF MRES teams were not informed, and it is thought that many items of identification could have been missed at this time.

One of the bodies had fallen into the garden of a Dutchman who was living very close to the scene of the crash. His name was Johann Wilms, of 61 Arnold Straße. (He personally buried two airmen without formal records.) This airman was removed shortly afterwards from the garden, but it was not known where the body had been taken when the investi-gators attended the scene. The first of the airmen buried by the Dutch-man to be exhumed was believed to be Flight Sergeant Feaver. It is stated that the Dutchman gave the description as 'one English wireless operator, named Frayer or Faver, aged 23 years old, professional labourer and an airman since 1941'. Papers or some kind of note must have been found on the body to reveal this information.

A second body had been located in a meadow of the Emscher Brock, and this was personally buried in a different grave by the same Dutchman. This second body had a wing on his uniform with a 'B' on it, indicating that this airman was probably a bomb aimer. No paperwork was found on the body, but the Dutchman advised that it had been there two days before he came across it and it is thought that any paperwork could have been looted from the body. A long oval piece of leather was sewn on the right-hand breast pocket of his uniform jacket with something written in ink. It is not known what, because of the state of the paperwork on the original report. This airman was exhumed and removed on 7 May 1946 on the order of the governor of Hamborn, and was then interred in the north cemetery of Hamborn; he was later exhumed again and removed to the Duisburg Wald cemetery. The remaining five airmen must have been located in the fuselage at the crash site or very near by it, although the exact description is not given prior to their burial in a field near the site.

On 15 July 1947, the investigation team attended the cemetery at Duisburg and entered Field No. 1 to exhume plots 340 to 344 inclusive. These graves contained all of the recoverable remains of the crew of PB357. All graves were exhumed by the team, which was witnessed by Flight Lieutenant L'Estrange, an officer already familiar from many earlier reports on other aircrews from the Duisburg raids. A cross above the grave site showed '4 unknown British Airmen', but we know there were five men here.

Graves were opened up from left to right. The first contained the remains of a flyer. The height and build could not be determined. The clothing showed the body of an air gunner, wearing an officer's shirt, white flying sweater and trousers. No equipment was located on the airman.

The next grave to be exhumed contained a body, but again it was impossible to determine the height and build. No other clothing, apart from officer's trousers, shirt and a white flying sweater, were located. Parts of this flyer's Mae West survival vest were discovered, together with tags on his vest showing the numbers 602. Civil braces were also found. This man would later be identified as the pilot, Flying Officer Crawford.

The third grave to be opened revealed the body of an airman. Parts of this man's flying trousers were located, together with an officer's shirt and a civilian sweater. Silk flying gloves, torn parts of a Mae West survival jacket, and electronically heated flying suit, were also found. This would indicate that this body was possibly that of an air gunner.

The fourth grave contained a body, dressed in officer's trousers, a tunic and officer's shirt, held on with RAF-issue braces. Parts of an electrically heated flying suit were also located on the body. No details were found regarding rank, name or service number.

The last grave to be opened contained remains of a flyer, again difficult to identify. No details on the build or height could be determined. Parts of an airman's tunic and officer's shirt were found, together with the remains of a Mae West survival vest. Nothing else was noted in the grave.

At the time of this exhumation, none of the airmen could be specifically identified. These five remains were removed and buried in Reichswald Forest Cemetery to rest until further details came to light that might prove the identity of these airmen. The two other airmen located in the cemetery at Duisburg Wald Cemetery in plot 336 were also removed. In July 1949 a letter sent by the Air Ministry to the Commanding Officer of the No. 20 MRES team advised that the respective graves in Reichswald cemetery were to be registered as unknown airmen. However, later on this was changed once the pilot had been identified and the description of the other two bodies the Dutchman had found closely matched two of those missing from PB357. The Air Ministry then took steps to record six of the airmen in a collective grave.

The pilot's body was identified, as the insignia on the uniform showed him to be a flying officer together with his RAF wings. His identity was also confirmed by the numbers 602 found on the vest, the last three digits of his service number. He rests beside the crew in his own grave.

It will be noted that, at age 35, Flight Sergeant Phillips, the rear gunner, was well over the average age of aircrew employed on Bomber Command operations. His skipper was 20 and the crew had flown thirty-two sorties.

The aircraft's wireless operator was Flight Sergeant Thomas Feaver. He was born in Middlesex, London, on 4 September 1922 and lived with his family. Following his schooling, he was employed as a labourer before enlisting with the RAF. He commenced service on 24 February 1941, at the age of 19. Thomas was a keen young man and began basic training in late September 1941, having been placed in reserve for a number of months. Having chosen to become a wireless operator after he was called up, Thomas undertook a wireless operators' course at the No. 3 Signal School on 1 January 1942. Other training establishments were also used for various courses, and Thomas also spent time at RAF Abbey Lodge and Topcliffe. Following months of training, he qualified as a wireless operator in late 1943 and was then posted to the No. 18 Initial Training Wing to begin instruction on the aircraft and put his skills to use. While here Thomas undertook an air gunners' course at the No. 10 air gunnery school and qualified as a gunner, achieving a pass mark of 75 per cent in his exam. Final training with a crew was completed at the No. 82 OTU in late August 1943, before he was posted to No. 31 Base.

The navigator of PB357 was Pilot Officer Eric Thomas Rivers (J89099), son of Russell Alexander Rivers and Edith Gertrude Rivers. He was one of three siblings, with a brother called Glenn and a sister Reta. They resided together at Princeton Road, Woodroffe, Ontario, Canada. His father passed away on 30 March 1936. Eric was born on 4 September 1917 in Woodroffe. He spent his early years living with his parents and, unlike many Canadians, he was not born and raised on a farm. His early years consisted of eight years at the Woodroffe public school, moving on to Nepean High School for the remaining six years of education, leaving when he was 21. Still listed as a student and not working, he enlisted in the RCAF on 10 March 1939 in a recruiting station based in Ottawa at the age of 21. On enlistment he stood at just over 6ft tall but with a 'poor' physical development; he had dark brown hair, light brown eyes and a sallow complexion. Other than this, he showed no medical problems that would prevent him from undertaking active service within the RCAF. On 19 March 1943 he was awarded the navigator's badge.

No. 90 Squadron

Lancaster LM165 WP-T

Pilot	Flight Sergeant Francis John Cook	KIA (RAAF)
Flight engineer	Sergeant Frederick Henry William James	KIA
Bomb aimer	Sergeant Kenneth Brian Howell	KIA
Navigator	Sergeant Kenneth Morrell	KIA
Mid-upper gunner	Sergeant William Paston Liddon Purnell-Edwards	KIA
Rear gunner	Sergeant John Robert Sunley	KIA
Wireless operator	Sergeant George Irving Read	KIA

Lancaster LM165 was a Mk I produced by the Sir W. G. Armstrong Whitworth Aircraft Company. The bomber was constructed at Whitley in Coventry under contract number 239/SAS/C4/C. This aircraft was based with No. 90 Squadron at RAF Tuddenham and became airborne at 2252 hrs for the second raid to Duisburg, but failed to return. All the crew were killed.

This bomber was involved in a mid-air collision with ME748 near the target, which sent both aircraft tumbling to the ground. This particular aircraft crashed in fairly open ground near the anti-aircraft barracks in the Morians Muhle area of Duisburg Meiderich. It is not known which aircraft hit which, nor is it known why they collided. Quite possibly they simply did not see each other, or one was damaged by anti-aircraft fire and lost control. There were lots of bombers in the vicinity converging on the same target and it was not uncommon for aircraft to collide, especially over the target area at night with so many bombers in such a confined space. The crashes at this location between both bombers took place at approximately 0145 hrs on the morning of 15 October 1944.

After the war, the investigating officers were still trying to piece together the facts about this aircraft and ME748, both missing from the night raid to Duisburg. The crews had not been located, and, in an attempt to find them, many members of the flak barracks who had dealings with the crashes were interviewed.

An eyewitness account of the actual crash was taken by investigating officers from the person in charge of the flak barracks at the time of the incident. His name is believed to be Willy Wriadreich (the surname is unclear on the original papers).

During the night of the 14/15 October 1944 at about 2400 to 0200 hrs there was a heavy air raid on Duisburg and Duisburg Meiderich. I heard a terrible noise, which could hardly have come from an exploding bomb. My suspicion that two bombers could have collided in mid air was confirmed when the air raid was over. When it became light at about 06:00 in the morning on 15 October 1944 I was still employed with extinguishing the burning barracks. I was informed that two crashed aircraft were lying on Neumuhler Straße and close to the carpenters' barrack. I remark that I write the exact facts and happenings about everything which happened during the night of 14/15 October. I have again thought over the whole night, which was terrible.

On 15 October in the morning, I went to the crashed aircraft, which were completely destroyed. The aircraft which was lying in the road on Neumuhler Straße had only one wing left, the other was missing. Also only part of the aircraft's body remained. Dead flyers were not lying within the aircraft. According to its construction, it ought to have at least seven crew. It puzzled me as to where this crew was. At first I had a suspicion they could have saved their lives by parachuting, but this suspicion was not confirmed, because the destruction of these aircraft pointed to the fact that a collision had happened at a great height. In the surrounding area of the aircraft there were about 800–900 parts of both aircraft lying around. In the field just by the grounds of the Flak Kaserne on Neumuhler Straße, I found the first dead flyer. Then there were more. These crashed airmen were all dismembered. I counted seven dead, who were lying scattered over the wide field, without head, without arms and legs. All of them were without uniforms, several only wearing a shirt. It was impossible to identify these dead, and none of them had either any identity papers or identity cards with them. Most of these casualties were badly burnt, and it appears these seven men found belonged to one whole crew.

As to the other aircraft that was involved in the crash, this one came to rest at the carpenters' barracks, and it was still burning in the morning. Here too there was only the aircraft body with the motors and one small piece of the wing. The aircraft should also have had a crew of seven. Searching the area, I found six men. Two of the dead flyers were in good condition; the other four were completely dismembered, head and arms missing, together with their clothing, which was all burnt. I have to add that the dead bodies also were scattered in the surroundings and not all together. The two complete dead flyers must have jumped out of the aircraft in the last minute, as they were not burnt.

From my chief of the Flak Kaserne I had got an order to report the dead flyers to Mulheim/Ruhr, as from there the recovery unit for dead bodies was despatched to collect the dead. In the afternoon of 15 October, a lorry with Russian prisoners of war commanded by an Oberfeldwebel arrived at the scene. The dead were just put on the lorry, the seven completely dismembered dead bodies from the field at Neumuhler Straße and the six dead, who were lying on the grounds of the Flak Kaserne. The two dead who were in good condition who had their identity papers with them – I can remember that very well – were laid to one side. The Oberfeldwebel then took over the papers. On my question as to where the crashed enemy comrades would be buried, I got the answer 'first I drive to Mulheim, there everything will be photographed, the papers will be handed over to the Red Cross. The dead will be buried either in Mulheim/Ruhr in the soldiers' cemetery, or in Kalkum. I am sorry I cannot tell you exactly.' I have forgotten the name of the Oberfeldwebel of the recovery unit, and I cannot remember, despite thinking over. An alternative to find out his name would be the former leader of the Flak Kaserne, Hauptman Didier. He is supposed to live in Düsseldorf. You can most probably find his address from the former canteen keeper of the Flak Kaserne and from the former pay master, as the canteen keeper knew him. I think Hauptman Didier and his former Kamptfeldwebel can give you the best information as to where and in which barracks the recovery in Mulheim had its residence.

Neither on the grounds of the Flak Kaserne nor in the field where the dead flyers were found, nor in the bomb craters were dead flyers ever buried. I would have known about it. The crashed flyers were soldiers and had done their duty; they should have had an honourable soldier's grave. At any time I can state by oath this information.

The one aircraft, lying on the street, had seven crew members, which I had found. The other aircraft at the carpenters' barracks was of the same type; there I found only six dead. One of the flyers ought to have saved his life, as, despite a thorough search, I could not find him. However, a month or so later in November 1944 – I cannot recall the exact date – it was very cold, I found the seventh crew member. My little dog, hunting rats, found him. He was hunting rats and then came to an area and would not leave until I followed him. In an almost destroyed house, in Morian Mulhe, I found the dead flyer. He had dropped through the roof and was lying under rubble. The head was unrecognizable, the boots he was wearing were scattered in the destroyed room. These are now in possession of the person living there.

This casualty was a sergeant I think. I handed again the identity papers to the leader of the recovery team. This time it was somebody else who undertook the duty. I do not know his name. The dead were brought to Mulheim or Kalkum for burial. There were three possibilities where the crashed flyers could have been buried. One of the dead flyers who were in good condition was approximately 19 to 20 years old; he had reddish hair, blue eyes and small snow white teeth. The upper front teeth were both gold plated, height approx 1.75 to 1.78 tall, quite slim. These is my statement for everything that happened during the night of 14/15 October 1944.

An engine was discovered at the scene by post-war investigators and was found to be from ME748, and other parts were found to have come from LM165, with the main bulk of the wreckage of ME748 being located at Neumuhler Straße, Meiderich, Duisburg. Some was also in the nearby fields, together with that of LM165, which was also very close by in open ground, situated on Neumuhler Straße itself. The crew of this aircraft are still missing and are all commemorated on the Runnymede Memorial.

After the end of the war, some local farmers who were ploughing the crash site stumbled upon two lots of human remains. The first lot were recovered when the engine, which was identified, was dug out by them. After recovery, the remains were interred in the Rheinberg Military Cemetery in plot VII-D-21. The second set was found while the fields were being ploughed near to the same spot. These were removed and also taken for burial in Rheinberg and interred next to the first plot. No identification was possible it would appear; these are buried as unknown airmen.

This particular case is confusing, as the documents mention one location for burial of the crew, but when enquiries were made they stated no airmen were ever buried here.

The airmen from this Lancaster were removed from the wreckage and interred in the nearby Duisburg North/Hamborn Cemetery by the Germans, according to the official report. However, when enquiries were made, another report mentions that no airmen were ever buried in this cemetery, with a sweep providing no results. An investigating officer, Flight Lieutenant Ramsden, was informed of this when he was searching for the crew of PB357, as again the documents stated they had also been buried here. He checked these cemeteries' records in 1946 and also searched the cemetery, and no trace of Allied aircrew were recorded.

It is also possible the documents were incorrect and recorded the wrong burial location. The services were heavily disrupted. Many airmen were noted as being buried in one cemetery only to be found in another. The other piece of information we know that is a little confusing is that nineteen unidentifiable bodies were brought into this Duisburg Stadt West

Friedhof cemetery in December 1944. Where these came from is not known. We know, for example, that the crew of PB357 were moved to the Duisburg North/Hamborn Cemetery temporarily in July 1946, as the mayor gave an order to have the bodies moved from their isolated burial sites. This, however, appears to have been only a temporary measure in order to have the bodies examined and not placed here for burial. It could have been that these crews were also moved and consolidated. My personal opinion, having studied the various documents, is that the crews of LM165 and ME748 were never buried in the Duisburg North/ Hamborn Cemetery and were buried directly into the Stadt West Friedhof (Duisburg Wald Cemetery), with the exception of Flying Officer Shaw, Flying Officer Shaw was located in an isolated spot, in the south-west cemetery in Essen, on Fulerumer Straße. He was interred into the area that was set aside for Allied airmen. It was established that this was the airman who was found in November by the eyewitness under the rubble in the house. He was in reasonable condition, which probably went a long way to assisting the MRES teams when he was exhumed. It is likely he ended up in the cemetery in Essen because he was found on his own, weeks after the crash. He was later exhumed and removed to Reichswald Forest Cemetery, Kleve.

In the case of Lancaster LM165, four names were identified with two bodies at the scene from identity papers recovered. If they were buried in the Stadt West Friedhof, they would have been interred into Field 1, which was then the old cemetery and the area used for Allied aircrews. Two other crews, PB357 and LM596, were found here after the war by investigators, as well as a number of unidentified airmen. It is likely these airmen or at least some of them constitute the remains of ME748 and LM165. The IRCC communicated the German information via telegram to the Allied forces that four airmen were confirmed as identified being Sergeant Sunley, Sergeant Purnell-Edwards, Sergeant Morrell and Sergeant Read, but it did not state burial particulars, so this also gives no leads.

We know two of these were identified from the scene of the crash, as the eyewitness states that the two flyers in good condition were placed to one side. It was also mentioned that in total they had located seven airmen when telegrams were sent quoting German information. The fate of the other unnamed airmen was not listed, and so the Air Ministry still classed them as 'missing' until further evidence came to light to prove otherwise. In the case of the four listed, they would be classified as 'missing believed killed' at a later date, until further information was found.

The fact that two of them had been identified after the crash and a list of names was established meant little, as the MRES teams investigating the case after the war could only assess them as 'missing airmen'. It was quite clear, however, they had located the crash sites of the two aircraft involved and had confirmed that the crew or a considerable part of the crew had been found or recovered from the aircraft at the time of the crash and been taken away for burial to an unknown location.

The investigation and search for the crew went on as late as June 1951, but was then abandoned, as the exhaustive investigation brought up no further indication as to the positive identification of the crew. A number of airmen from other cemeteries would have been located, but, as no identification was possible, they are still listed as missing, despite most likely now resting in Reichswald Forest Cemetery or Rheinberg Military Cemetery. All unknown airmen were interred by the RAF in these cemeteries as 'Unknown Airmen' and 'Known unto God'.

The Pilot, Flight Sergeant Francis John Cook, enlisted with the RAAF on 9 October 1942 at the No. 3 recruiting centre at Rock Hampton, Brisbane, at the age of 19, enrolling with the hope of becoming a pilot. Francis was the son of Alexander David and Hilda Mary Cook, of Anakie, Queensland, Australia, and he was born on 8 March 1923. He was educated in local schools and attended the Sapphire state school and Bradley's College in Rock Hampton, sitting the intermediate public exams and state scholarship examinations between 1936 and 1940.

Upon leaving school his main occupation was that of a general clerk, but he had been involved in the military for a short time before requesting discharge to join the RAAF, in order to remuster as aircrew. Francis had served with the Army, 1 Australian Field Section, and had held the rank of Private, No. Q114323, serving from April 1942 to October that same year. He had a general interest in sports outside of work that included tennis, football and cricket.

No. 692 Squadron

Mosquito XVI MM184

Pilot	Flying Officer Frank H. Dell	Evader
Navigator	Flying Officer Ron A. Naiff	KIA

This is the story of the only Mosquito that was shot down on the night of 15 October 1944 while on a diversionary raid in support of the main raid to Duisburg.

MM184 became airborne late in the evening on 14 October 1944 from RAF Gransden Lodge with the intended mission of dropping a 4,000lb bomb load on to Berlin as part of a distraction and nuisance raid in support of Operation Hurricane. Frank Dell had done this trip to Berlin a handful of times before without incident. The aircraft was routed south-east across the North Sea into the north of Belgium and then the Netherlands, where it would turn east for Berlin via the north of Duisburg and Munster, passing Brunswick before reaching Berlin itself. However, the aircraft failed to make it past Munster.

MM184 became a victim of a preying German nightfighter, shot down by Uffz Hans Dürscheid at 5,600 meters. The Mosquito was attacked from behind, and the crew knew little about it until they were hit by the machine gun and cannon fire from the German fighter, just after flying through a wall of searchlights.

The Mosquito MM184 crashed in the Duisburg–Munster area at approximately 0211 hrs following the attack. Hit by enemy fighter and with bullets ripping into the airframe, the Mosquito quickly broke apart, and only the pilot, Frank Dell, escaped with his life by sheer luck. His navigator was unable to get to his parachute in time, and was still in the aircraft when it blew up at high altitude, breaking up as it went down.

Parts of the wreckage were scattered over a large distance; however, RAF records state that the aircraft crashed one mile south-west of Munster. The navigator, Flying Officer Ronald Arthur Naiff, is commemorated on Panel 208 of the Runnymede Memorial, as his body was never formally located after the war by the MRES investigation teams. The Germans did claim that an airman was removed from the wreckage of the Mosquito and buried locally, but no positive identification could be obtained by the MRES teams after the war, so he remains listed as 'missing'. It is, however, likely that he rests in the Reichswald Forest Cemetery as an 'unknown' airman.

In March 2010 I met Frank at his son's home, and he gave me this account of his experience when he was shot down that evening:

Approximately four days after collecting the Mosquito we were detailed to fly this mission to Berlin, and it was all part and parcel of acting as a decoy in an attempt to draw away the nightfighters from the heavy bombers that were going to bomb Duisburg.

Not long after take-off, as we were climbing up through 10,000 feet or so, we found that whenever we altered course, the aeroplane shook as though going into a stall. This happened even though the airspeed was well above the aircraft's stalling speed. It occurred to me that when the aircraft was assembled, the factory had never tested it with a full load, especially as we had the 4,000lb on board and thus I believe it had a fault of some kind.

On that night, the plan was to cross the North Sea and fly eastwards towards the direction of Munster, Hanover and then on to Berlin. The idea was to pass to the north of the Duisburg region before crossing the area of Munster in the hope of drawing away Luftwaffe nightfighters from our heavy bombers, which were bombing Duisburg at that moment. We were at approximately 28,000 feet, nearly at our maximum operating altitude, and again, once in the cruise, whenever I had to change course the aircraft shook.

We had a clever device on the aeroplane called Boozer. It consisted of two radio receivers with two lights, one tuned to the German ground radar frequency and the other tuned to the German nightfighter frequency. The ground radar frequency had a yellow warning light and the nightfighter frequency had a red warning light. When you flew over Germany, the yellow warning light was on pretty constantly, but if a radar-controlled searchlight, the blue ones, pointed straight at you, the yellow light would illuminate very brightly. If a nightfighter was closing in on you, the red light would come on very brightly.

We passed Duisburg, just to the north, on our way towards Berlin, and I looked down and I saw it burning. The weather was clear in this area, but for part of the journey we were in fact above cloud. Not long after passing Duisburg, we altered course towards Munster, and as we were coming up to Munster, coloured flares were being dropped and kept coming down. This was dangerous, as the nightfighters would then lie in wait for passing aircraft to attack. On the outskirts of Munster we ran into a great wall of searchlights, they were weaving around and searching for aircraft. It was so bright that my cockpit was illuminated and I could have read a newspaper at 28,000 feet. Looking out to my left, I could quite clearly see a couple of Mosquitoes going along, with another three or four out to my right.

Just before getting into the situation, my amber bright light came on, which suggested the searchlights were looking at me personally, with either a searchlight or an anti aircraft gun. The standard drill was to alter course as soon as one of these lights came on brightly, either to the left or right, thirty degrees or so; you then started counting, one second for every thousand feet of altitude. So, as we were at 28,000 feet, we counted for 28 seconds and then resumed our course again. Normally you would then look back over your shoulder and see shells bursting in the sky, where you would have been.

As I altered course, the aircraft shook like mad. The control column was shaking and the Mosquito just reared up into a climb and flicked over onto its back and began to enter a violent spin, becoming uncontrollable. The aircraft must have spun down for at least five or six turns and then I had no idea what happened. There was a giant crash, and it soon broke apart, and this was probably due to the 4,000lb bomb breaking loose. I must have been thrown through the Perspex roof of the aircraft, as, when I came to my wits, I was just bundling through the air towards the ground, out of the aircraft. Meanwhile, just before the incident, my poor old navigator had gone down into the nose of the aircraft in order to set the wind that he had reconfirmed by his navigation. This was in order to set up the bomb sight ready for when we arrived over Berlin. It was during this time we were hit, and as we were spinning down violently, he was stuck in the nose and had no means or ability to get his parachute, which was stored in the cockpit, or even get out of the aircraft.

As I was falling through the sky, I felt around to see if I still had the seat of my aircraft attached to me, as I had been wearing my shoulder harnesses and straps, but that was not there, but my parachute pack was, and so I pulled the ripcord and the parachute opened and that was that. By this time the searchlights had gone out and everything was quiet.

My parachute must have opened above 20,000 feet, and with a light southerly wind I may have ended up and landed approximately five miles to the north-west. Upon exiting the aircraft, it took approximately three seconds for my parachute to deploy, and having taken about twenty-five minutes to drift slowly through the night sky on my parachute, I landed in a farmer's ploughed field and then shed myself of my parachute. The next day I hid up in a wood, but this wood turned out to be the location from where the Germans were launching V2 rockets. I recall being in pain. I had split both of my eyebrows open, and had torn the end part of my nose. My left leg was in pain and my battledress had been ripped at the back from top to bottom, and my left sleeve had been torn out, but my legs worked, although I felt as though I had played in the roughest game of rugger ever.

The RAF advised in such situations that, after landing, one of the first things you should do is to open your escape pack and find the Benzedrine tablets, which were in a plastic wrapper, as these would help to overcome shock and sharpen you up; in particular, to take some in case of capture as, when suffering from shock, things may be said that otherwise would not be mentioned. My emergency pack, which consisted of chocolate, glucose tablets, Benzedrine tablets and water purifying tablets, was in my tunic. In the darkness, having arrived in the ploughed field, I opened the escape pack and took out the plastic packets and took some of the tablets, then set off walking. I began walking in a generally westwards direction towards Holland, but only at night time, as we had been advised to do.

The next day, when hiding in the wood where the V2 rockets were, I took stock of the situation and opened my escape pack only to find the tablets I had taken the previous evening were not Benzedrine tablets. They were water purifying tablets, one per pint! I also sewed up my battledress and put my sleeve back onto my jacket. While there, I thought the world was going to end, as the Germans fired one of these V2 rockets and the entire place shook.

I did not walk far on the first night after landing, possibly approximately 25 kilometres or so on the second night, and another 25 kilometres on the third night. After walking for a number of nights, I passed a signpost to Ahaus, which pointed in a north-west direction, but by this time, the fifth night, I was becoming very tired and did not cover much ground. It was then I located a small barn, and this was where I was found the following day. The village of Ahaus is a small German village located very close to the Dutch border, and it was near here that I found shelter in the house of the Breukelaar family in the Varsseveldseweg in Aalten.

As I had been walking in the rain for much of the fifth day, I was soaking wet, and came across a barn, and so I went inside and found a ladder and climbed it to the area where there was a small space with hay. In the darkness I took my wet clothes off and hung them on the beam to dry, then ducked down into the hay pile to get some rest for the evening. Early the following morning, at approximately 0900 or 1000 hrs, I was rudely awakened by the sound of a fighter plane diving down and firing its guns at something very close to the farmhouse. A minute or two later, I heard some cautious footsteps coming into the barn and up the ladder into my hay loft, where I was hiding.

I heard whispered conversation and then realized that in fact there were two people who had come up into the area where I was, and it was then they had discovered my clothes hanging up on the beam. Having thought to myself, I decided I had best reveal myself and come out of hiding to claim my clothes. I had a strong feeling that these two people had come in, having been frightened by something that caused the fighter to come down and attack.

I came out of the hay pile and confronted two 16-year-old boys. They appeared greatly alarmed to see me, although one of them spoke a little English, and he said to me in broken English while pointing at me: 'You Tommy. Pilot!' I replied 'Yes.'

He told me: 'Sssshhhhh. You be quiet. German soldiers in the farmhouse.'

It transpired that the German soldiers had been coming along in an army truck and had been spotted by the passing aircraft and so were attacked. The truck had been wrecked by the gunfire, and the Germans had jumped out and run for their lives. Their nearest shelter was the front door of this farmhouse, and so they had burst in, and these two 16-year-old boys had become frightened and run out of the back to seek shelter in the barn.

After approximately half an hour or so, the German soldiers had pushed off and the two boys left to report the situation to the farmer; one of them was the farmer's son. The boy who spoke broken English was in fact the son of the schoolmaster in the town, and he told me: 'Tonight I go to my father, who is schoolmaster. Schoolmasters know many people, he may help you.'

The following day, a member of the Resistance came and took me under his wing. The two boys were very frightened though at this time, as there were notices in the town that the Germans had placed mentioning that all men found to be helping any Allied airmen would be shot, and that any women found involved in this activity would be sent to a concentration camp. It was the underground people who assisted me and placed me with various families in hiding. When I was taken to the Prinzen family, it was a dangerous situation for them, as they had ten children and to be found meant the family would suffer at the hands of the Germans. I and other airmen, who were being kept there, spoke to the Resistance, and we were moved to one of their farms away from their children.

By this time we were receiving RAF drops, which included canisters of weapons, guns, hand grenades and such like. The underground people interrogated me to ensure I was who I said I was, and the last question was did I know Morse code. It came to light that the underground workers were about to receive these canister drops and none of them knew the Morse code and so would be unable to communicate with the aeroplane, which flew over low to drop the supplies. I was then appointed the Morse code operator and equipped with a signal lamp. The bombers would come over low, using the navigation aid 'Gee' to fly to our location and would then signal us with lamps, and we would respond, and so the aircraft would drop these canisters from approximately 500 feet by parachute at night time. Each time we were supplied by a Stirling bomber, and sometimes when it came over, the canisters were not packed tightly enough and they burst open when the parachute opened, sending weapons and equipment all over the place. I was involved with the Resistance during my stay there and was given a gun, but it meant that, if I was caught, I would be shot.

At one point when I was with another family in temporary accommodation, I was with this Dutch family and sitting at the table with the Resistance worker and his wife. A German soldier who was billeted at the premises then came into the room after coming through the front door and he sat down at the opposite end of the table to where the wife was sitting. I was at the side of the table and next to the Dutch man, the German sitting next to him. The German soldier then dropped his cap, after going to place it down onto the table; he knelt down to pick it up, but in the process I could quite clearly see the butt of his pistol protruding through the top of his tunic. At this moment the Dutch man indicated to me that it was time for both of us to leave. This was one of the moments that I came close to being caught.

Towards the end, liberation was near and the Resistance organized two or three ways to get us out, but the problem was that we were on the wrong side of the river Rhine. The fighting at Arnhem had already taken place, and the British and Canadian armies had already reached the south side of the river Rhine and we were ten miles or so out of the area on the wrong side. Each of the possibilities proved too difficult to carry out. It was not just us that they had to get out of the area; there were approximately 400 paratroopers still in hiding from the drops, and these also had to get out somehow. One of the rescue operations they arranged was that a number of boats were used to cross the river, each holding about fifty or sixty men. The first one successfully crossed the river, but the second one was intercepted by the Germans and an awful lot of the men were killed, and so, following this, they cancelled the third crossing, and it was this one that I was supposed to be in.

We were then advised to stay where we were until the army advanced over the river, and eventually, in March 1945, they crossed over and arrived after a lot of heavy fighting in the area. One morning the farmer knocked on our little trap door and informed us that all of the Germans had pulled back and they could see a 'Tommy tank' approaching. Myself, together with an Australian and an American, climbed out and walked down the road towards the tank, which actually turned out to be an armoured car. It was waving its 6lb gun around and, as we walked up to it, it took no notice of us, so I banged on the side of this thing and eventually the steel lid on the gun turret opened up, and out came a face with a beret on and a huge handlebar moustache.

I informed the man that my name was Frank Dell of the RAF and I had been in hiding with these other fellows, and the soldier replied in typical English: 'Jolly good show, jolly good show.' The soldier turned out to be from the household cavalry, who were the reconnaissance boys at the head of the armoured division, and very aristocratic. He then radioed back, and they sent up a truck to collect us, but by this time there were seven of us altogether. I was extremely sad when we had to leave, as they only gave us five minutes to say our goodbyes and we had become part of the family, as we had been there with them for many months. It just did not seem right; we had to leave so quickly.

The German nightfighter pilot that claimed Flying Officer Frank Dell's Mosquito was a young man named Hans Dürscheid, the son of Johann and Anna Marie Dürscheid, born on 25 April 1917 in Cologne. There are various spellings for his name, one other being Doerscheidt.

On the night of the attack of Mosquito MM184, Dürscheid was flying a Messerschmitt BF110 twin-engined nightfighter and was part of a force hunting the bomber stream that was attacking Brunswick and Duisburg. Hans Dürscheid was killed in a crash at Bonn-Hangelar airfield on the night of 24/25 October 1944.

No. 61 Squadron

Lancaster ME595 QR-Y

Pilot	Flying Officer Norman Hoad	Survived POW
Second pilot	Flying Officer S. Cadman	Survived POW
Flight engineer	Sergeant Cyril Webb	Murdered
Navigator	Flying Officer Bill Ball	Survived POW
Bomb aimer	Flying Officer Bill Pullen	Survived POW
Wireless operator	Sergeant George Boyd	Killed
Mid-upper gunner	Sergeant Norman England	Survived POW
Rear gunner	Sergeant Embury	Survived POW

ME595 was the only heavy bomber to be lost on the raid to Brunswick that took place in the early hours of 15 October 1944. It was based with No. 61 Squadron at RAF Skellingthorpe. The aircraft was constructed under contract number 2221. Initially this aircraft wore the QE-Y markings, but these were changed later on to QR-Y, which were the markings it was wearing when it failed to return. ME595 had approximately 528 flying hours on its airframe when it was lost. It had been heavily damaged some months before but had been repaired and put back into service until it was lost over Brunswick.

The aircraft became airborne on the late evening of 14 October. The Lancaster was shot down as it crossed the target area on its bombing run and crashed between 0245 and 0300 hrs at Rieseberg, which is approximately 6 kilometres north-west of Konigslutter, a short distance east of Brunswick itself.

All eight members of the crew, including the second dickey pilot, managed to abandon the stricken bomber before it went down, but two of the crew were killed. One was murdered by his captors after being taken

POW. The other was injured when the aircraft was hit by flak. His fellow crew members attempted to give him a chance, and so they assisted him out of his station, strapped on his parachute for him and pushed him out of the rear door. However, the parachute somehow opened in the aircraft as he was being helped to the door, and it failed to deploy properly. He did not survive the jump. Both airmen are now buried in the Hanover War Cemetery side by side.

The pilot of the aircraft, then Flying Officer Norman E. Hoad and now a retired Air Vice Marshal kindly agreed to grant me an interview and provided written accounts, so I can now present his recollections of that fateful evening on the raid to Brunswick.

That evening our target was the city of Brunswick. It had been raided a number of times throughout the war by the RAF, but it had failed to really do it, and I think this time they wanted to do it properly and put the tick in the box. I had a second pilot that evening with me in the cockpit, Flying Officer S. Cadman, who was on his first raid as a 'second dickey' and was there to watch what was going on and learn the ropes prior to taking his own crew on operations.

The flight to the target was rather straightforward and nothing out of the ordinary; it was only as we turned onto the bombing run on the approach to the target that we ran into problems.

The bomb-aimer then took over, supplying me with commands to follow to steer the aircraft to line it up with the target, as from the cockpit I could not really see anything, whereas down in the nose he had a good view of the overall picture. I was busy looking at the instruments and everything appeared to be going well. The bomb doors had already been opened and the bombs were exposed in the underbelly of the Lancaster to the night sky.

That evening the flak was somewhat interesting and rather heavy, with it rocking the aircraft. Flak bursts could be seen with a glowing orange flash at the centre. Up until the bombing run we could take action and try to avoid it, but now that we were on the bombing run with the bomb doors wide open, it was impossible to do anything, as the bomb-aimer was doing his best to line us up with the target and he instructed me how to fly the aircraft. I had to ignore everything that was going on around me outside and solely concentrate on following the bomb-aimer's instructions. I think that evening part of our bomb load consisted of a 4,000lb cookie and other general-purpose bombs and incendiaries, which we called 'cookies and cans'. The bomb-aimer was giving me instructions like right, left, etc., there was a fair amount of flak around outside and that's when we were hit.

Suddenly there was a large salvo and large explosion underneath the aircraft, towards the rear from where I was sitting, with a huge bang, and it shook the aircraft violently, causing it to shudder. This hit blew parts off of our aircraft. Then very quickly there was a fire, and lots of smoke began filling the bomb bay area. It turned out that a number of the incendiary bombs we had on board had been hit by the flak as they lay exposed in the underbelly of the aircraft, and they began to burn furiously in the bomb bay. Being incendiaries, they burned very hot and the fire began to spread.

The bomb-aimer was now trying to jettison the bombs, but could not get them to leave the aircraft. The electrics had been damaged when we were hit by the flak, and there was no way of getting rid of the now blazing bomb load, and all attempts had failed.

There was confusion on board, as smoke began to fill the aircraft. The flight engineer, Sergeant Webb, went back to give the boys a hand with an extinguisher in an attempt to put out the fire, but they were wasting their time, of course, and they told me so over the intercom. The mid upper gunner, who was also injured, got down to help the wireless operator, who had been hit and badly injured by the flak; the crew were helping each other out.

Now realizing the seriousness of the situation, I gave the order to bail out, realizing that at any moment the cookie could go off. I got an acknowledgement from everyone over the intercom in respect of my order. The first to bail out was the tail gunner; he put on his parachute and bailed out via the rear turret.

The wireless operator was very seriously wounded and he could not fit his own parachute or walk properly; the mid upper gunner pulled him from his station, fitted his parachute to him and then carried him down the fuselage to the rear door. However, his parachute cord had somehow been pulled in the process and it unpacked inside the aircraft; all that could be done was to gather it up and assist him out. All the while this was going on I was still holding control of the burning aircraft.

Once at the rear door, the mid upper gunner tossed out the wireless operator and then jumped himself. Sergeant Boyd never survived the jump, owing to the parachute having already been opened, and it is thought that it never deployed properly, killing him as he hit the ground. That took care of everyone from the rear end of the fuselage. The navigator then got up from his position and went forward past me and the others and went out through the front hatch; the bomb-aimer had already gone by this time too.

It was very crowded up the front of the aircraft on this particular evening, as we had the second pilot on board with us, and everyone that was left was trying to make their way down past me and into the bomb-aimer's position down the steps. The engines were performing marvellously and they gave no problems whatsoever, but by this time the rest of the aircraft was on fire in a spectacular way. I was still in my seat flying it as the last members of the crew walked past me down the gangway, the second pilot and the flight engineer went out of the hatch, which left only me in the now empty but burning aircraft. All of this took place in a very short amount of time. I was trying to hold the aircraft, which was now falling out of control and beginning to lose altitude at a rate of knots, and I knew I had to get out. I then left my seat and let go of the controls and the aircraft began to do all sorts of aerobatics but I made my way down the steps to the nose of the aircraft with my seat parachute attached and saw that the hatch had been left open. By this time it was a struggle for me as the aircraft was losing altitude at a rate of knots and I was in a desperate situation. There was a further problem though. As I made my way down the steps I fell and lost my balance, landing head first into the bomb-aimer's compartment with my head out of the escape hatch, but I got stuck as something got tangled up. I could see though the flames, which looked quite pretty. Dragging myself back up inside, I untangled myself and turned myself around and rolled back up, heading out of the hatch head first.

Don't, whatever you do, pull the ripcord too soon! Once clear of the burning aircraft, count one, two, and three slowly, and then pull. The words of the instructor had clearly made an impact, for, despite the noise and confusion of getting out of the burning Lancaster, that is exactly what I did. As I fell clear of the burning Lancaster I was hit by a wall of ice cold air but restrained the urge to pull the ripcord, recalling clearly what the instructors had told us. Now I was clear and I was falling through the night sky. I slowly counted out the delay needed to ensure clearance and then with relief pulled the ripcord, but nothing happened for what seemed like an eternity. In fact, it took that long for the canopy and shroud lines to deploy, and then I felt an enormous shattering jolt as the chute opened and my flying boots were jerked off of my feet! Suddenly, it was quiet and I hung there gently swinging in the stillness of the night over Germany falling through the sky.

Remembering my drills, I looked up and reached for the shroud lines and found that, by pulling down each side in turn, I could, indeed, steer my descent and maintain a little control. It was dark and I could not see much as I fell further towards the ground. I was still at some height and it was some time before I could vaguely make out features on the ground. However, as my eyes adjusted to the dark and I got lower, I began to see a patchwork of the ground below me. No details could be seen, but I seemed to be drifting towards an area that was very much darker than the rest of the ground, which I decided must be a wood. It was too big for me to steer away from and quite suddenly I could see I was going to land in the tree tops. There was no chance of carrying out any sort of controlled landing, so, shielding my head as best I could and with legs together and slightly bent, I crashed into the trees. I did not come to rest immediately, but fell through the smaller higher branches and gradually came to rest, breaking off branches as I fell. I hung there in total darkness and in total and absolute silence.

Instinctively, my first thought was to get out of my parachute harness, but, in the act of punching the quick release box to free myself, something stopped me. Suddenly it had struck me that I had no idea how high up I was. I was sitting virtually in a nest of broken branches, so I decided to pull myself into the main trunk and climb down from there. Remembering, too, escape and evasion training, I tried to pull the parachute harness and canopy down from the tree tops, but it was so entangled that there was no way I could make any impression, so, reluctantly, it had to be left as a mega-marker of my presence.

Pulling myself into the body of the tree, I soon found the main trunk; fortunately it was some kind of conifer, so identifying the main trunk was not difficult. Once I was sure of this, I freed myself down from the chute and tentatively began to climb down. It went on for some time, but it was relatively easy to lower myself, as most of the branches stood out horizontally, with the trunk getting thicker as I went down. At last I had reached the ground, and, while I have no accurate idea of how high I had been when I landed, I would, undoubtedly, have been lucky to have escaped serious injury had I just allowed myself to drop.

Once I was on the ground, it seemed like a good idea to get my breath and take stock of the situation. To help the process I felt inside my overalls for a cigarette, only to remember I had shared my last one with my wireless operator on the dispersal pan at base while waiting to climb aboard ready for take-off! It was still pitch dark, and there was not a sound to be heard, but with my parachute advertising my presence, it seemed wise to get as far away as possible from my present position before daylight. Direction at this time was not important: all that could come later!

I soon found that this was easier said than done, for movement in bare feet and in near total darkness was an experience that no amount of evasion training had prepared me for. Suffice to say, it was painful, noisy and slow. After what seemed an age, I was stopped in my tracks by the sight of a line of lights stretching across the direction I had been moving. Clearly, it was a search party, and it was equally clear that there was no point in trying to make a run for it. I froze with indecision and, while I was trying to make up my mind as to what to do, the lights were very obviously getting closer as well as the yelping of the dogs. Suddenly, it was clear I had no choice but to dive into the undergrowth and freeze. Once at full length on the ground, I pulled the loose twigs and leaves over myself as best I could and waited.

The racket made by the search party and the dogs got even louder, but from my full length position I could see nothing whatsoever. Then, to my horror, I felt a dog nose into my hiding place. It sniffed me up and down and pawed at me, but, thankfully, did not give voice, and at that moment his handler shouted something and to my everlasting relief, the hound bounded off. Why I escaped I will never know, for I must have been pouring with adrenalin, but escape I did. The searchers moved on, and, as they faded into the distance, I lay there while my heart rate slowly returned to normal.

It was some time before I gathered my composure, but eventually it became clear that once again I was on my own. I got out of my hiding place and again began moving slowly through the woods and trees in the opposite direction from which the search party had been coming. Eventually I realised I could begin to see more, as the night faded towards the dawn, but I was still in the thick of the wood, so I decided to go to ground for the day and work out some kind of a plan of action.

The first requirement was to find out where I was. Until I knew that, all bets were off. We had been shot down on an easterly bombing run heading towards Brunswick. It was very likely, therefore, that I was on the ground somewhere west of Brunswick, but by how far was anybody's guess. From that area there were three possible evasion routes: north into Denmark, south toward Switzerland or west into Holland. There were pros and cons to each, but in terms of distance the western route seemed to be the best option, with the exception of one formidable snag. The eastward advance of the western Allied armies had bogged down following the debacle of Arnhem, and the entire front line lay right across my shortest route home. In no way would it be sensible to try and filter my way through the German Army. If, therefore, the western option was to be taken, the best course lay in getting into Holland and once there to try to contact the Dutch resistance for help.

This very elementary appraisal took longer to write than to decide and once I was clear in my mind that, subject to establishing exactly where I was, the Dutch option seemed to be the best, I settled down to spend the day in hiding. Evasion training dictated movement by night only and to stay out of towns and built-up areas. In the event, this proved to be easier said than done, but it was clearly my intent at first. I now took the opportunity to take stock of myself and possessions. My flying overalls were clearly recognizable for what they were, so I took them off and buried them in the woods; my battledress jacket was hidden by a lightweight kind of anorak that I always wore for flying, so that was kept on. Had I been more of an expert I might, with hindsight, have fashioned some kind of foot wear from my discarded overalls but it simply did not occur to me. By far the most precious of my possessions was my escape kit; this was a small pocket sized plastic box containing helpful bits and pieces. The most important was a silk map of western Germany and from this I later established I was in the area of a small town named Konigslutter. There was a tube of Benzedrine tablets, a small stick of shaving soap and a safety razor, some Horlicks tablets, a button compass and some water purifying tablets. All of these items were invaluable in their own way, though in the event I had to give up trying to shave to keep myself looking reasonably respectable, as shaving in ice cold water was just not on.

All that day I lay low and catnapped. In the evening I set off gingerly through the undergrowth, with neither sight nor sound of any activity, and by luck rather than judgement I came upon a woodland track and rightly or wrongly I decided to follow it to speed up my movements. The going was very much easier, and some hours later I began to hear the occasional sound of motor vehicles. The track I was on led me to what turned out to be a proper road, and I then decided to follow this too, despite being advised to keep away from things like this. However, there was plenty of cover and I reckoned I could dodge into it whenever I heard anything. The next piece of luck was wholly fortuitous, in that a roadside signpost inscribed 'Konigslutter' gave me the fix that I so badly needed in order to ascertain my position. From where I was I could just about make out the letters, but there was no possibility of finding it on my map in the dark whatsoever, so I decided to hole up until I could.

There was occasional traffic on the road, but, clearly, it was very much a byway and not a heavily used road. However, later in the day, when I had established my position on my map, I found that it ran roughly east–west, so I decided to use it as a general guide for the direction I needed.

It would be tedious in the extreme to recount the events of the next few days even if I could. The fact of the matter is that, after fifty-six years, my recall is by no means total, to say the least. Some detail remains bright and clear, but the sequence of daily events is lost in a haze of disconnected doings that do not add up to a continuous story. My own physical condition at the time probably accounts for some of the vagueness. Lack of food, no proper sleep, the mental and physical stress of trying to keep going, all must have contributed to this state.

What can be recalled clearly, however, was my realization that I was not covering ground fast enough to reach Holland before my strength ran out and I had to do some-thing, but the problem was what? The idea of stealing a motor vehicle was dismissed out of hand, and I rapidly came to the conclusion that I would have to steal a bicycle. I toyed with the idea of waylaying a cyclist, but, thankfully, rejected it in favour of a stealthy search through a village or small collection of houses. This meant abandoning the strict rules for successful evasion, but I knew that unless I could speed up progress I would fail in my attempts to evade. Happily, I located a bicycle propped up against a garden fence. It was not the most handsome of machines, but to me it was worth its weight in gold. I had not ridden one for years and my efforts were not helped by the fact that it had backward peddling brakes. It took me some time to get used to the hang of riding it and using the brakes, and having no lights did not help, but I was mobile and proceeded to make good use of the fact.

How far I rode that night I have no idea, and several times during the night I had to choose which direction to take in the road. Several vehicles passed by, but by and large it was head down and keep going. The following day I lay up and, after taking two Benzedrine tablets, set off again in the evening. The weather was not good; it had been blustery although dry until that night, when steady continuous rain set in. Riding along the road with no lights and my head down in the pouring rain, I was only vaguely aware of my surroundings when suddenly, with a bone-shattering jolt, I was thrown off of my bike. It turned out that I had ridden straight into a road block! When I had picked myself up, I found that the front wheel was now bent and the tyre was badly punctured. I tried riding it, but very soon found that the gain was not worth the effort, and sadly I had to abandon it.

I was now back to foot power. My Horlicks tablets had long since gone and I was down to just two Benzedrine tablets, and now I thought to myself that I had to get food and footwear and if I could not locate another bicycle I would have to break in somewhere to see what I could find. In the event it was not until the next night that I came across an isolated house.

I lay up for some time and when I was satisfied that nobody was about, I approached it and broke into it. I was hoping to find a pair of wellington boots and something to eat, but, unhappily, I was out of luck, although I did help myself to a mackintosh coat. This could have been my downfall and a fatal mistake after I was captured, as my interrogators told me that by wearing civilian clothing over my uniform I had put myself beyond the protection of the Geneva Convention on the treatment of POWs. I did not know this at the time, and my purpose had been mainly to use the coat as weather protection and to wear it as a kind of disguise to any civilian eyes that might see me.

The rest of the tale can be swiftly told. I did not find another bicycle, and my daily rate of progress became ever slower. I still moved mainly at night in the dark, but one morning I simply left it far too late to find cover and found myself in the middle of the flat open countryside. In the end I had to make do with a haystack. It was approximately 0730 hours when I went to ground and after covering myself up with the hay as best I could, I went thankfully to sleep.

The next thing I knew I was being prodded sharply in the midriff. Upon opening my eyes I found myself looking at the business end of a rifle and a bayonet and for me the war was over. The problem for me now was ensuring my survival from it.

'How do I know you are who you say you are? You were picked up wearing civilian clothing and you persist in giving me only your alleged name, rank and number. By these actions you have put yourself outside the protection of the Geneva Convention and unless you tell me where you have been and what you have been doing since you were shot down, I shall have no option but to hand you over to the Gestapo. You have until two o'clock to make up your mind!'

With this I was dismissed back to my cell by my interrogator, a Luftwaffe major. It was the third time I had been brought before him, and each time he had tried persistently and persuasively to get me to answer his questions about myself, my squadron and the base from which I had flown. None of the questions was unfair: I would have asked the same kind of questions had I been in his place, and it was not until the third session of questioning that his manner changed from fair and reasonable to one of threatening menace. In truth I found it somewhat embarrassing to keep repeating the mantra of number, rank and name only, and on one occasion I went so far as to say I was sorry I had to keep repeating myself, but if I went further I would be held responsible for my actions by my own authorities when I returned home after the war.

When I got back to my cell, I confess I began to consider my options. His threat, for that is what it was, was worrying me and doubtless intended to do so. He was not altogether right to say I had been picked up as a civilian in civilian clothes. While evading I had broken into a house and, for warmth as much as a form of disguise, I had indeed taken a mackintosh coat. I wore this over my uniform, so, I suppose he was technically right in his accusation, but at no time had I ever denied I was an Englander. Despite my filthy and shoeless state, my uniform was proof enough to validate my name, number and rank reply to all interrogations.

All this took place some days following my capture by two men of the Volksturm – the German equivalent of 'Dads' Army'. The business end of a rifle and bayonet prodding me in the midriff was a distinct discouragement to heroics, and their raucous shouts of 'Raus, Raus' was enough to convince me that discretion was the better part of valour. I crawled out of the haystack I was hiding in and stood facing them to await their next move. One of them pointed his rifle at me and shouted 'Russki, Russki' in a demanding sort of way, to which I made no reply. I had no German but it was clear one of them thought I was a Russian. The pair of them started to argue among themselves, and the upshot of it was that I was marched off and taken by a van to the nearby small town.

I later found out that it was a place named Stadthagen and while here I was taken to a shop marked Apotheke, where the boss began to question me. I had no idea what he was saying, so I thought it was best to come clean. To do this, I stripped off the mackintosh coat I had stolen and astonished them all by showing my uniform, which was now visible for all eyes to see. Shouts of 'Englander' and 'Terror Flieger' were easily understood!

By this time, however, the shop had filled up with local people, all keen to see what the fuss was about and to find out what was going on, and I began to feel distinctly vulnerable in my position. While I was there, there was a great deal of discussion going on, and it seemed they had come to an agreement to hand me over to the authorities, and in due course I was taken to a Luftwaffe base and placed in the cells. Before leaving Stadthagen I had been given food and for the first time I made the acquaintance of black bread, but despite my hunger I found it almost impossible to eat.

I have never found out which airbase I was taken to, but it must have been Wunstorf or Celle, I think. At all events, I was placed in the station 'Cooler', and during my first night a number of Luftwaffe pilots came in to see me. Most had some English, and I was regaled with their tales of derring-do. This suited me well, for it required nothing of me, and I took the opportunity of scrounging a packet of cigarettes. At this time it appeared things were looking up for me.

The very next morning two Luftwaffe airmen came and collected me and took me by van to Hanover. Though at the time I did not know it, I was on the way to Dulag Luft –the Luftwaffe central clearing point and interrogation centre for Allied airmen who were shot down over Germany. It was located in Frankfurt at a place named Wetzlar.

Upon reaching Hanover, I had my first sight of a blitzed town. There I was frog-marched through piles of rubble and devastation; the hostility of the locals was all too evident towards myself. In a curious sort of way, the guards who were with me acted as protectors, and I was much relieved when we reached what was left of the railway station. It was crowded with would-be passengers, and I was taken into a kind of canteen, which was dispensing bread and soup to all and sundry. This was welcome. After a longish wait, a passenger train pulled in, and, after a prolonged argument with the Reichbahn official, we were allowed to clamber aboard for what turned out to be our journey south. At the time I had no idea how long the journey was to be or where we were going. All I can say about it is that it went on for the rest of that day and all that night, with frequent and interminable stops. At Hanover we had picked up a third guard, who turned out to be a sergeant, and at no time was I ever left with less than two of them. Had they known it, the last thing I would have been able even to contemplate was escape.

The wear and tear I had suffered since being shot down had left me somewhat low, and the uncertainties of what lay ahead were enough to keep my mind fully occupied. At Frankfurt we changed to a feeder line for the short run to Wetzlar. There a lorry took us to Dulag Luft, where my guards handed me over, and I was dumped into a cell and there I sat.

That evening, a mug of hot mint tea was pushed through a hatch, and, after a restless night, the same thing happened the next morning, accompanied by a hunk of black bread. I sat there all morning, and around midday a bowl of thick soup and a few steam cooked potatoes, in their jackets, were delivered the same way. Nobody came to see me, and I began to experience just what solitary confinement meant. A sort of urinal or toilet provided the only facility, but there was no way of washing or doing anything to freshen myself up. Hot water pipes provided heat, but they were turned on and off in a way that varied the temperature in the cell from stifling heat to shivering cold. I have never been able to make up my mind whether this was by accident or part of the softening-up procedure. At all events, it was an effective way of putting on the pressure.

On about the third day I was collected from the cell and taken off through a rabbit run of corridors for interrogation. It was then I met the Luftwaffe major for the first time. I think his name was Eberhart.

'Good morning Flying Officer Hoad,' he said. 'How were things at Skellingthorpe before you left?' 'I am sorry I can't answer your questions,' I said, and the whole process of questioning got under way, which, after the third session, led to me being sent away to ponder his threat about the Gestapo.

I do not mind admitting that while waiting for my two o'clock appointment I fell prey to considerable unease ... I would maintain my refusal to go beyond number, rank and name.

Just before the appointed time, my guards took me back to the major's office and he greeted me by asking, 'Well, what have you decided?' I cannot recall the exact words I used, but it was to the effect that my position was the same. I repeated what I had said in the first session about the war being nearly over and that I would be back with my own people soon. There I would be held responsible for anything that I had revealed.

He looked at me for some seconds without speaking and then he said 'I am not going to waste any more time on you.' With this he gestured to my guards and they prodded me to follow them. I was taken through what seemed to be an endless series of passages and I was very uncertain where I was being taken. One thing was clear. I was not being taken back to my cell, and I began to anticipate the worst. Eventually, however, we emerged into the open air, walked across a sort of courtyard and into an entirely different building. Once inside I was handed over to two new escorts and, in English, told to follow them. We came to a large door, which was opened by them, and I was pushed through. I was totally astonished to find myself looking at most of the members of my crew. Bill Ball, the navigator, Bill Pullen, the bomb-aimer, the two gunners and Flying Officer Cadman. He had been put with me for his familiarization flight into operations. Needless to say, there was much to talk about, and I found out from them where I was and what was likely to happen. They had all been put through the interrogation process and the follow-up procedure common to all new arrivals at Dulag Luft. Thanks to the Red Cross, they had all been issued with essential clothing and fed a mixture of German rations and food from Red Cross parcels. In my turn, a blissfully hot shower and the issue of a pair of army boots, together with a khaki great-coat, began to restore how I felt about things in general.

A couple of days later, we, together with several dozen fellow POWs, were herded aboard a train for our journey across Germany to our ultimate destination at Stalag Luft III Sagan in Lower Silesia. Our train was made up of cattle trucks, each one clearly marked eight horses / forty men. Our trip to Sagan took days, was bleakly uncomfortable and a chilling introduction to life in the bag.

That was it. As far as I and any of the others were concerned, the other two crew-men had simply disappeared and I, for one, have spent the last fifty-four years wondering what happened to them. I now know that after the war the Air Ministry formed teams

*of investigators charged with the task of tracking down the fate of the, literally,
thousands of RAF crew members who had disappeared on operations over Germany
and elsewhere. They discovered that my wireless operator did not survive his jump with
the half-opened parachute and was killed on landing. The flight engineer's story was
rather different. After landing successfully, he managed to evade capture for four days
but was then apprehended by the Luftwaffe, and they shot him. By outstanding detective
work, the investigating team tracked down the two sergeants responsible, arrested them
and their Commanding Officer, and had them put on trial as War Criminals. In May
1947 all three were hanged.*

*Both of my boys were buried in separate locations, but the Commonwealth War
Graves Commission later had both of them reburied side by side in the Hanover War
Cemetery. Three years ago my wife and I went to Hanover and laid our posies of
Flanders Poppies on their graves.*

Sergeant George Patrick Boyd prior to the war was a gas fitter. He
enlisted in the Air Force shortly after his brother Frank Boyd, as he said
he did not want his younger brothers fighting his war for him. His
brother Frank was a rear gunner who flew thirty-four missions and was
awarded the DFC.

George was the eldest of three brothers born to George and Elizabeth
Boyd, and lived with his family in Sandwich in Kent. His father worked
for the Royal Mail and had previously served twenty-two years in the
Army and as a consequence George had spent a lot of his childhood
overseas, particularly in India. At the time of his enlistment his brother
Dennis was serving with the Royal Navy and Frank was in the RAF. Both
survived the war. A fourth brother, Patrick, was born during the war,
being only 3 years old when George was killed in action. He served many
years later.

George Boyd volunteered for service within the RAF and was enlisted
on 1 October 1940 at the No. 1 reception centre with the Uxbridge reserve.
He was sent for training to Blackpool and began with the No. 3 Signal
School on 27 November, where he stayed until the middle of 1941.
George qualified as a wireless operator on 3 September 1941, but was
then posted abroad, for a short period of time serving in Bombay.

The first sighting of Sergeant Boyd was made by a 12-year-old boy named
Herrmann Altenbach, who is now a farmer. He discovered the flyer lying
in the middle of a farmer's field a short distance to the south-west of the
village of Glentorf in full flying uniform, together with his opened parachute. He was found later that same day, after the heavy raid on Brunswick.

A short time later the Germans came and took him away after noting down his particulars and buried him locally in a small German cemetery named Glentorf Cemetery. Glentorf is a small village located to the north-east of Brunswick, and just 4 kilometres north of the aircraft's crash site at Rieseberg.

There was a far more tragic story in terms of the flight engineer Sergeant Cyril Webb, who was captured a number of days later after landing by parachute. He was apprehended by a road patrol man named Hermann Behrens, who then informed the local police, and so he was taken away by officers to the police station at Gross Schwulper. He was subsequently murdered shortly after his arrest. This murder was investigated after the war by Captain B. T. J. Turner Bridger, of the Coldstream Guards.

The alleged crime being investigated was the murder of an English airman named Sergeant Cyril Webb (162973) on 18 October 1944 at approximately 2300 hrs, following him having been taken prisoner earlier after he bailed out on 14 October after being shot down. Eventually those accused were Hermann Wilhelm August Dinge, George Gawliczek and Josef Bussem. The incident in question took place on a small bridge in between Wendezell and Volkenrode, near Brunswick. All of these men were from the airfield near where Sergeant Webb had landed by parachute.

Initially the inquiry proved rather complex for the investigating officer, as, it was difficult to distinguish the facts from the rumours that had become rife after the incident in the local community. The hideous crime had become widely known, not only throughout the personnel at the Volkenrode airfield, where the accused were working at the time of the incident, but also in every household in the adjoining village of Volkenrode. Rumours had become grossly exaggerated and what was imagined to be fact actually turned out to be only rumour. The other underlying issue is that two of the suspects, Gawliczek and Bussem, had been in touch with each other in Paris before the interrogation, and it was thought that these men had conferred between themselves and agreed on the story that the airman was shot while trying to escape.

The first of the accused was Major Wilhelm Dinge, Commander of Volkenrode airfield. He had joined the NSDAP in 1931 and also be-longed to about six other party organizations, although he did not hold any particular official position in any of them. In 1934 he became a 2nd

Lieutenant in the SA reserve, where he was in charge of the SA at Stadt Oldendorf. However, he was dismissed from there on 1 May 1937, as he fell out with the brigadier over refusing an order that was given to him. Some of the witnesses to whom the investigating officers spoke said he was strict and brutal in command; however, others stated that he was temperate and 'would not have given an order like that'. He was summed up as being artful and prepared to lie profusely.

Wilhelm was born in Germany at Tiddische, Kreis Helmstedt, on 27 January 1892 and was married with a wife and daughter. At the young age of just over 14 years, he attended the Non-Commissioned Officers' training school at Neubreasach near the river Rhine, where he served for two years until he was transferred to the NCOs' training school at Juelich. He left the school with the rank of corporal, and was transferred to the Infantry Guards unit stationed further away in Berlin on 1 April 1911, serving with them until 1916. From there, Dinge continued his military career, joining the German Air Force as a pilot until the end of the war in 1918, surviving two crashes and being wounded in action three times between 1914 and 1918. He left the Army as a lieutenant, a rank he was given for outstanding service in the face of the enemy and for having served a total of twelve years. He came to Brunswick on 21 October 1921.

Stabsfeldwebel Georg Gawliczek was a regular soldier who had a reputation at Volkenrode airfield of being brutal. His deposition was deemed to be so full of blatantly obvious lies that it was thought best to leave it as it was and not to reinterrogate him. He was born on 2 January 1909 in Mittellazis in Poland, which was German territory when he was born. Gawliczek was married but had no children. He lived at Langen-hagen in Hanover and was a member of the Roman Catholic Church.

Upon leaving the elementary school in Middle Silesia at the age of 14 years old, Gawliczek became a butcher. He stayed in this occupation until the age of 19, and then joined the local police force in 1929. He stated that he had volunteered for the police as he wanted to assist the weak and suppress crime, but also that there was limited employment in the area at the time he joined. Gawliczek left the police force in 1934 having gained the rank of sergeant. He had many transfers, the last being to the airfield at Volkenrode in 1943. He stayed there until the end of the war, when the Americans captured him, placing him in a POW camp in France. Gawliczek was shown to have a rather simple mind and to be mentally slow.

Stabsfeldwebel Josef Bussem was said to have lacked the courage to stand up to his convictions and stated to officers that he did not know that he was doing wrong when he undertook to discharge his 'duty'. On more than one occasion he attempted to convince himself and others that he was not guilty of the crime by using the words 'an order is an order' continuously. It was deemed that his deposition could be relied upon, except for the points that he referred to in his original statement.

Bussem was of German nationality. He was born on 29 April 1917 in Hagenbach in the Rhine province and was educated at a standard elementary school. By trade he was a driver. He joined the German army on 3 November 1936, and served for eight years, holding the rank of sergeant at the time of his capture. He had been promoted on 1 November 1942. Bussem was transferred to Volkenrode aerodrome to work as a motor transport driver.

On the night of 14/15 October 1944, Sergeant Cyril Webb had bailed out of his stricken Lancaster ME595 and parachuted to earth, after being shot down by anti-aircraft fire. He landed near Didderse, which is located approximately 20 kilometres north of the city of Brunswick. From here he was on the run, and it was not until three days later, on 18 October at about 0800 hrs on a dry and mild morning, that he surrendered himself to Mr Hermann Behrens, a local road sweeper at Didderse, after coming out of the woods by the road.

Sergeant Webb gave himself up with no weapon, not wishing to participate any further in the war and wanting to become a prisoner of war. He was wearing his trousers and RAF jacket, but was without any boots or head gear. He made signs and gestures to Mr Behrens indicating he had jumped out of an aeroplane and had hurt his foot. As he could not walk properly because of his injured foot, the road worker stopped a passing milk van and loaded him on to it; this took him to the local bakery. Webb was left in the bakery and later handed over to the local burgomaster, Mr Wilhelm Stoter (a baker by trade but also the burgomaster).

Mr Edward Aumann, a local policeman for both Gross Schwulper and Didderse, was notified by Mr Stoter of the incident. He went to collect Cyril on his pushbike and took him to Gross Schwulper. His particulars were obtained and recorded in the police records, after which he was locked up in a cell in the fire station for safe custody. The walk back to Gross Schwulper was approximately 4 kilometres, which took about an hour in total, with the airman pushing the bike while the policeman walked alongside, both walking on the path and not in the road. The airman had bandages around his feet and was not in possession of any boots. This was between 1300 and 1400 hrs.

After receiving the prisoner and making his report, the policeman telephoned the Volkenrode airfield and notified them of the airman's capture, stating that he had detained a British airman and had him in custody. Mr Hermann Behrens also reported that the airman had his feet in bandages and that he required the support of a stick. Before the airfield was informed, the burgomaster was told of the capture.

The airfield staff informed the police that they would attend to collect the airman, and later that day two men of the German Air Force in full uniform arrived to take him from the hands of the police. This was at approximately 2000 hrs. Before the airman could be handed over, there was an air-raid alarm, and everyone made their way to the shelter nearby until the all-clear was sounded at about 2200 hrs. The airman's few belongings were removed from him. These were later left in the major's office. They included a picture of the airman's girlfriend and mother. The fate of Sergeant Webb had already been sealed, and it was now only a matter of hours before he would be murdered in cold blood.

At the end of September 1944, Major Wilhelm Dinge, who commanded Volkenrode airfield, attended a conference in Celle, which was presided over by General Wolff. Major Dinge stated that, at this conference, General Wolff issued instructions to the effect that in future no enemy airmen or parachutists were to be taken prisoner alive, and that the armed forces were not to intervene if the civilian population desired to lynch those enemy airmen.

About a fortnight after this conference, Major Dinge passed on General Wolff's order to his officers and non-commissioned officers who were based at Volkenrode airfield. A witness, Mr Kurt Muethel, who was himself present, alleges that Major Dinge was careful to avoid any personal attachment to Wolff's order but merely conveyed the meaning of the order to his hearers and stressed the authority of its originator. However, he is alleged to have terminated his speech with words similar to: 'So, in future, I do not wish to see prisoners brought to this aerodrome alive.' Nevertheless, it was thought that Major Dinge did not delight in forwarding Wolff's order.

In general terms the order was along the lines of: 'As from today, enemy parachutists will not be made prisoner of war any longer and will be shot dead. These criminals who murder our women and children do not deserve to be made prisoners of war.'

Oberst Lueder, the commander of Broitzen airfield near Brunswick in 1944, also attended Wolff's meeting. However, he almost certainly did not pass on the general's order to his own subordinates. This information was given to the investigating officer by Hauptmann George.

On 18 October 1944, Major Dinge received Aumann's telephone call regarding the airman from Gross Schwulper, and thereupon ordered his secretary, Mr Diesenberg, to bring him a roll call of his NCOs. From the list, he selected and sent for Kurt Muethel, who was the interpreter sergeant. On arrival, Muethel was first informed by Diesenberg of the nature of the job about to be assigned to him and was then shown into Major Dinge's office, where he received a direct order. Initially Muethel agreed to carry out the order; however, this was to change when he discovered the full details. Major Dinge wanted the airman collected, stating: 'A prisoner has to be collected from Gross Schwulper.' When Muethel answered 'Yes sir', he was told: 'You know, of course, Muethel, what that means.' Muethel was shocked, and informed Dinge that he could not carry out such an order.

Following interrogation, it was noted that Muethel claimed that Major Dinge did not give him a straightforward direct order to shoot Cyril Webb, but first of all commanded him to collect the airman and then reminded him of General Wolff's order. To Muethel, this was tantamount to saying 'go and shoot the airman' and he informed the major that he could not obey. A heated exchange followed, including words to the effect that Muethel was a coward. Major Dinge dismissed him with the words 'I shall not forget this.' Muethel then waited outside in Diesenberg's office. It was noted that, when he refused the order, he was calm and showed no emotion.

Muethel, a man in his fifties, had participated in both world wars. He was an educated man and admitted in court that he could not comply with the order that was being asked of him. However, he knew that he could have possibly been disciplined for refusing the order, as he was punished during the First World War for not obeying orders. In the outer office Muethel made a sarcastic comment to Diesenberg, saying: 'This job was meant for a butcher such as Gawliczek.' Gawliczek had been a butcher before joining the armed forces. Diesenberg seized hold of the unintended suggestion and informed Major Dinge, who then agreed to use him. Gawliczek, and Feldwebel Bussem, the motor transport sergeant, were then summoned by Diesenberg, by telephone, to come to the major's office. Diesenberg reported to Major Dinge a short time later that both NCOs had arrived. Both were shown into his office to receive the directive, and a repeat of General Wolff's order, followed by Diesenberg.

Major Dinge was said to have informed the men: 'Go to Gross Schwulper and collect a prisoner, but don't bring him back.' Bussem commented to the major: 'That means we take him to the camp at Breutsenb?' Dinge repeated: 'No, not to Breutsenb. You know Wolff's order. I do not wish to see the airman here.' Both men then left the office, but appeared shocked and turned pale when receiving the order.

Major Dinge's statement, however, conflicts with this, as it suggests that Diesenberg was not present when the orders were issued. Dinge also states that he mentioned that the airman should be shot only if he attempted to escape, and that the two men were responsible for the life of the prisoner. However, he also stated that the prisoner should be taken to a POW camp nearby.

This is not what witnesses suggested he told the two men, however. Other comments in the room by Dinge were to the effect of: 'Get a Tommy gun, if you don't shoot this airman, you will have to be expected to be shot yourself.' Both NCOs were advised by Dinge in a serious way that 'the higher authorities attached a great weight to the carrying out of these orders and that if the orders were disobeyed, heavy punishments were to be expected'. Dinge was said not to have added anything to General Wolff's order.

However, in the case of these two NCOs, Major Dinge had included a sentence which read: 'If you fail to carry out this order, you will be shot.' Major Dinge admitted during interrogation that he might have uttered these words at the time, as 'threats of shooting', and declared that these words were a normal routine of his administration to ensure his commands were punctiliously obeyed.

During interrogation the major gave the sequence of his own orders as: 'Go and fetch the airman from Gross Schwulper and remember General Wolff's order, but do not use your weapons unless he tries to escape.' He stated that he gave this order to both men in a very serious way, leaving his desk and going up to them when they returned to his office a second time after getting dressed appropriately to report they were ready.

On receiving the order, Bussem was convinced something wrong and criminal was being demanded of him. However, he thought he was bound to have to carry out the order, as it had been given by his superior, and he was told that if he did not carry it out he would be shot. Bussem had been called into the army in 1936 at the age of 19; he had been brought up with the ideas of National Socialism and been taught that all military orders had to be complied with. It was heard in court that he had never been instructed that it was his right to refuse to carry out an order. He was of the opinion that, if he did not carry it out, then he too would be shot. Bussem asked Major Dinge a number of times whether he should instead take the airman to the nearby airfield at Broitzem, but this was refused. His lawyer attempted to portray to the court that Bussem did all he could to avert the killing of the airman and was trying to get out of the order that was issued.

The major also stated that in the German army it was customary to obey the last command received and to consider previous contradictory orders as cancelled. In other words, he was saying that his sole command was 'go and fetch the airman from Gross Schwulper and do not use your weapons unless he tries to escape'.

Muethel remained in Diesenberg's outer office throughout and recorded that Gawliczek and Bussem were both ill at ease as each emerged from the major's office.

Bussem then collected his motorcycle and sidecar, got as far as the entrance to the airfield, and met Gawliczek. He then discovered that the motorcycle did not have enough petrol to complete the journey. The motorcycle was to be used, as ordered by Major Dinge, because only one prisoner was to be collected and because they had to economize on petrol. He then abandoned his motorcycle and telephoned Johann Clemens the ambulance driver, and ordered him to pick them up. All three men went to Gross Schwulper, and it was Gawliczek who signed the paperwork for the airman from Aumann, while Clemens helped Sergeant Cyril Webb, into the rear of the ambulance. Gawliczek informed the court that Webb did indeed have bandages on his feet, but that it did not impede his walking, but other witnesses stated he could not support himself properly and was hence being helped. The prisoner was otherwise in good condition. He was placed in the rear of the ambulance, but it was not locked, as the lock had broken. The other men sat in the front.

During the return journey, Clemens learned of Major Dinge's order and refused to have any part in the crime, saying he was going to drive straight back to the airfield. Bussem stated that during the short journey he attempted to convince Gawliczek that he should not kill the airman in accordance with Major Dinge's order, but to no avail. Gawliczek told him to shut up and that an order was an order. This was supported by the ambulance driver, who witnessed this while driving the ambulance, stating that Bussem was speaking his mind.

Just short of the airfield, Gawliczek ordered Clemens to stop the ambulance. Then Bussem went and collected his motorcycle, while Gawliczek waited approximately 150 metres from the gate entrance. Sergeant Webb was then transferred to the sidecar of the motorcycle with the help of the ambulance driver, who supported him, as he could not comfortably move to the other vehicle on his own. Clemens then drove his ambulance back to the airfield, after being dismissed by the two men, and returned to his billet.

The others drove the motorcycle to a bridge between Volkenrode airfield and Wendezelle; however, they went back and forth, while deciding what to do with the airman and discussing between themselves the options. Bussem stated he was sweating as they drove to and fro up the highway, thinking how he could save the life of the prisoner, but considered their own lives should not be sacrificed for that of the airman, as they had to contemplate the risk of being shot if they did not comply with the order given by Major Dinge.

After about fifteen or twenty minutes, during which time they crossed the bridge back and forth three times, the motorcycle was brought to a halt a number of metres from the bridge on the right-hand side. Apparently the airman had indicated to both of them by means of hand signals that he wanted to relieve himself. The air was cold that night and the sky was cloudy and dark, with no moon and no frozen ground. It was reported some light snow had fallen earlier on, but it was not snowing when they stopped.

At the trial Gawliczek repeated his story that the airman had attempted to escape, which resulted in him being shot. However, Bussem informed the court that he had decided to tell the truth and told a different account of what actually took place that night. Bussem stated that, after the motorcycle was stopped, all parties got out, relieving themselves, and the prisoner was standing by the bridge, shortly after going to have a look over it into the canal. Gawliczek, who was standing approximately 10 metres from the airman, then raised his machine carbine and aimed it at the prisoner and pulled the trigger, but nothing happened, and the gun jammed. He told Bussem to pull out his pistol in case the airman made an attempt to escape. He then tried to unblock the stoppage and again raised the machine carbine at the prisoner, while advancing to within 5 metres of the airman. At this point the prisoner looked round and saw the carbine being pointed at him, became frightened, hurriedly returned to the side car and sat down in it, and never attempted to leave it again. Gawliczek then withdrew his pistol and aimed the gun at the prisoner and fired two shots into the back of his neck, killing him.

The airman's head had fallen backwards when he was shot, and he was bleeding as he sat in the sidecar. The blood was running on to the edge of the sidecar, and that is how the pool of blood became visible on the road. From the time they exited the car to when Webb was shot was roughly ten minutes. Gawliczek then ordered Bussem to fire his gun also, stating 'Carry on – shoot!' So Bussem fired three rounds into the airman's back, and then they both pulled him from the sidecar and hauled him over the parapet of the bridge and threw his body into the canal. Bussem remarks that he did this without looking at the airman's head, fearing the ghastly sight that confronted him.

Gawliczek had claimed that the airman had run off from the motorcycle towards the bridge, that he himself had shouted 'halt' and had then fired a number of shots from his revolver in the direction of the airman after his machine carbine had jammed. Both Bussem and Gawliczek had collaborated on this story and told this at first to the investigating officer, but Bussem had changed his account in court.

After the deed was complete, both men returned to the airfield on the motorcycle, arriving there between about 2100 and 2130 hrs and they dropped the airman's belongings into the orderly room and telephoned Dinge. He advised them to hand in a report and to come and see him in the morning.

The interrogators deemed that, whatever the accused might say, it was certain that their one intention had been to shoot Sergeant Webb, with how and where being the only decisions left to take. It was certain that the motorcycle had been stopped on this bridge and that Sergeant Webb, either in the seat of the sidecar or having alighted from it, was shot in the back of the neck. Which of the two men carried out this act was unclear, as neither of the suspects admitted that the prisoner was shot in this way in their interviews.

Both remarked that they fired at Sergeant Webb as he was running away, that he fell over the bridge and into the canal, and that they were not certain that they had hit him as it was dark at the time. Both of them had forgotten that Sergeant Webb had both of his feet in bandages and wore no boots, yet they had both helped him into the sidecar themselves. Gawliczek also mentioned that they did not go down into the canal bank to look for Webb as it was too dark, which contradicted Bussem's remark, as he stated they did go down and look for Sergeant Webb.

On the morning after the incident, Clemens was ordered to drive his vehicle away from the airfield as there was an alert and vehicles had to be dispersed. Between approximately 1000 and 1030 hrs he left and drove towards a nearby wood in Wendezelle. He had heard the previous night that someone had been shot on the bridge and was curious, so he drove to the bridge on the way to the woodland to investigate for himself and stopped to have a look. Clemens confirmed that on the carriageway of the bridge, on the left-hand side in the middle of it, in the direction of Wendezelle, he observed a large pool of blood about a metre in diameter, which pointed to Webb having lain there for a few minutes after death. The pool of blood was approximately 1 to 1.5 metres from the parapet of the bridge.

Sergeant Webb was presumably dropped into the canal. It was also noted that Gawliczek had possibly handed papers to Diesenberg that belonged to Sergeant Webb. The final report back to Major Dinge was handed to him the following morning at approximately 0830 hrs. It read: 'On the 18 October 1944 Sergeant Bussem and I received an order from Major Dinge to collect an airman from Gross Schwulper. On the way, this airman tried to escape, and was shot whilst doing so.'

Bussem came into the major's office and informed him that the airman had been shot at or was shot dead while trying to escape, with Gawliczek coming in sometime later on and repeating the result. Major Dinge asked no questions about the deed and dismissed it with nothing further to say, but then he completed another report of the incident to higher authorities and also informed the local police station at Watenbuttel. Dinge relayed this information, as he was not sure if the airman was dead or on the run in the countryside. It was the responsibility of the police to search for escapees and not that of the airfield staff. No particulars of the airman were taken.

Almost two months after the incident, on 5 December 1944, the body of Sergeant Webb was found floating in the canal about half a mile from where he had been shot and thrown over the bridge. A Mr Kabelitz, who was a police waterways official, hauled the body from the water, but could find no papers on him, although an identity disc was located on his trouser belt. He then recorded these particulars in a written report and sent this to his headquarters.

A short time later, Volkenrode airfield was notified of the recovery, and the body was collected by them later that day. The same evening, Andreas Heyer instructed two airfield personnel, who were believed to be medical staff, to dig a grave for Sergeant Webb in the north-east corner of Volkenrode old cemetery, where he was unceremoniously interred in a sheet of canvas and without a gravestone.

Following part of the post-war crime investigation, the body of Sergeant Cyril Webb was exhumed from the single grave in which he had been placed. This and the post-mortem were carried out on 18 April 1947 by Lieutenant Edward William Roy Trounson of the RAMC in the company of the war crimes investigator Captain Turner Bridger.

The findings concluded that there were no wounds to the feet; however, there were a number of fractures to the bones of the spine, and that the airman had been interred for at least a year. It was summed up that the bone damage to the spine was not caused by gunshot wounds; however, a fracture to the bone at the base of the skull was also noted, but again this was inconclusive in connection to gunshot injuries. The state of the clothing on the body was such that it did not indicate any other wounds, and the post-mortem was unable to ascertain the exact cause of death because of the length of time the body had been in the ground. No bullets were located in the body. The conclusions of the post-mortem were that bullet wounds could have contributed to the injuries found, but it was not certain that this was the case, as they could have been old injuries incurred prior to death.

It was concluded, after evaluation of the depositions and the case, that Major Wilhelm Dinge did order that no enemy airmen were to be taken prisoner when he addressed his officers and NCOs at the end of September or beginning of October 1944, an order he attributes in the first instance to General Wolff of Luftgau XI, and that he ordered Bussem and Gawliczek to dispose of Sergeant Webb on 18 October 1944. It was recommended that he be tried for instigating the murder of Sergeant Cyril Webb. Gawliczek and Bussem were together also concerned in the shooting of Sergeant Cyril Webb, an airman who had laid down his arms and surrendered, and it was recommended they jointly be tried for his murder.

It was also considered that General Wolff was also primarily responsible for this crime, as he had issued the original order at the conference in Celle, but at the time of investigation there was no evidence to support this beyond reasonable doubt, and such further investigation was necessary before action could be taken against General Wolff.

All three accused were held in custody after investigations had begun. Trials began on 27 August 1947 and lasted until 4 September 1947, with the accused all pleading 'not guilty' for the charged offence. After a short trial, all three men were found 'guilty' by the military court. The suspects informed the military court that the prisoner was trying to escape. The court did not believe them.

On 4 September 1947 all three men were sentenced to death by hanging. Numerous appeals for clemency were lodged against the sentences, but it was seen that there were no grounds to justify overturning the sentence, and they were subsequently rejected by the courts.

The hangings were carried out in the courtyard of the Hameln prison on 14 November 1947, with Gawliczek being the first to be executed at 1012 hrs, followed by Bussem at 1122 and lastly Dinge at 1403. The bodies were then interred in the graveyard next to the prison.

No. 434 Squadron
Halifax MZ920 WL-C

Pilot	Flight Lieutenant Donald Zachary Taylor Wood	KIA (RCAF)
Flight engineer	Sergeant Geoffrey Davies Grant	KIA
Bomb aimer	Flying Officer W. Stirling	Injured (RCAF)
Navigator	Flying Officer William Robert Ewing	KIA (RCAF)
Wireless operator	Flight Sergeant Stamtis	Survived (RCAF)
Mid-upper gunner	Sergeant Owen Parsons	KIA (RCAF)
Rear gunner	Pilot Officer Donald McLeod Ward	KIA (RCAF)

Halifax MZ920, a Mk III, was based with No. 434 Squadron at RAF Croft, No. 6 Group, and was one of a number of aircraft on the raid of Duisburg to be lost, but it was a mechanical failure rather than combat that resulted in a tragic accident and loss of life. On 14 October 1944 eighteen heavy bombers were detailed to bomb Duisburg in the first heavy raid as part of Operation Hurricane. The Halifax successfully bombed the target and returned home back to base, bringing its crew back to safety. The aircraft took off at 0601 hrs, and came back at 1205 hrs, where it was made ready again a few hours later for the night-time raid back to Duisburg. The bomber was flown on the morning attack by Wing Commander A. Blackburn; however, the following raid would be made by a different crew, skippered by Flight Lieutenant Donald Wood, who had already flown the morning assault in Halifax NP144, landing at 1143 hrs.

The crew of seven, under the command of Flight Lieutenant Wood, received their battle order for their second trip of the day back to Duisburg, and allocated Halifax MZ920 for the trip. Shortly before 2220 hrs the engines were fired up and the aircraft made its way to the active runway among the many other bombers all assigned for the target that evening, leaving the runway dead-on 2220 hrs. Just over one hour later the aircraft ran into trouble as it made its way towards the target, and, at its operating altitude of 20,000 feet, a problem occurred on board. While the crew were still over England, there was a mechanical malfunction in the starboard outer Hercules XVI engine, whereby some of the studs that held the cylinders down came loose or sheared away, allowing lubricating oil and boosted mixture to escape on to the hot engine, where it ignited.

The flight engineer attempted to extinguish the fire by using the built-in engine fire extinguisher, but this failed, so the pilot attempted to dive the aircraft in order to put out the fire, which by now was spreading and beginning to fill the fuselage and cockpit with thick smoke. When the dive failed to douse the fire, the pilot tried to divert to Church Lawford aerodrome in an attempt to land, and the order was given to abandon the aircraft. But there was a further problem. The crew members in the front of the aircraft, trying to escape, pulled the escape hatch inwards and then attempted to throw it back out through the hatch to jettison it. It got stuck, blocking the hatch itself, rendering it useless. In the meantime the fuselage had filled with smoke and flames were preventing the crew from moving backwards to the rear door. So the crew at the front of the aircraft were trapped and unable to get out. Two members of the crew were, however, able to leave via the rear exit and bail out.

Shortly before the aircraft reached the runway and safety of Church Lawford aerodrome, parts of the wing began to drop off, and eventually most of the starboard wing detached after the main spar had burnt through, causing the aircraft to fall out of control and to crash approximately one mile from safety. Following the incident, a full investigation was carried out and, in future, modifications were used to prevent such engine malfunctions from occurring. However, the investigating officer did state that at the time of the crash the aircraft were still not protected against fire.

The crash was witnessed by a number of local inhabitants. One even cycled to the site as he observed the aircraft coming down in flames. Others saw a huge crater and many flames; bombs were scattered over a wide area and the main Coventry to London road was closed because of unexploded ordnance. The RAF and local police were very quickly in attendance.

Following the crash, the area was made safe, and the deceased airmen were recovered from the wreckage. Then a guard was mounted until 25 October until everything could be cleared away. Funerals were also held at this time, with the RCAF airmen being buried at Blacon in Chester, while Sergeant Grant was removed to his hometown in Wales.

Of the two survivors who bailed out, Flying Officer W. Stirling was injured and was admitted to St Cross hospital at Rugby before being transferred to the RCAF hospital at Marsden Green, near Birmingham, on 18 October 1944. Following recovery, he was transferred to No. 419 Squadron on 2 November 1944 and then, on 13 December 1944, he was posted to the RCAF R depot, which was used as a transit camp for re-patriated airmen. It is thought he was sent back home to Canada. It was this airman who was believed to have come down hitting power lines, fusing them and knocking out electricity in the local area, hence his injuries. The other airman who survived, Flight Sergeant O. Stamtis, was also transferred to the RCAF hospital at Marsden Green.

The pilot of the stricken Halifax was Flight Lieutenant Donald Zachary Taylor Wood of the RCAF. He was the son of Stuart Taylor Wood and Gertrude Maude Wood, being born on 17 March 1918 in Winnipeg, Canada. Donald was also the husband of Mignonne Helene Wood of Ottawa, Canada. Donald had a large family circle and he surprised his family early on in the war when he married his girlfriend, who gave birth to his only daughter, named Cheryl Ann. Sadly he was to see his daughter only once before he was posted overseas and subsequently killed in the accident. He has an interesting background, with his great, great, great-grandfather being Zachary Taylor, the twelfth president of the United States, and his great-grandfather being the captain of the *Tallahassee*, the famous Confederate ship. When the time came for Donald to attend school, he excelled from an early age, completing his senior matriculation in June 1935 and then going on to attend the Royal Military College in Kingston, Ontario, from 31 August 1935, where he graduated with a diploma in chemical engineering on 13 June 1939. From the college he enlisted in the Royal Canadian Navy Volunteer Reserve in September 1939, where he held the rank of sublieutenant, being awarded the War Medal and the Canadian Volunteer Service Medal and Clasp following service on the HMCS *Stadacona* and HMCS *Fraser*. He left there on 17 March 1940 to transfer to join the RCAF and enlisted on 15 May 1940 at a recruiting office in Halifax, Nova Scotia.

The rear gunner was Pilot Officer Donald McLeod Ward. Born on

30 August 1923, he was one of three sons of Mr Wyley Ward and Mary Ellen McClary. His father had been born in New Brunswick and his mother was born and brought up in Charlottetown, both of Canadian citizenship. He lived with his parents at 316, 5 Avenue, Verdun, Quebec, and attended the local St Willibrord School from 1931 until 1940, achieving Grade 9. Upon leaving school in 1940, he worked for the Canada Car Company, joining them in the September and remaining with them until October 1942, working as a general fitter. He left to take up employment with Canadian Vickers Ltd, also as a fitter, but then left in the same year to join the RCAF. Upon enlisting with the RCAF at a recruiting centre in Montreal on 24 November 1942, he chose flying duties as his point of interest and had a desire to become a pilot, although he also told the recruiters that he would be prepared to undertake any aircrew position. He had completed some previous military service with the 17th Duke of York Hussars in 1939; however, he served only three months, as he was discharged after being found to be underage.

The mid-upper gunner was Sergeant Owen Parsons, the son of James John Parsons, a bread salesman, and Beatrice Mary Hewitt. They were both UK citizens who later moved to Canada. Owen was born on 5 May 1920 in Winnipeg, Manitoba, and lived with both his parents at 111 Perth Avenue, Winnipeg. He graduated from high school in 1934, reaching the eighth grade. After leaving school he was employed with the Canada Bread Company Ltd for three years from 1936 until 1939 as a bread checker, after which he sought employment with Burnell and Portage as a machine operator. He had many general interests, including model aircraft building and working on engines, and took part in sports such as swimming and baseball. On joining the RCAF on 16 September 1940, he enlisted for ground duties, specifically asking for aero engine mechanics, but he became a security guard with the rank of aircrafts' man prior to undertaking his mechanics, and machinist course, from which he graduated with marks of 84 per cent in his exams. He spent the next few years serving as an aircraft mechanic, with attachments to different placements, including Calgary and Toronto. But after some time in the trade, he transferred to aircrew flying duties and underwent training as an air gunner, starting his course on 16 September 1943 and completing it with the award of the air gunner's badge on 28 January 1944, at which point he was promoted from leading aircraftman to sergeant.

The navigator on board was Flying Officer William Robert Ewing, born on 7 August 1920 on a farm near Winnipeg, Manitoba, to Robert

Stanley and Eva Gertrude Ewing, who were both Canadian citizens. Robert had been born in New Brunswick; Eva was his second wife. William was one of four children, of which a brother and sister were stepchildren. His full-blooded brother was George Ewing, born a short time after William on 22 June 1922. William's schooling would appear to have been rather mixed. Between attending primary school in 1926 and completing his final course at university in 1942, he went to six different schools and colleges. He spent his secondary schooling reaching eleventh grade, then studied a science course for two years, finishing in 1938, after which he took a secretarial course in 1938–9. Finally he undertook a three-year chartered accountancy course, but failed to complete it, as he enlisted with the RCAF in 1942, after just two years of the course.

Upon enlistment on 8 June 1942 with the RCAF in Winnipeg with the rank of aircraftsman, he specifically chose flying duties, in the hope of becoming a pilot. However, he was to transfer partway through his pilot training course to become a navigator instead.

The flight engineer was Flight Sergeant Geoffrey Davies Grant. He was the son of Isaac and Sarah Mary Grant of 20 Woodland Street, Mountain Ash, south Wales. He joined the RAF on 4 October 1943 and qualified as a flight engineer. Prior to his career in the Air Force he had worked as a fitter at Deep Duffryn Colliery. He was a prominent member of St Margarets Boys' Club, Mountain Ash, having captained both cricket and football teams at the club. During his last leave, which was only one week prior to the accident, he had become engaged to 19-year-old Sylvia Beauchamp.

MZ920 came down just over a mile from the RAF base at Church Lawford in a farmer's field. Many of the buildings in the nearby farm were utilized by the Air Force for their trucks and equipment for many days until the wreckage had been cleared.

A local resident who took time to track a number of the relatives and make enquiries as to what took place on this fateful evening arranged a local memorial to be erected in memory of the crew who perished at the spot.

No. 101 Squadron

Lancaster LL774 SR-U

Pilot	Pilot Officer Colin Charles Hunt	KIA (RAAF)
Flight engineer	Sergeant Andrew James Hannah	KIA
Bomb aimer	Sergeant Dennis Noble	KIA
Navigator	Sergeant George John Fretter	KIA
Mid-upper gunner	Sergeant Gerald Purcelle Neville	KIA
Rear gunner	Sergeant Robert Gwilym Williams	KIA
Wireless operator	Flying Officer David Myers	KIA
Special ops	Flying Officer Benny Yellin	KIA (RCAF)

This particular Lancaster was delivered to No. 101 Squadron on 28 April 1944 and remained with this squadron until 15 October, when it was shot down and lost on the night raid to Duisburg.

LL774 took off from RAF Ludford Magna at 0016 hrs on the morning of 15 October, but neither the aircraft nor its brave souls were ever seen again. It was due back at base at approximately 0523 hrs. As well as being part of the main force, this squadron was given the additional and unique role operating radio counter-measures employing the ABC device to jam enemy transmissions. In this battle with Luftwaffe nightfighter control, German-speaking operators were carried in some Lancasters to intrude on enemy voice transmissions. On the night of 14/15 October there were nightfighters active in the target area, and LL774 could have been attacked by one of them, or it could have been hit by anti-aircraft fire. It is not known.

Once all investigations for other aircraft missing from this raid were complete, five aircraft and crews remained unaccounted for, LL774 being one of those five. Once it was identified that, out of these five missing aircraft, two had been lost on the daylight raid and two on the night raid, and crash sites had been identified for the other four but not for this aircraft, it was confirmed that LL774 was not one of the aircraft that went missing over Duisburg. No other crash sites turned up at Duisburg, and, following in-depth investigations, nothing was ever located that suggested or confirmed that this crew crashed in Duisburg. Neither the aircraft nor its crew has ever turned up anywhere, and to this day nothing is known of its whereabouts.

An interesting note is that most of the case documents held by the Germans included many names from these five crews. These were hopelessly mixed up, but in none of the documents was there any mention of any crew members' names from LL774. This indicated strongly to the investigating officers that, although LL774 was reported missing from the Duisburg night raid, it had not crashed anywhere near Duisburg and certainly not over the target area. It was possible it came down en route to the target or on the route home somewhere, possibly into the North Sea. This particular case was considered closed by the Air Ministry after careful and in-depth investigations, and the crew of Lancaster LL774 have no known graves and no known crash location. It is possible they lie in a Commonwealth War Graves Commission cemetery as unknown airmen, having perhaps formed part of the list of unidentified airmen located by investigation teams. Searches by the MRES teams eventually ceased in 1950. All eight crew members are commemorated on the Runnymede Memorial.

Pilot Officer Colin Charles Hunt was the son of Charles Thomas Hunt and Zella Rutledge Hunt, of Croydon, New South Wales, Australia. Colin was born on 27 May 1920 in a small town named Burwood. He was killed at the age of just 24 while piloting his Lancaster to bomb Duisburg.

Colin was one of five siblings, the others being Terry, Brian, Berly and Eunice. Colin's father, who was known as Tom, was initially a school teacher, but later became a dentist. The family lived together in Croydon, a suburb in New South Wales, and all family members were prominently involved in the local Methodist church. The Hunt family was initially descended from a Richard Hunt who was sent to Australia as a convict in 1817 but then became a successful grazier. Many of the Hunt family until recently were involved in various grazing pursuits, and Colin's father eventually became managing director of the family grazing business.

Following school, Colin became a bank officer with the Commonwealth

Bank of Australia, Ashfield, but then spent a short time serving with the Royal Australian Army with the 14th Field Regiment, where he obtained the rank of sergeant. Following time with the Army, Colin joined the RAAF reserve on 27 October 1941 at the Sydney recruiting centre, but was not enlisted until 25 April 1942. He was enrolled at the No. 2 recruiting centre, Sydney, at the age of 21; the conditions of service stipulated he had to serve for the duration of the war plus twelve months. He was selected for pilot training. After taking his medical, Colin began his initial training with the RAAF at the No. 2 Initial Training School, where he learnt the basic skills and discipline of military life. Flying training began on single-engined Tiger Moth biplanes at the No. 11 Elementary Flying School, Benalla, New South Wales. Much of his time was spent grasping the basic concepts of flying, which included handling, navigation and basic aerobatics. He began his flight training on 10 August 1942 and completed the course, at which point he was posted to the Service Flight Training School on 22 November 1942.

During his time at the Elementary Flying School, Colin was involved in an accident on the ground while in charge of an aircraft. On 12 November 1942, at 1750 hrs, he failed to observe a proper lookout while in command of a Wackett Trainer, call-sign A3/19, and collided with another Wackett Trainer, call-sign A3/124, causing substantial damage to each aircraft. Colin received a forfeiture of pay to the sum of £5.00 following a brief trial.

Colin's time in Australia after qualifying as a pilot was short-lived, as he was posted to Europe, where he initially spent time increasing his flying experience and gaining further skills, including conversions to multi-engined aircraft and finally heavy bombers. Having left Brisbane on 5 May 1943, he arrived in the UK just over two months later at the No. 11 Personnel Receiving Centre, before being posted to the No. 6 Advanced Flying Unit in August. The Advanced Flying Unit presented further challenges, as much time was spent on multi-engined flying, cross-country flying and night flying. The types flown by Colin included the Avro Anson and Airspeed Oxford. RAF Chipping Norton was home to the unit. The crew were finally transferred to No. 101 Squadron on 8 September 1944, where they would undertake active operations a few days later.

The special equipment operator on board that evening was Flying Officer Benny Yellin, a Canadian serving with the RCAF. Benny was the son of Sam and Rosie Yellin, and was one of four brothers. He was born in Montreal, Quebec, on 30 April 1924, but, although he was of

Canadian citizenship, both of his parents were Russian, both having been born in a town named Bialystok, and both marrying in Poland. His father, Sam, was self-employed and had a clothing repair company named Yellin Goldman Clothing Contractors. His family were of Jewish descent.

Benny was educated to seventh grade at Fairmount School until 1936, but from here continued his secondary education until 1940 at the Baron Bygg High School, where he completed his eleventh grade. He had an ambition to become a diesel mechanic and sought to achieve this by attending the Montreal Technical College, undertaking a course in Diesel Engineering and Mathematics.

After he had completed his education, Benny's first job was as a fitter at the Fairchild's Aircraft Company, although this was short-lived, as he was employed for only three months before being made redundant. However, he gained further employment within the aircraft industry and took a job with Noorduyn Aviation at Longue Pointe as an assembler, but then in December 1941 he took a transfer to the Canadian Association of Aircraft as a fitter. This finished three months later, and so he moved again to the Fleet Aircraft Company, London, Ontario, where he was employed as a wing repairer. Benny resigned from here upon his own will to work for his father as a purchasing agent. On 24 February 1943, at the age of 19, he enlisted with the RCAF for standard aircrew duties at the No. 13 recruitment centre, Montreal, Quebec.

Sources and Acknowledgements

The Volunteer
Written by Sgt Ernest Peter Bone, gunner, No. 626 Squadron, RAF
Wickenby.

The Birth of Operation Hurricane
Operation Hurricane I and II – National Archives, Kew, London.
REF: AIR 8/1357. ASO summary NO 1424 for 14 and 15 October
1944 – RAF Museum, Hendon, London. Summary of Bomber
Command Operations 14 and 15 October 1944 – RAF Museum,
Hendon, London. Bomber Command War Diaries.
Dead Before Dawn, Frank Broome.

Wakey, Wakey Chaps
RAF Wickenby Squadron ORB and museum records. Extracts from
the personal diary and letters of Sgt Ernest Peter Bone. Extracts from
various letters with Trevor Jenkins. Extracts from a letter with Dick
Westrop. Extracts from the personal diary and letters of F/Lt Roy
Yule. Operation Hurricane I and II – National Archives, Kew, London.
REF: AIR 8/1357. No. 425 Squadron ORB, National Archives, Kew,
London, AIR 27. No. 153 Squadron ORB, National Archives, Kew,
London, AIR 27. No. 626 Squadron ORB, National Archives, Kew,
London, AIR 27. No. 166 Squadron ORB, National Archives, Kew,
London, AIR 27. Diary extract of Syd Stewart DFC. Information
provided by Sgt Harry Irons. ASO summary NO 1424 for 14 and
15 October 1944 – RAF Museum, Hendon, London.

Good God, Not Again.

Extracts from the personal diary and letters of Sgt Ernest Peter Bone. Records of the 14/15 October 1944, Luftwaffe Command Unit, from Bundesarchive, Freiburg. ASO summary NO 1424 for 14 and 15 October 1944 – RAF Museum, Hendon, London. Information supplied by Dr Theo Boiten, Nachtjagd operations for 14/15 October 1944. No. 419 Squadron ORB, National Archives, Kew, London, AIR 27. No. 166 Squadron ORB, National Archives, Kew, London, AIR 27. No. 425 Squadron ORB, National Archives, Kew, London, AIR 27. Extracts from the personal diary and letters of F/Lt Roy Yule. No. 300 Squadron ORB, National Archives, Kew, London, AIR27. Information from Sascha Weltgen, Dinslaken, Germany. Records of 14/15 October 1944, Luftwaffe Command Unit, from Bundesarchive, Freiburg. Video of the raid, IWM, OPX 236–239. Information supplied by Dr Theo Boiten, Nachtjagd operations for 14/15 October 1944. *RAF Bomber Command Losses 1944*, W. Chorley (Midland Publishing, 1997).

The Destruction of Duisburg

Operation Hurricane 1 and 11 – National Archives, Kew, London. REF: AIR 8/1357. ASO summary NO 1424 for 14 and 15 October 1944 – RAF Museum, Hendon, London. Summary of Bomber Command Operations 14 and 15 October 1944 – RAF Museum Hendon, London. *The Bomber Command War Diaries*, Martin Middlebrook, Chris Everitt (Midland Publishing, 1996). *RAF Bomber Command Losses 1944*, W. Chorley (Midland Publishing, 1997). Account from F/O McKinnon and crew of No. 425 Squadron, Squadron operational record book for 14/10/44, National Archives Kew, London, AIR 27. Personal account of Sgt Ernest Peter Bone. Personal account of Sgt Harry Irons. Bomber Command War Diaries. Bundesarchive, Freiburg, Germany – reports for damages.

The Search for the Missing

Air Historical Branch, MOD, Bentley Priory, Stanmore. Reports from MRES files of deceased airmen from 14/15 October 1944. Report of F/Lt Tennison, MRES team. National Archives of Canada.

Lancaster NF928

RAF Bomber Command Losses 1944, W. Chorley (Midland Publishing, 1997). Service record for F/Lt Ray Clearwater, National Archives of Canada. MRES investigation report for NF928, located in the service record of F/Lt Ray Clearwater, National Archives of Canada. Personal account and letters of F/O Frank Augusta. Personal account of Fritz Van Laak, Dinslaken, Germany. Personal account of Mr Grube, Dinslaken, Germany. Commonwealth War Graves Commission cemetery records. Family records and service record of George Walton, courtesy of Gary White, grandson. Family records for F/Lt Ray Clearwater, courtesy of Bob Richardson and family. Accident report records for 16 May 1942 AFU, RAF Museum, Hendon, London. Service record and family records for Sgt Richard Wolsey. No. 12 Squadron operational record book, National Archives, Kew, London.

Lancaster ME788

Account of ditching courtesy of the RAF Wickenby Museum. *RAF Bomber Command Losses 1944*, W. Chorley (Midland Publishing, 1997). No. 12 Squadron operational record book, National Archives, Kew, London.

Lancaster LL909

Loss card, RAF Museum, Hendon, London. *RAF Bomber Command Losses 1944*, W. Chorley (Midland Publishing, 1997). Service record and investigation reports for F/O Harold Gartrell, National Archives of Canada. Records supplied by the Air Historical Branch, MOD, Bentley Priory, Stanmore. POW records, National Archives, Kew, London. Family records supplied by Christine Broughton, daughter of Sgt Ross Allen. Personal account of F/O Richard Randall, National Archives of Canada. Research assistance from Sascha Weltgen, Hermann Mollenbeck, Dinslaken. Personal account and interview from Mr Schafer, Sterkrade. MRES investigation reports from Lancaster PD319. Commonwealth War Graves Commission cemetery records. No. 12 Squadron operational record book, National Archives, Kew, London.

Lancaster HK599

Loss report card, RAF Museum, Hendon. Records supplied by the Air Historical Branch, MOD, Bentley Priory, Stanmore. Commonwealth

War Graves Commission cemetery records. Service record for Justin
Francis Loughnan, Australian National Archives. POW records,
National Archives, Kew, London.

Lancaster ND805

No. 115 Squadron operational record book, National Archives, Kew,
London. Service records and investigation reports for F/O David
Mayson Price, F/O Clyde George Redden, P/O Douglas Stewart
Haggis, P/O Dale McGowan Hamilton, National Archives of Canada.
Includes MRES investigation reports. Commonwealth War Graves
Commission cemetery records. Records supplied by the Air Historical
Branch, MOD, Bentley Priory, Stanmore. POW records, National
Archives, Kew, London.

Lancaster NG133

No. 550 Squadron operational record book, National Archives, Kew,
London. POW records, National Archives, Kew, London. Service
record and MRES investigation reports for F/Sgt John William Brown.
Records supplied by the Air Historical Branch, MOD, Bentley Priory,
Stanmore. Eyewitnesses spoken to on Gest Straße in Baerl.

Lancaster PD319

No. 550 Squadron operational record book, National Archives, Kew,
London. Records supplied by the Air Historical Branch, MOD, Bentley
Priory, Stanmore. Service record for F/Sgt Clarence Walter
Beckingham, National Archives of Australia. Relatives of Sgt Albert
Laidlaw, Evelyn and Peter Miller. Son of P/O Harry Black, Norval
Black. Relatives of F/Sgt Clarence Walter Beckingham, Christine and
Chris Cole, William Beckingham, Australia. No. 550 Squadron
Association. Commonwealth War Graves Commission cemetery
records. Service record and investigation reports for F/O Harold
Gartrell, National Archives of Canada – LL909.

Lancaster NF959

Records supplied by the Air Historical Branch, MOD, Bentley Priory,
Stanmore. Commonwealth War Graves Commission cemetery records.
No. 300 Squadron operational record book, National Archives, Kew,
London. Airmen records supplied by Thomas Rajkowski, Germany.

Lancaster KB800

Personal letter supplied by W/O Nicolas Walter Karpassiti, DFC. *RCAF Overseas*, 6th edition, Oxford Press, Toronto. Service record for F/O Jules Napoleon Robert Therreault. National Archives of Canada. Service record for P/O Harold Sigal, National Archives of Canada. Service record for P/O Robert Gordon Manwell, National Archives of Canada. Service record for Lucien Charles Le Vasseur. No. 419 Squadron operation record book, National Archives, Kew, London. Mr Huffen, owner of the farm where the aircraft crashed. Records supplied by the Air Historical Branch, MOD, Bentley Priory, Stanmore. POW records, National Archives, Kew, London.

Lancaster NE163

Loss card, RAF Museum Hendon, London. Service record for Sgt Harry Jeffries – Patricia and George Jeffries. Service record for F/O Thurston Culshaw, National Archives of Canada. Service record for F/O John Mervyn MacMillan, National Archives of Canada. Personal letters and correspondence with Chris Grande, relative of F/O Thurston Culshaw. Correspondence with Patricia and George Jeffries, relatives of Sgt Harry Jeffries. Squadron records for No. 626 Squadron, RAF Wickenby Museum. Records supplied by the Air Historical Branch, MOD, Bentley Priory, Stanmore. Personal letters from Trevor Jenkins. Personal letters from Ernest Peter Bone. Service record and correspondence of F/Lt Reginald Major Aldus, supplied by Chris Bill, relative.

Lancaster LM596

Service record of F/O James Commodore Campbell, National Archives of Canada. Service record of F/O Robert Albert Charland, National Archives of Canada. Service record of P/O William Frederick Palmer, National Archives of Canada. Service record of F/O Ross Cuthbert Clouston, National Archives of Canada. Service record of P/O Roland Marcel Joseph Champagne, National Archives of Canada. Details of F/O John Allan Orr, Tom Bint, David Stapleton. Details of Sgt Sidney John Akhurst, Bill Akhurst, relative. No. 626 Squadron records, RAF Wickenby Museum. Records supplied by the Air Historical Branch, MOD, Bentley Priory, Stanmore.

Lancaster KB780

No. 428 Squadron records, National Archives, Kew, London. Service record of F/Lt William Harold Janney, National Archives of Canada. Service record of F/O Archie Verdun Batty, National Archives of Canada. Service record of P/O Walter Henry Killner, New Zealand Military Archives. Service record of P/O Paul Reviere Jones, National Archives of Canada. Service record of P/O Francis John Harrison, National Archives of Canada. Service record of P/O Albert Sydney McFeetors, National Archives of Canada. Correspondence and log book for P/O Albert Sydney McFeetors, supplied by Raymond McFeetors, son. Correspondence for P/O Walter Henry Killner, supplied by Annette Facer, daughter. Witness report – Ron Cassels, Ghost Squadron. Correspondence for Sgt Leonard Brotherhood, supplied by Andrew Leech, relative. New Zealand Defence Force archives. Records supplied by the Air Historical Branch, MOD, Bentley Priory, Stanmore.

Lancaster NG190

No. 166/153 Squadron records, National Archives, Kew, London. Service record of F/O Joseph Ross Eugene Brouillette, National Archives of Canada. Service record of F/O Glenn Crawford Bellamy, National Archives of Canada. Service record of F/O Alfred Alexander Picard, National Archives of Canada. Service record of F/Sgt William Greene, National Archives of Canada. Service record of F/O James Lindsay, National Archives of Canada. Records supplied by the Air Historical Branch, MOD, Bentley Priory, Stanmore. Extracts from the service record of F/Lt Clearwater relating to NG190, National Archives of Canada.

Lancaster JB297

No. 166/153 Squadron records, National Archives, Kew, London. No. 166/153 Squadron association records. Extracts from the service record of F/Lt Clearwater relating to the graves at Dinslaken, National Archives of Canada.

Lancaster PD224

Service record of F/O Andrew McNeill, National Archives of Canada. Service record of F/O Edward Roger Lambert, National Archives of Canada. Service record of F/O Bryn Evans Roberts, National

Archives of Canada. Service record of F/Sgt Leonard Schaff, National
Archives of Canada. Service record of F/Sgt Joseph William Powell,
National Archives of Australia. Records supplied by the Air Historical
Branch, MOD, Bentley Priory, Stanmore. No. 166 Squadron records,
National Archives, Kew, London. *RAF Bomber Command Losses 1944*, W.
Chorley (Midland Publishing, 1997) with updates on the internet.
Desmond Amos, brother of Albert Amos.
No. 166 Squadron Association.

Lancaster ME748
No. 166 Squadron records, National Archives, Kew, London. Records
supplied by the Air Historical Branch, MOD, Bentley Priory, Stanmore.

Lancaster LL956
No. 625 Squadron records, National Archives, Kew, London. Service
record of F/O L.A. Hannah, National Archives of Canada. Family
records courtesy of David Langner, relative of F/O L.A. Hannah.
Service record of F/O L.D. Bennett, National Archives of Canada.
Details supplied by Margaret Brader, owner of the farm where the
aircraft crashed.

Halifax MZ674
Bomber Command museum and memorial of Canada. No. 425
Squadron records, National Archives, Kew, London. *The RCAF Overseas*,
6th edition, Oxford Press, Toronto. Service record for F/O Dell
Alfred Butler, National Archives of Canada. Service record for
P/O Francis Harvey Eade, National Archives of Canada. Service
record for P/O Charles Maurice Crabtree, National Archives of
Canada. Service record for P/O Leonard Hunter Hogg, National
Archives of Canada. F/O Augusta, interview details.

Halifax MZ453
No. 429 Squadron records, National Archives, Kew, London. Personal
account from the pilot, F/O Frank Augusta.

Lancaster PB357
No. 7 Squadron records, National Archives, Kew, London. Records
supplied by the Air Historical Branch, MOD, Bentley Priory,
Stanmore. Service record for F/Sgt Thomas Edward Feaver, courtesy

of Frances Rogers, relative. Service record for P/O Eric Thurston
Rivers, National Archives of Canada. Family records for Sgt Arthur
Henry Frost, courtesy of Susan Frost, relative.

Lancaster LM165
No. 90 Squadron records, National Archives, Kew, London. Service
record of F/Sgt Francis John Cook, National Australian Archives.
Records by the Air Historical Branch, MOD, Bentley Priory, Stanmore.
German eyewitness account, National Archives of Canada.

Mosquito MM184
German service record courtesy of Chris Goss. Personal account of
F/O Frank Dell via interview. Records by the Air Historical Branch,
MOD, Bentley Priory, Stanmore.

Lancaster ME595
No. 61 Squadron records, National Archives, Kew, London. Personal
records and service records for Sgt George Boyd, courtesy of Paddy
Boyd, brother. Personal accounts from interview and diary records for
F/O Norman Hoad. Court case documents and war crime
investigation for Sgt Cyril Webb, National Archives, Kew, London.
Glentorf cemetery details and reports, courtesy of Ruediger
Kaufmann, Germany.

Halifax MZ920
No. 434 Squadron records, National Archives, Kew, London.
Information supplied by David George, local researcher to the crash
site. Service record of F/Lt Donald Zachary Taylor Wood, National
Archives of Canada. Service record of F/O William Robert Ewing,
National Archives of Canada. Service record of Sgt Owen Parsons,
National Archives of Canada. Service record of P/O Donald McLeod
Ward, National Archives of Canada.

Lancaster LL774
Service record of F/O Benny Yellin, National Archives of Canada.
Service record of P/O Colin Charles Hunt, National Archives of
Australia. No. 101 Squadron records, National Archives, Kew, London.
Family records for P/O Colin Hunt, courtesy of Chris Hunt and
family, Australia.

A special thanks to Sascha Weltgen, Peter Monasso and Paddy Boyd.

I also need to extend thanks to all of the relatives, various museums, squadron associations and veterans who have contributed to this book. There are far too many to mention, so apologies if any have been missed out.

Index of Units

Index of Personnel